Nimbus Publishing Limited
3731 Mackintosh St, Halifax, NS B3K 5A5
(902) 455-4286
nimbus.ca

Printed and bound in Canada
NB1028

Author photo: Sandra Kipis, 2011
Cover and interior design: John van der Woude Designs

Library and Archives Canada Cataloguing in Publication

Whitehead, Ruth Holmes
The Black Loyalists : southern settlers of the first free black communities in Nova Scotia / Ruth Holmes Whitehead.

Includes bibliographical references and index.
Issued also in electronic formats.
ISBN 978-1-77108-016-3

1. Black loyalists—Nova Scotia—History. 2. Black loyalists—Nova Scotia—Biography.
3. Nova Scotia—History—1775-1783. 4. Nova Scotia--History--1784-1867. 5. United States—History—Revolution, 1775-1783. I. Title.

FC2321.4.W55 2013   971.6'00496   C2012-907368-7

Nimbus Publishing acknowledges the financial support for its publishing activities from the Government of Canada through the Canada Book Fund (CBF) and the Canada Council for the Arts, and from the Province of Nova Scotia through the Department of Communities, Culture and Heritage.

Black LOYALISTS

SOUTHERN SETTLERS OF NOVA SCOTIA'S FIRST FREE BLACK COMMUNITIES

RUTH HOLMES WHITEHEAD

NIMBUS PUBLISHING

NIMBUS.CA

*For all the descendants of the Black Loyalists everywhere,
who wish to know what life was like for their ancestors
as slaves and as free people in the "Before Time."*

*In memory of Isabelle (Miss Molsey) Simmons, Louisa Sellars,
and Eliza Logan Cherry.*

Contents

Introduction

*I*t's the third of May, 1783. In Barrington, Nova Scotia, a seven-year-old boy named Thomas Doane is fidgeting at the graveside where his father is being buried. When finally he looks up and out to sea, he is transfixed by what he is seeing. Bracketed by the headlands of the harbour, passing by in silent stateliness like great cumulus clouds on a summer's afternoon, the British fleet out of newly surrendered New York City, on its way up the coast to Port Roseway, is delivering a thousand Black Loyalists to freedom in Nova Scotia.[1] These men and women would found the first free black communities in the province.

During the following months, and over the next two years, more than four thousand black men, women, and children would come to Nova Scotia as a direct result of the American Revolution (1775–1783). They came as freeborn persons, as former slaves who had seized freedom from the chaos of war, or as indentured servants. Some came still enchained to their enslavers. They came fleeing the British surrender of thirteen American colonies: the Massachusetts Commonwealth (which then included Maine), New Hampshire, New York, Connecticut, Rhode Island, New Jersey, Pennsylvania, Delaware, Maryland, Virginia, North Carolina, South Carolina, and Georgia. During the course of the war, as these colonies fell one by one to the victorious

Americans, mass evacuations of British forces and supporters to their remaining centres of power began to take place.

As early as 1775, slaves were being promised freedom if they deserted rebellious colonists to come behind the British lines. Many of them took advantage of this offer, following the British Army or sailing with the Royal Navy, as the lines of battle and power surged up and down the Atlantic Coast. Historians now refer to these people as the Black Loyalists—a term that seems to have been extended to cover all the blacks who emigrated to Nova Scotia, New Brunswick, and Quebec, whatever their circumstances, between the years 1775 and 1785.

The colonies of Newfoundland, Nova Scotia (which at that time included what is now New Brunswick), Île Saint-Jean (later Prince Edward Island), and Quebec had remained loyal to King George III of England throughout the revolution. In the south, East Florida never left British control (West Florida was retaken by the Spanish toward the end of the war). Midway between the two lay the city of New York. By August 1776, the British were entrenched in New York, holding it until the end of the war. Thus, by 1783, the bulk of Black Loyalists, enslaved originally all along the east coast from Georgia on up through Maine, were concentrated in New York, the port from which many would later sail to Nova Scotia.

They would not be the first Black Loyalists to come to Nova Scotia, however. Boston had fallen to the American forces before the British seizure of New York; hence a number of black Bostonians evacuated directly to Halifax. According to historian James Walker, "The first known group of free Black Loyalists to arrive in Nova Scotia was the 'Company of Negroes,' evacuated from Boston with the other British forces in 1776. No sooner had they arrived in Halifax than the suggestion was made that they should be used as ransom in exchange for Loyalist prisoners held by the Americans. Such was apparently to be their reward for sharing the hazards and hardships of the New England campaign."[2]

For all practical purposes, the American Revolution ended in October 1781, with the surrender of General Cornwallis to General Washington at Yorktown, Virginia. Sporadic fighting continued in other places for several months. As the British were evacuating Savannah and Charlestown from July through the end of December 1782, more persons poured into New York.

By April 1783, the first transports had begun taking thousands of British and Hessian troops home to Great Britain and Germany. With them went many who had been loyal to Britain, black and white, with their families and the little they had been able to salvage from the wreckage of war. Refugees also made directly for Nova Scotia, sailed for the West Indies, or took ship to Quebec. Others went to St. Augustine, East Florida, where they were promised peace, provisions, and land.

Florida was not to remain a refuge for long, however. The English colony of West Florida was retaken by the Spanish prior to the signing of the peace treaty in 1783, and East Florida by that same treaty was ceded back to Spain, with its refugees and old settlers given until 1785 to complete evacuating the territory. Many of these opted for the same promises of provisions and land in Nova Scotia, far to the north.

A number of excellent books have told the story of the part played by black men and women in the American Revolution. Others have written about the arrival of the Black Loyalists in Nova Scotia, and the departure of many of them, in 1791, for a new life in Sierra Leone—all good general surveys. This book, however, is much more specific, taking a look at those founding members of the Black Loyalist communities in Nova Scotia whose stories began in the southern provinces of South Carolina and Georgia (which was carved out of South Carolina in 1732). I chose the South Carolina Black Loyalists to focus upon particularly because that province, before the American Revolution, had the largest black population of any in North America; many contemporary Nova Scotians who are descended from Black Loyalists have ancestors who were enslaved there. South Carolina is also where I was born, and a number of my own ancestors there were slave owners who lost people to Nova Scotia. As a former registrar at the Charleston Museum, I knew the research infrastructure. It seemed a good place to start looking at individual Black Loyalists, following them through the war that led to their arrival in Nova Scotia. This book is an attempt to recover their history—and that of their contemporaries—for their descendants, many of whom live in Nova Scotia today.

How their names have survived is an interesting story in itself. All people are a treasure house of information, of personal memories. If we are fortunate, ancestors pass some of this down to us. Nowhere on earth, however, has the generational transmission of history been cut more devastatingly than in the "forcible migrations" whereby an estimated ten million persons of African birth were brought as slaves to the New World. Torn away from their heritage, their extended families, their languages and culture, these men and women have left to their descendants often little more than a handful of memories.

Restoring this lost family history is hampered in the United States, in many cases, by the lack of surnames in historical documents before 1863—the year the Emancipation Proclamation declared slavery illegal. (Slavery had been abolished in the British Empire in 1834.) The Black Loyalists who left New York in 1783, therefore, provide a unique window for their descendants, and for historians and genealogists in general, for two reasons. First, they had surnames and, second, they were documented with these surnames from the time of their leaving New York with the British.

Once again, this fortuitous circumstance arose because of the war. General George Washington, commander-in-chief of the Continental Army, demanded at the end of the American Revolution that all people formerly considered "American property" and now living behind the British lines be returned. General Sir Guy Carleton, newly appointed commander-in-chief of the British forces, met with Washington in May 1783, but refused this request in a letter dated May 12, saying he had no right to "deprive them of that liberty," which had been granted by proclamations of various British officials and generals, beginning with Lord Dunmore, royal governor of Virginia, in November 1775.[3] Carleton announced that he'd ordered a list kept of each black person leaving New York with the British convoys. This document, which came to be called the Book of Negroes (see Note at end of introduction), in most cases gave a first and last name, the person's age and physical description, as well as the name and location of his or her former enslaver, with details as to when each had "left him." Names of blacks still enslaved or of indentured black servants leaving with the fleet were also to be included in this list of free black émigrés. Because of this unique list, which fixes each person in time and space at one particular moment in their lives, many descendants of these Loyalists can track their families from 1783, when they first arrived in Nova Scotia.

Using, in addition, census records, muster rolls, poll tax records, court cases, and church records of births, deaths, and marriages, family trees can be established for some Black Loyalists in Nova Scotia *seventy years earlier* than any comparable record can be created for most blacks in the United States. This material also enables some tracking of Black Loyalists coming to Nova Scotia in ways other than those mentioned in the Book of Negroes. Less well known, for example, are the Black Loyalists who were shipped from East Florida or Jamaica to Guysborough, Nova Scotia, in 1784, whose names appear in a Guysborough muster. Almost no records of their lives prior to their arrival have survived, but many were originally enslaved in South Carolina or Georgia, before post-war evacuation took them further south and north. A number of Carolinians, such as David George and his family, or the Reverend John Marrant, are not listed in the Book of Negroes, but were discovered through other sources documenting their origins.

This is not the only good news. Using their former slave owner's names and locations, some Black Loyalists can be tracked *backwards* in time from 1783 to their enslavement and escape in an American colony. In some cases, using wills and inventories of the estates of previous owners, family histories can be taken back another twenty years or more, and sometimes all the way home to Africa. Because it is known where they were, and by whom they were enslaved, and when they were born, the lives of many can be fleshed out beyond all previous expectations. After fifteen years of searching, I am still astonished by the amount of data available. A biographical entry for every person I've found has been prepared, and will eventually be made accessible, possibly on the Black Loyalist Heritage Society's website.

Everyone's story has a beginning, and to understand the lives of these Black Loyalists, it is necessary to start with their circumstances before the war—circumstances that were a direct result of the African slave trade. Consequently, I first examine European involvement in the West African slave trade through the journals of slave ship captains, slave fort administrators, and others. These materials include a first-hand account by someone who accompanied a Muslim slave trader on a months-long journey through the interior of Africa to collect slaves for sale to the English on the coast. In the early twentieth century, historian Elizabeth Donnan amassed four huge volumes of records on the slave trade—a blessing to researchers, the first two of which I have relied on heavily. The original accounts are so vivid that I may have erred on the side of presenting extracts from too many people, but as one South Carolina slave, Warwick Francis, said, "I am an Eye Witness to it."[4]

Black life in South Carolina is next presented. From its initial founding in 1670, Carolina was involved in the slave trade. Some of the Lords Proprietors to whom Charles II initially granted the colony were members of the Royal Company of Adventurers Trading into Africa. Slavery there first took root when the thin coastal margin of colony was still the frontier of Carolina—beyond it was wilderness. In the early days of the colony, slave owners often worked side by side with their slaves. Marriage between blacks, Native Americans, and whites was legal. Moreover, slaves were often freed after a term of service, manumission made possible simply by the owner signing a statement of emancipation—later each case had to be approved by the legislature (usually they refused), and the emancipated slave had to leave South Carolina. Prior to the American Revolution, however, as slave labour helped the colony morph into a place of wealth and ease, Carolina substituted the relative freedom of the frontier for a much more severe and rigid legalism, designed to control the ever-growing population of the enslaved. The slave statutes, for example, those laws regulating slave life, are grim but telling documents that shed light on how slavery evolved in the colony.

Excerpts from the memoirs of three Black Loyalist ministers who came to Nova Scotia, one of them born free and two born enslaved, provide windows into life in the colony. Other resources are the runaway-slave advertisements of the period: rich mini-vignettes of daily life. Enslavers' personal and business documents offer another avenue, in particular the voluminous correspondence of Henry Laurens, which spans many years (1747–1792). I have included a few of his comments on his own slaves to illustrate how an enslaver felt and acted within a slave-owning society. The oral history of a family living in Christ Church Parish (across the harbour from Charleston) provides glimpses of lifeways preserved and passed down from African ancestors during the late nineteenth and early twentieth centuries—lifeways vastly unchanged from those of Black Loyalists.

Chapter 3 profiles eight Black Loyalists (including a baby), using the available data to reconstruct their lives as much as is presently possible. During the course of this research, I remember telling my father, "I've done minimal biographies now for about eight hundred people, but there's so much information turning up. I could write whole essays on about two hundred of them!" He looked at me pityingly, and said, "I *really* think you need to narrow your focus." So I've chosen to profile certain Black Loyalists who settled at Birchtown, Port Mouton, Guysborough, Halifax, and Annapolis Royal or Digby. They represent the spectrum of black people who came to Nova Scotia: free men and women, some still employed by the British Army; indentured servants; people still enslaved. Their enslavers also come from a variety of backgrounds: male and female, married and single, rich and poor, planters and artisans; their homes in rural areas, small towns, or Charlestown itself.

The middle portion of the book covers both the war that would provide freedom for the Black Loyalists, and the ways in which they escaped to Nova Scotia. Here, I was helped by the series of documents collected in *Naval Documents of the American Revolution*, published by the US Department of the Navy. Unfortunately, this undertaking does not yet cover all the war years, but the volumes completed to date—running well over a thousand pages each—are the next best thing to having been there. K. G. Davies' multi-volume work containing calendars and transcripts of documents in the National Archives of Great Britain (*Documents of the American Revolution, 1770-1783: Colonial Office Series*) provided excellent primary data, and some fascinating side trips. The British Headquarters Papers (in the same archives) and contemporary South Carolina newspapers added greatly to my research on the war years.

Another research highlight was the Royal Navy muster rolls, which list the names of black people who made it to sanctuary on board the King's ships as well as the names of those captured to be sold as booty as soon as the ship reached an appropriate port. Such musters added to my knowledge of the interactions between Black Loyalists and the Royal Navy, and provided corrections or elucidations of some of the data in the Book of Negroes. In addition, ships' daily logs provided added texture and background.

The final three chapters take a look at life after the signing of the Treaty of Paris in 1783. The first describes the evacuation of New York, detailing the voyages of a few of the ships that carried Black Loyalists to England and Germany, Quebec and Nova Scotia, or the West Indies. The second examines the early years of the Black Loyalists in Nova Scotia and the history of their largest founding communities. These include Birchtown, Annapolis Royal, and Digby, largely abandoned for Sierra Leone in 1791; the doomed community at Port Mouton, destroyed by fire on a spring night in 1784, with many of its people being relocated to Birchtown, Chedabucto, or Saint John; and the

Tracadie land grants given to local Black Loyalists in 1787. The final chapter looks at the recent rise of interest in Black Loyalist history, and the resulting books, museum exhibits, and videos, as well as the findings of archaeological digs. Birchtown in Shelburne County, once (for a short time) the largest town of free blacks in North America—fifteen hundred people—has become a primary centre for this sort of study. The creation there of the Black Loyalist Heritage Society and the work of its individual members has done a lot to bring the history of Black Loyalists into public knowledge.

To sum up, this book presents a picture of what life was like for Black Loyalists, before they escaped slavery in early South Carolina, Georgia, and Florida and after they settled in Nova Scotia. My intention is to illustrate how some very brave and enterprising men and women found a way to pass through the heart, ironically, of a War for Liberty, *to* liberty and human dignity. They had a passion for freedom, and they acted upon it. This book is for their descendants, who, over the succeeding generations, have made a life for themselves in Nova Scotia.

A note on Book of Negroes: Its full title is "Book of Negroes Registered & certified after having been Inspected by the Commissioners appointed by His Excellency Sr. Guy Carleton K.B. General & Commander in Chief, on Board Sundry Vessels in which they were Embarked Previous to the time of sailing from the Port of New York." Because I mention it eighty-nine times in this book, I use the shortened form, Book of Negroes, and I use it without quotation marks. It is not to be confused with Lawrence Hill's novel, *The Book of Negroes*, which uses it as inspiration for a novel about a single fictional Black Loyalist.

A note on the combatants: The term *British* is used for everyone on the side of King George III except for the American Loyalists, whom their opponents called Tories. (They weren't any more British—or less American—than were their opposite numbers, most being Americans of British descent.) The term *Loyalists* seems a reasonable one for them, since that is what they called themselves. Black persons assisting the British army or navy during the war, taking refuge behind the British lines, are herein referred to as *Black Loyalists*. The term *Americans* or *rebels* refers to all those opposing King George III.

Part
ONE

THE SLAVE TRADE AND THE PROVINCE OF CAROLINA

*C*harlestown Harbour, early December, 1782: The British Navy is loading ship after ship with people who want to leave South Carolina. Those civilians who sided with King George III are all aboard now with their families, their allowance of baggage, their slaves, their dogs, a favourite parrot in a cage. Up the side come the Black Loyalists, freed from slavery by coming in to the British forces, perhaps bringing with them a change of clothes, some bedding, a few tools, a small bag of cornmeal. Then are brought aboard people still technically the property of King George III: the slaves captured in war or taken from the sequestered estates of rebellious Americans. They have almost nothing except the rags on their backs. And lastly, on December 14, the ships begin boarding the regiments of the British Army and their Hessian allies, evacuating a former colony at the tail end of the American Revolution.

For those of African birth—and out of the more than three thousand blacks evacuated, a great many had suffered the experience of the African slave trade first-hand—being taken aboard a troop transport surely brought back the time when they had been brought to the Province of Carolina from West Africa in the hell of a slave ship's hold. The darkness below decks, the smell of tar and bilge, the sound of water against the hull, the beginnings of seasickness from the heave of the ship and the heat of so many bodies packed together, not to mention their anxiety about the unknown, would have caused a cascade of memories. As their vessels began to make sail down the ship channel, they could see out the gunports Sullivan's Island, the ground they would have first set foot on to complete quarantine. Many must have sat speechless in those first moments on board, re-experiencing their African past, their capture and forced march to the sea, their placement in irons, the long wait in slave-factory dungeons until the ship arrived that would take them across the ocean. They had been victims of one of the biggest "forced migrations" the world has ever seen, part of a terrible trade in humans already several hundred years old, and one which would continue for nearly a century in South Carolina.[1]

The fifteenth century saw the first rush of European explorers to Africa south of the Sahara. One of the most fascinating seeds for this interest in exploration originated in the African empire of Mali in the early 1300s. Mali's ruler, Abu Bakari II, filled with curiosity and the desire for epic adventure that was to win for him the praise name "The Voyager King," decided to equip a fleet of two thousand ships and sail with them across the Atlantic. He wanted to know what was on the other side. Abu Bakari departed his kingdom from somewhere on the west coast of Africa, and as late as 1324, had not returned, vanishing into speculation. He left his wealth and power, as well as his sense of adventure, to his regent, Mansa Musa (1312–1337), who as a devout Muslim decided in 1324 to make a pilgrimage to Mecca. While passing through Egypt, Mansa Musa astounded the Mediterranean world with the massive amounts of gold he had brought with him from Mali. His huge retinue and his lavish spending turned heads and fired imaginations: there was gold in Africa, south of the Sahara. While in Cairo, this Malian ruler gave an interview to the Arab historian and geographer Shihab al-Umari, who in 1340 preserved for history the account of Abu Bakari and his quest into the South Atlantic.

To men of the Mediterranean littoral, Abu Bakari had done the unthinkable, launching himself due west into the unknown and terrifying World Ocean, following a dream of clouds and birds and land beyond the seas. Mansa Musa gave Europeans other themes to ponder, ideas that amplified the lure of exploration: uncharted regions of Africa as realms of mysteries, of wealth and wilderness. And flowing through all of their imaginings, a river of gold, gold, gold. Eyes and thoughts turned west and south. Europeans took up the story of Mansa Musa and preserved it: an image of the king, for instance, appears on the map of Angelino Dulcert, published in 1375. In the same year, a portrait of Mansa Musa was included in the 1375 Catalan atlas, and—just to make sure no one forgot the salient point—he is portrayed holding an enormous gold nugget.[2]

Thirty-five years later, intrigued by similar stories of African gold, a prince of Portugal began to push the boundaries of the world as known to Europeans. Dom Infante Henrique, third son of King João I and his English wife, Phillipa of Lancaster, took part in the conquest of North African Ceuta (now a Spanish enclave in northern Morocco). Here, in 1415, he evidently became interested in accounts of Muslim trade with sub-Saharan Africa—a trade that the Portuguese conquest had effectively ended. Prince Henry, as he is referred to in English, went home to Portugal, set himself up at the port of Sagres, and eventually began to finance voyages of exploration down the coast of West Africa. Due to reefs and tricky currents, and the primitive naval technology of the times, it had been thought impossible to pass Cape Bojador, just south of the Canary Islands. Prince Henry persevered, however, sending fifteen expeditions between 1424 and 1434 alone. His support, not only for expeditions but for ship-building innovations and better map-making, eventually enabled Portuguese ships to pass the southernmost tip of Africa and find a way to the Indies. The West African trade was thus fully opened. Gold was now being acquired from Africa in quantities large enough for the royal mint in Lisbon to issue a pure gold coinage, the *cruzados*. The rest of Europe couldn't help but notice. Gold, ivory, and slaves began to find their way north from Africa, in ships of other nations.

RISE OF THE ENGLISH SLAVE TRADE

The earliest English voyage to West Africa that both engaged in the slave trade and left records got underway nearly a hundred years later, under the command of Captain John Lok: "In the year of Our Lord 1554 the eleventh day of October, we departed the river of Thames with three goodly ships, the one called the *Trinity*, the other called the *Bartholomew*, the third was the *John Evangelist*, the first day of November at nine of the clock at night departing from the coast of England."[3] The captain had set out to trade for gold and ivory; the fact that he brought home slaves appears to have been almost an afterthought. Although Lok seems to have respected the Africans he met, he cautions, "they that shall have to do with them, must use them gently: for they will not traffic or bring in any wares if they be evil used." His actual trade in slaves is mentioned only briefly: "They brought with them certain black slaves, whereof some were tall and strong."

Gold and elephant ivory would continue to be part of the cargo of Guinea ships, but Captain Lok's "gentle usage" would quickly be replaced by cold and pragmatic calculations, as both Africans and Europeans realized the enormous profits to be made by the sale of human beings. Ten years later, the voyage of another Englishman, Sir John Hawkins, proved much more brutal. Accompanied by the *Salomon* and the *Swallow*, Hawkins left Plymouth on October 18, 1564 in the *Jesus*. He reached Madeira by November 4, and by November 25, was off Cabo Blanco, a Portuguese trading station on the coast of Africa, noting, "The people of that part of Africa are tawny, having long hair without any apparel, saving before their privy members. Their weapons in wars are bows and arrows." At Cape Verde, he observed that "these people are all black, and are called negroes, without any apparel, saving before their privities: of stature goodly men." Hawkins went into the Callowsa River, "where the Portuguese rode [at anchor], and dispatched his business, and so returned with two caravels, laden with negroes."[4] After a brutal encounter with locals during a second slave raid, he left Sierra Leone with his cargo of slaves and sailed for the West Indies. John Hawkins pioneered the English Triangular Trade: Africa, America, Europe. His snatch-and-grab method of acquiring cargo, if practised in England, would have been considered theft, rapine, and murder. These same practices in Africa, applied to raiding for slaves, were just taking care of business.

In the centuries that followed, however, Englishmen, ever practical, sat back and let African kings and nations do their slave hunting for them. The English made trade alliances, purchased land, built forts, and enlarged these forts into towns, eventually expanding into a full-blown colonialism and taking over huge chunks of the continent—all in the pursuit of marketable human flesh. These men weren't pirates; they were chairmen of the board.

They had paperwork to cover every eventuality: contracts, for example, setting out exactly what they expected of their ships' captains, whom they required to post bond. They had insurance agents and brokers and lawyers; they commissioned map-makers and surveyors to chart land and sea. In the process, they invented a new meaning for the verb *to slave*.

The year 1660 is the next important one for this story. The throne of England had been restored to the Stuart line in the aftermath of the English Civil War, and Charles II crowned in London. As Alexander Hewatt wrote a century later, about the Carolina colony's inception, "Domestic peace being re-established on the solid foundation of regal and constitutional authority, England, amidst other national objects, turned her views toward the improvement of commerce, navigation, and her colonies."[5] The resultant founding of the colony of Carolina in the New World, and the creation of the Royal Company of Adventurers Trading into Africa, later reinvented as the Royal African Company, were a direct result of the Restoration. In 1660, Charles II granted a monopoly on the slave trade to the Company of Royal Adventurers—literally to himself, as he had invested private monies in it—giving the company "the whole, entire and only trade for buying and selling bartering and exchanging of for or with any negroes, slaves, goods, wares, merchandize whatsoever." His brother James, Duke of York, later James II of England, was one of the directors; his mother also put money into the venture.

Three years later, in 1663, Charles II granted the New World territory that would, in 1729, be divided into North and South Carolina to various Lords Proprietors: Edward Earl of Clarendon, George Duke of Albemarle, William Lord Craven, John Lord Berkeley, Anthony Lord Ashley, Sir George Carteret, Sir William Berkeley, and Sir John Colleton. A new economy began to fall into place. The Company provided slaves and Carolina provided a market, although at first the colony got most of its slaves at one remove, from the West Indies.[6]

The English slave trade burgeoned. Between 1672 and 1689, the Royal African Company is estimated to have transported ninety thousand to a hundred thousand slaves out of Africa. Royal African profits consolidated English financial power in London, the company's home base. The company's insignia was the elephant and castle. All their human merchandise was branded DY, for the Duke of York, or *RAC*, for the company itself. And their gold underwrote the monarchy. Indeed, between 1668 and 1722, the company even provided gold to the English mint. Coins made with this African gold, which were called "guineas," bore an elephant below the image of king or queen.[7]

By the end of the seventeenth century, England led the world in trafficking slaves. This is how the business worked: When a ship set out from England, the owners would draw up a contract with the ship's captain. Next would come letters of instruction. Nervous about their money, owners had to micromanage captains before the ships left England, for they knew that it might be months before they heard from them again. In 1725 a consortium of Bristol shipowners, for example, sent Captain William to Andoni, on the Bight of Biafra, north of the island of Fernando Po, with the following instructions: "So soon as you begin to slave let your knetting be fix'd breast high fore and aft and so keep 'em shackled and hand Bolted fearing their rising or leaping overboard." And once his cargo of human flesh was loaded, the owners sent him across the Atlantic to the island of Nevis to wait for further orders. If he missed his landfall, he was to "make the best of your way to So. Carolina and d'd all the slaves to Mr. Jos. Wragg who shall have directions for the farther proceedings."[8]

Negotiating with local rulers, Europeans gradually acquired land and permanent infrastructure. An account of one such English fort or factory (the name for those establishments where their "factors" purchased people brought in by local slave-traders and stored both goods and slaves) was set down by John Atkins, a Royal Navy surgeon who visited Guinea before 1735. "Within the castle," he notes, "is a smith's shop, a cooperage, store-houses, a chappel, and houses for the officers and servants. The general's lodging communicates with the chappel; a capacious hall, which served to preach and dine in, pray or drink, serve God or debate on Trade; hence they can over-look what the company's servants are doing, and how comply with their respective duties."[9]

Others were headed for less pleasant accommodations: "The Slaves when brought here, have Chains put on, three or four linked together, under the Care of their Gromettas, till opportunity of Sale; and then go at about 15 Pounds a good Slave, allowing the Buyer 40 or 50 per Ct. Advance on his Goods." Atkins also describes the fort's large dungeons, "with an iron grate at the surface to let in light and air on those poor wretches, the slaves, who are chained and confined there till a demand comes. They are all marked with a burning iron upon the right breast, D.Y., Duke of York." Many times, he says, people would be held in these underground chambers for months until a ship came to take them away. The fort's "Negro Servants"—or gromet-tas—kept these dungeons full, continuously trading upriver and inland, paying for slaves with rum, with iron, with textiles, chunks of coral, and barrels of cowrie shells.[10]

Where were all these enslaved people coming from? DNA research may clarify this somewhat in the coming century, but they appear to have come mostly from the West African coastline and interior, with the occasional person dragged from as far away as East Africa or Madagascar and a small number coming from South Africa. Tied or yoked together, they were brought down to the coast by boat or on foot, with overland journeys lasting sometimes months or even years.

An Englishman named Mungo Park, who travelled between 1795 and 1796 with a slave coffle (or caravan) in West Africa, describes some of the hardships of these overland journeys. Park landed at the mouth of the Gambia River in June 1795; by the autumn of 1796, he had reached the town of Kamalia, "northeast of the headwaters of the Gambia." There he arranged with a Muslim slave trader, Karfa Taura, to allow him to accompany Taura and his group of slaves down to the sea. At one point on the journey, a slave collapsed from illness or exhaustion, and his enslaver decided to swap him for a young girl owned by a local. Park notes, "The poor girl was ignorant of her fate until the bundles were all tied up in the morning, and the coffle ready to depart, when, coming with some other young women to see the coffle set out, her master took her by the hand and delivered her." He then goes on to observe, "Never was a face of serenity more suddenly changed into one of the deepest distress; the terror she manifested on having the load put upon her head, and the rope fastened round her neck, and the sorrow with which she bade adieu to her companions, were truly affecting."[11]

Mungo Park eventually reached the coast and sailed on the *Charles-town*, a slave ship bound for South Carolina. He never forgot, however, the nobility of the men and women he travelled with: "During a wearisome peregrination of more than five hundred British miles, exposed to the burning rays of a tropical sun, these poor slaves, amidst their own infinitely greater sufferings would commiserate mine, and frequently, of their own accord, bring water to quench my thirst, and at night collect branches and leaves to prepare me a bed in the Wilderness."

After the slave ships were fully loaded, of course, they set off to the New World, but first it took even further months to fill those holds, slave purchase by slave purchase. Their living cargos, as they were acquired, were confined below decks in a fug of smells, a hell of heat. After being loaded aboard, enslaved people lived without fresh air, light, or space, were often shackled, and endured a severe lack of drinking water or sanitation. Moreover, if wind and weather kept the ship behind schedule once it finally put out to sea, food as well as water often ran out. Disease flourished under these conditions and frequently proved fatal to the ship's crew as well as the slave cargo. While sailors more often died of malaria and yellow fever, slaves were particularly susceptible to dehydration. We've all had the experience of getting into a car that has been left to sit in the summer sun. Imagine, then, confinement in temperatures of between 48° and 54°c—for weeks and months. Kenneth Kiple and Brian Higgins have described what happens: Once a person has lost 10 percent of her body water, acute dehydration develops, marked by severe thirst, muscular fatigue, anorexia, and withdrawal. The tongue swells until one cannot swallow, the eyes sink into the skull, and delirium begins, ending in death. Lack of water on slave ships was exacerbated by the dehydration from sweating, vomiting from seasickness, and dysentery brought on by by the filthy conditions in a slave ship's hold. "As the body progressively loses sodium," Kiple and Higgins note, "muscle cramps characteristically develop along with mental apathy, and vomiting is common. The risk of shock in dehydration is increased enormously with sodium depletion: as the blood pressure plunges, the loss of sodium pulls potassium out of the cells... Potassium loss finally produces heart failure."[12] The bodies of the dead were thrown overboard, particularly when the ship was anchored, as the practice attracted sharks and thereby prevented frantic slaves from flinging themselves into the sea.

Another danger a captain might encounter was a slave mutiny (or even a crew mutiny). Captain Joseph Harrison wrote in 1758 to his ship *Rainbow's* owners: "We arrived here on the 25th inst. in company with Capt. Perkins from Bonny, and Capt. Forde from Angola...I expect to sail from hence for

South Carolina in five days, having on board 225 slaves, all in good health except eight...I have buried all my officers, except my first and third mates and gunner. Having lost since left Liverpool, 25 white people and 44 negroes. The negroes rose on us after we left Mr. Thomas's; they killed my linguister whom I got at Benin, and we then secured them without farther loss."[13]

"These Mutinies," according to slave-ship captain William Snelgrave, "are generally occasioned by the Sailors ill usage of these poor People, when on board the Ship wherein they are transported to our Plantation." Rape was commonplace. Slave-ship captain John Newton—in later life rector of St. Mary Woolnoth in London and composer of the hymn "Amazing Grace"—recorded one aboard his own vessel, *The African,* in 1753: "Wednesday 31st January...Buryed a girl slave (No. 92). In the afternoon while we were off the deck, William Cooney seduced a woman slave down into the room and lay with her brutelike in view of the whole quarter deck, for which I put him in irons. I hope this has been the first affair of the kind on board and I am determined to keep them quiet if possible. If anything happens to the woman I shall impute it to him, for she was big with child. Her number is 83."[14]

William Snelgrave recommended kindness as an antidote to slave mutiny, but this was one seldom employed, with inevitable consequences. In another account, "a Ship belonging to Liverpool coming from the Coast of Africa, with about 350 Slaves on board, and when in Sight of the Island Guadaloupe, the Slaves, as 'tis supposed, being admitted to come upon Deck to air themselves, took an Opportunity on the 28th of May...and kill'd the Master and Mate of the Ship and threw fifteen of the Men overboard, after which they sent the Boat with two white Lads and three or four others to discover what Land it was."[15] All these people wanted was to go home. Thousands attempted it; few ever succeeded. Desperation drove many to take their own lives.

But the slave trade had tragic consequences beyond the obvious horror of its effects on individuals, on African populations, and on African history. One was the transport, using humans as biological containers, of the most serious malaria virus (*Plasmodium falciparum*) to the New World, with the result of hundreds of thousands of deaths. Malaria is still a problem in many Central and South American countries. The slave trade also aided in the adaptation of *Aedes aegypti,* the yellow fever mosquito, to the New World. Michael D'Antonio explains how this happened: "*Ae. aegypti* was spread by the slave trade, and the voyages had a profound effect on its lifestyle. It would lay its eggs in the water cisterns of sailing ships and learned to live almost exclusively on the blood of its human shipmates. By the time *A. aegypti* disembarked in the Americas, it had become virtually domesticated—like the Norway rat or the common American cockroach."[16] The newly adapted mosquito promptly took to spreading disease: devastating epidemics of yellow fever, as well as dengue and dengue hemorrhagic fever.

Furthermore, the Africans who survived the voyage were largely those whose bodies were more adept at retaining salt and thus able to combat the severe dehydration that was such a factor in deaths aboard slave ships. Some sub-Saharan African populations had a natural predilection for retaining salt, and the slave trade saw to it that black populations in the New World retained this ability to hold on to salt to a much greater extent. There is speculation that this may underlie problems of hypertension in New World blacks today.[17]

SLAVERY IN SOUTH CAROLINA

The landscape of the Carolinas is similar enough to West Africa that the colony may not have been the shock to these Africans that Nova Scotia, for example, would be to their South Carolina Loyalist descendants. At first glance, it would have appeared as wilderness, flat for miles inland, warm, buggy, and bordered by the ocean. It had alligators, mosquitos, palmettos, and snakes. True, there were no mangrove swamps, but there were still resonances with the African west coast. The Province of Carolina, in fact, may have seemed a much more strange and exotic place to its first English settlers.

In letters home, the early European arrivals depict Carolina as a paradise of plenty, a riotous *richesse*, "the Air of so serene and excellent a temper, that the Indian natives prolong their days to the Extremity of Old Age." Europeans write of sweet, clean springs of water, navigable rivers and creeks, a temperate climate, and land—land stretching beyond the limits of human imagination. In "odiferous and fragrant Woods, flourishing in perpetual and constant Verdures," could be found great mossy oaks, the long-leaf pines whose trunks were perfect for ships' masts, magnolias, sweet-gums, laurels,

medicinal sassafrases, cedars and myrtles, peach trees and mulberries, wal-
nuts and hickorys, chestnuts and beeches—and, wandering beneath, so many
herds of deer, "that the whole Country seems but one continued Park." Beauty
saturated the senses (and affected the prose of those early reports): a dazzle-
ment of red and green parakeets, the shrill silver singing of cicadas, and, after
dark, "great numbers of Fire Flies, who carry their Lanthorns in their Tails in
dark Nights, flying through the Air, shining like Sparks of Fire, enlightning
it with their Golden Spangles." Wealth was there for the taking. All one had
to do was to domesticate and harvest this new country. Or so said the initial
recruitment propaganda.[18]

The Lords Proprietors, given Carolina as their own little fiefdom by
Charles II in 1663, sent a "first fleet" of colonists out from England and Ireland
in the autumn of 1669, overwintering in Barbados, where further settlers were
recruited, before travelling on to the mainland in the spring. Of all the islands
in the Caribbean, Barbados was the closest port of call from Africa, and slavery
was well-established there. The history and culture of the island helped shape
the future of the Carolinas: Barbados continued to send over a multitude of
new colonists, passing on through them its wholesale dependence on black
labour and its stringent slave laws, as well as its cuisine and architecture, both
well-adapted to a hot climate. Elizabeth Donnan notes that slave labour in
Carolina was "a foregone conclusion from its earliest settlement." Not only
were many of the early settlers from the West Indies "familiar with the potential profits from negro labor" but also "four of the Lords Proprietors [the Earl of
Shaftesbury, the Earl of Craven, Sir George Carteret, and Sir John Collecton]
were members of the Royal African Company. Under these circumstances, it is
hardly surprising that immediate provision for negro labor was made and that
there was here no period of dependence upon indentured service."[19]

Early encounters with Native Americans along the South Carolina coast
went well. Nicholas Carteret, one of those who sailed from Barbados on
February 26, later wrote an account of their experience. They made landfall,
he said, somewhere between Cape Romain and Port Royal. The voyage had
taken seventeen days. As soon as the wind died down, they launched a longboat and sent a few men on shore to confer with local tribes, who seemed
friendly and greeted them in broken Spanish, saying "Bony Conraro Angles"
("Bien encontrado, Inglés," meaning "Well met, Englishmen"). Leaving

Sewee Bay with a local tribal leader, the colonists cruised along the coast looking for a good spot to settle down. This *cacique* (chief) of the Kiowa district, looking for allies, recommended the English choose his territory in which to dwell, and they did so.[20]

The initial settlement was in what is now Old Town Creek on the west bank of a river the English called the Ashley after one of the Lord Proprietors; the site itself was named Albemarle Point after the duke. Disembarking in April, just in time for the season of mosquitos and sandflies, the colonists began clearing land and built a palisade and moat around their initial habitation. After two years of work, however, it became obvious that nine-acre Albemarle Point was too cramped and less defensible than the large peninsula to the east—the land between the Ashley and the harbour formed by the confluence of the Cooper and Wando Rivers, which had more immediate access to the sea. By April 1672, the newly formed colonial grand council was directing its surveyors to chart the twelve thousand acres of land that would become the city of Charlestown.[21] Jean Boyd, a newly arrived Huguenot, wrote home to his sister in 1691, "In truth I had imagined that I would find the town of Charlestown built differently and much larger than it is." He noticed cacti growing in the streets and "crocodiles" up to 22 feet long, as well as such "monstrous poplars that the governor has a canoe of a single tree which is 8 feet wide and 45 feet long."[22]

The year 1690 saw the passing of legislation that actually dealt with the treatment of slaves, as distinct from other people; however, this legislation was separate from the acts that dealt with the city and was aimed more at plantation slavery. For example, slaves were not allowed off an estate without permission. It was read into law that any slave striking a white person would be severely whipped. Second-time offenders were again flogged, their noses slit and their faces burned. A third offense brought death. As the slave population grew, so did these so-called Slave Statutes, law after patchwork law, in an effort to contain and control what the colonists recognized as a threat: the presence of a black majority that had every reason to hate both their situation and their enslavers.[23]

The importation of slaves was rewarded with acreage: larger grants at first, tapering later to smaller ones. Colonists in the first fleet got 150 acres, with an additional 150 added to their grant for each male relative or servant brought in, and 100 acres for adult female relatives or servants or males under sixteen. Indentured servants received 150 acres when their time of service was up. This headright, as it was called, was reduced as the years passed, and by 1692 or 1693, it had stabilized at 50 acres for each person brought in, regardless of gender or situation.[24]

The first slaves recorded as having arrived in the Province of Carolina are a man named John, his wife, Elizabeth, and their son, John Jr., who travelled "in the first ffleet." Their names appear in a warrant for land dated November 23, 1672, made out to Colonel William Sayle's estate. Another Sayle slave, William, imported in September 1670, is listed in the same document. Colony surveryor John Culpepper was allotted 370 acres in December 1672, "for himselfe and Crow a Negro arriveing in ffebruary 1671 and Judith his Wife and one servant namely Alice Thomas, arriveing in December 1671." On December 2, 1672, Mrs. Jane Robinson was awarded 170 acres for herself and her slave Grace, having arrived in February of that year. Captain John Robinson was allowed 200 acres of land for himself and "One Negro namely Yackae arriveing in ffebruary 1671." These seven names—John, John Jr., Elizabeth, William, Crow, Grace, and Yackae—begin the roll call of the enslaved in Carolina.[25]

Slave labour in the Carolinas was fuelled by more than the importation of Africans, though. The English were also enslaving local Native Americans, a practice with a bearing on the lineage of many Black Loyalists. Intermarriage between Africans and Native Americans was common, especially since the Africans imported into the colony at first were largely male, while most of the Natives taken into slavery were women and children (captured men were usually killed).

This local slave trade was itself fuelled by a virus. Cattle herds in eighteenth-century Europe began dying from a devastating plague—probably rinderpest, a single-strand RNA virus in the family *Paramyxoviridae*. It first appeared in Europe in 1710, raged unchecked for four years, and then made periodic comebacks, with a major outbreak in 1750. France, for example, lost half its cattle. English tanners and leather-workers, forbidden to import leather from continental Europe, turned to the New World, fostering a trade in deerskins to supply their needs. The economy of Carolina initially did well by this demand for skins. But just as with the fur trade in more northern colonies, as skins were culled in one area, hunters began encroaching on the territories of other peoples, taking deer and slaves, "each person being traded for a gun."[26]

This second slave trade, however, and the combining of slave populations that resulted, proved helpful to the newcomers. Africans learned the land from their fellow Native American slaves, who taught them how, where, and when to hunt, fish, trap, and otherwise make use of New World animals, as well as what to expect from weather and seasonal change. Native Americans also passed on their knowledge of plants, including where, when, and how to recognize, harvest, prepare, and store different botanicals for use as food as well as for textiles and dyes, tobaccos and medicines.

Moreover, Native American slaves were able to provide the geographical knowledge needed for escape routes. Enslaved blacks began to flee south to Florida—and the Spanish who promised them freedom—early in the colony's history, and it is likely that they first heard of this haven from those Native Americans who shared their captivity. The Spanish gave the escapees land at Fort Mose—"in 1738 the northernmost outpost protecting the capitol of Spanish Florida" as well as the "first free black town in the North American colonies." Interestingly, the captain of the Fort Mose garrison was Francisco Menendez, a West African Mandingo by birth who himself had escaped from the Carolinas, with the aid of the Yamasee Indians. But even before the settlement of Fort Mose, runaway slaves were welcome in Florida. As Deagan and MacMahon note, "King Charles II of Spain sanctioned the policy of granting runaways religious sanctuary in 1693 with a royal proclamation 'giving liberty to all…the men as well as the women…so that by their example and by my liberality others will do the same.'"[27]

By 1698, the black population in Carolina had risen to the point that enslavers were beginning to fear insurrections. The English introduced more legislation to preserve a balance of power in the population, offering land to the Protestant populations of Germany, Switzerland, and the Netherlands, as well as to French Huguenot exiles. African slaves, however, remained the mainstay of the colony; they were, as C. C. Pinckney would say in 1785, "to this country what raw materials were to another."[28]

Disease was one of the factors that convinced the Europeans that they needed a primarily African labour force. The worst killers, ironically, were illnesses they themselves had imported along with their slaves—malaria and yellow fever. Dr. John Lining, living in South Carolina between 1728 and 1761, was the first to record the relative absence of these diseases among those of African descent. Many West Africans were able to fight off malaria due to sickle-cell changes in their hemoglobin. These sicknesses made using Native American or other European labourers impractical: malaria and yellow fever killed them by the thousands. An African-born labour force had a much higher rate of survival than indentured servants brought over from England or Ireland, or than the Native peoples who had no natural immunities to African or European pathogens. "Sub-Saharan Africa became first the primary and then the exclusive source of slave labor for the labor-intensive European colonies in the Americas," writes Elizabeth Donnan, "largely because no alternative source was available."[29]

The conversion of Landgrave Thomas Smith from an employer to an enslaver is a case in point. Smith, second cousin of the Duke of Albemarle, chartered a ship in 1683, and sailed from England for Carolina. He brought with him a number of white servants, as well as his wife, small sons, mother-in-law, brother-in-law and his wife, and a sister-in-law. Smith registered for his land grant in June 1684, but by the autumn, half his family and his entourage, including his wife, were dead in one of the first major outbreaks of malaria in the colony. After Smith had pulled himself together and remarried, he began using slave labour on his plantation at Back River, and in his town house on East Bay Street, Charlestown.[30]

In 1698, the colony began seriously addressing the spread of disease with the establishment of quarantine, passing legislation whereby "vessels were forbidden to pass a point one mile east of Sullivans Island until the pilot had ascertained from the captain whether there were contagious diseases on board." Then, in 1712, laws were passed enforcing an even more severe form of quarantine, as "great numbers of the inhabitants of this Province have been destroyed by malignant, contagious diseases, brought from Africa and other parts of America": a health officer was appointed who visited all vessels before anyone else was allowed on board, ordered masters to send their sick to the pest-house, and held vessels in quarantine for twenty days if anyone on board had died of a contagious disease."[31]

Another reason for employing African slaves was the South Carolina heat, which could be extremely debilitating for Europeans. "During the summer months," comments Alexander Hewatt, writing in 1779, "the climate is so sultry, that no European, without hazard, can endure the fatigues of labouring in the open air."[32] Dr. George Milligen-Johnston describes conditions after a dry spring in 1752, with afternoon temperatures at 37°C in the shade, and 54°C in the sun: "The atmosphere seemed in a glow, as if fires were kindled round us, the air being so thick and smoaky, that the sun appeared as a ball of redhot metal, and Shined very faintly. In breathing, the air felt as if it had passed through a fire, and the nights were as distressing as the days.... Though we lay on thin matresses upon the floor, with all the windows and doors open, we were constantly bathed in Sweat."[33]

The final reason to use slave labour was, of course, money and power. It was cheaper to house and feed slaves than to hire servants, and slaves would then produce little slaves, ad infinitum. Slaves, moreover, couldn't leave or refuse to work, and one could make them do anything one wished. An enslaver's power was absolute, even over life and death. This corrupt couplet of necessity and possibility was irresistible. Even Quakers, who spoke out against slavery in England, were seduced into trying it after a few years in the South Carolina sun. And it *had* to be African slave labour because the Native Americans were disappearing. By 1770, Lieutenant Governor William Bull was writing, "I cannot quit the Indians without mentioning an observation that has often raised my wonder. That in this province, settled in 1670 (since the birth of many a man now alive) then swarming with tribes of Indians, there remains now, except the few Catawba's, nothing of them but their names, within three hundred miles of our coast; no traces of their emigrating or incorporating into other nations, nor any accounting for their extinction by war or pestilence equal to the effect."[34]

An anonymous person complained to a South Carolina newspaper on March 9, 1738, that "negroes may be said to be the Bait proper for catching a Carolina Planter, as certain as Beef to catch a Shark." Local slave traders were ready to provide that bait—men, women, and children—from a very early stage in the colony's history. Samuel and Joseph Wragg were two of the first on record. In 1726, Samuel Wragg became the agent for the Carolina colony in Great Britain. His brother Joseph Wragg stayed in Charlestown, looking after that end of the family business. Wragg was interviewed in May of 1726 by the London Board of Trade, stating he had been slave-trading to South

Carolina for 17 to 18 years, and whereas the colony formerly had but few slaves, in those years their numbers increased to near 40,000.[35]

Some of the first advertisements for cargoes of slaves from Africa and the West Indies in the *South Carolina Gazette* (which began publishing in Charlestown in 1732) include the following:

> *July 15, 1732. To be sold, On Wednesday next, the 19th Instant, by Benjamin Godin and John Guerard, a Parcel of Gold Coast Slaves lately imported from Barbadoes, for Rice, or Currency on Credit till January next.*

> *September 30, 1732. To be Sold on Thursday next, being the 5th of October, by George Austin, for ready Money, a Choice Parcel of Negroes, lately imported in the Ship* Edward, *to be seen on board the said Ship at Eliott's Wharff.*

> *December 6, 1732. To be sold by Benjamin Godin and John Guerard, on Thursday the 22st Instant, a Parcel of Negroes, imported directly from Gambia in the Ship* Molley *Galley, Capt. John Carruthers.*

Charles Hill, Benjamin Godin, John Guerard, Benjamin Savage, George Austin, Henry Laurens, and William Glen were just a few of the many slave traders working in the city of Charlestown in the first half of the eighteenth century. Here is a page from the "Account Book of Austin and Laurens, 1751," listing a single day of sales in the firm of George Austin, and Henry Laurens, whose trading would make them both very wealthy men:

> *4 July 1751   49 Negroes*
> *Thomas Broughton, 6 New Negro Men Payable in Cash; for which we take his Rect. on Acct. and one half per Note dated yesterday Payab. in three Mth.[months]*
> *Thomas Shubrick, 1 Man and 2 Boys Payable in Cash or a Bill of Excha[nge]*

*Willm. Elliott, 2 Men and 4 Boys Payable to us in Cash in a few
days*

Peter David, 1 Man Payable per his note of yesterday at 1 Mo.

*Danl Heyward, 6 Men and 1 Boy payab. ⅓ in Cash and ½ on the
3d October next per his Bond dated yesterday 1740 1 Man per
Bond payable 1st Jany*

*Peter Simmonds (of Santee) 3 Men payable part per an order on
John Watson and remaindr per his Note payab 10th Ins.*

*Doct. John Linning, 2 Men payab. per Bond this date on 1st
November next with Ints. [interest]*

*Isaac Lecesne [Lesesne], 2 Men, ½ Cash ½ per Note payable in one
Month.*

Cash – 1 Man per Mr. Remington

1 ditto per Mr. Izard

Christ[opher] Gadsden, 3 Men per Note paybl.

*Sold as above 44 Men and Boys and 2 Women and remains…3
Men this 4 July.*[36]

Of these ten purchasers, eight—Broughton, Shubrick, Elliott, Heyward, Simmons, Lining, Lesesne, and Izard—as well as seller Henry Laurens, enslaved people who later escaped to Nova Scotia during the American Revolution.

In June 1755, Laurens informed Thomas Mears at Liverpool, "We have very good prospects of Crops this Year both of Rice and Indigo, by our computation shall make at least 500,000 weight of the latter barring accidents. This spirits up our People to give good prices for Slaves, many having planted largely in expectation of buying new Negroes to give them a Lift in their Crops so that a Cargo or two more would just now do extreamly well but our People growl in the Gizard a good deal at paying more than £260, this price they would be contented with which is equal to £37.2.10 Stg [Sterling]." He also wrote to the firm of Smith and Clifton at St. Christophers (St. Kitts, West Indies) in July, telling them that a good market was expected and he'd like to go halves with them in a shipment of "healthy people." War had been declared in London on May 18, 1756, which led to a drop in the purchase of slaves in Charlestown. Laurens was now trying to sell some sick people who had come in from Bance Island: "the Five Slaves that dy'd were all from Bance Island, another lies so very Ill there is very little Hopes of her and Eight more so mauger and sickly that they can't appear in the yard. Several have very bad sore Eyes, Others the Yaws."[37]

The trade continued to be brutal throughout the century, and many slaves arrived in Charlestown ill or maimed. Notices advertising runaways often mention wounds acquired during capture in Africa and transportation to the colony. One of these reads as follows: "Run Away from my plantation at the Horse-Shoe, about the 12th June last, two new negro fellows, bought lately from a cargo of Brailsford & Chapman's...one of them has a wound not quite well on one of his temples, and another occasioned by a shot on one of his buttocks." Other accounts mention Judy with a "Hack Mark on her Neck," and Cloe, who had been bayoneted from behind.[38] Henry Laurens occasionally noted such injuries in his ledgers of incoming cargo (for example, "one Man was maim'd by a shot in his ancle"). But wounds could be mental as well as physical. In 1769, Laurens had a job lot of people penned up in Charlestown awaiting sale. One of them was a very young girl who wanted to die, "poor pining creature," so small and thin that she managed to hang herself with a little vine. Laurens used her suicide, "which shews that her carcase was not very weighty," to complain about the substandard group of slaves his correspondent had foisted on him.[39]

Eventually, even Henry Laurens had had enough of the trade's innate cruelty: "I have been largely concern'd in the African Trade. I quitted the Profits arising from that gainful Branch principally because of many Acts from the Masters and others concern'd toward the wretched Negroes from the Time of purchasing to that of selling them again some of which, altho within my knowledge were uncontrollable." He told John Lewis Gervais in 1774 that it was, in fact, "repugnant to his disposition." Yet in some of his early letters to slave-ship owners, such as Isaac Hobhouse in Bristol, he shows little distaste for the trade, describing certain slave sales as "the most advantageous market," or, worse, as "charming": "We fear your Snow the *Mears* Capt. Allen has misd a most charming market with us."[40]

Laurens may have also been dissuaded from continuing in the trade by the new political climate in Britain's American colonies, which was making the importation of slaves riskier. In September of 1770, Laurens wrote to John Holman, a slave factor who lived on the Isla de Los off the West African coast: "I refer you to Captain Savery [who was carrying this letter to Africa] for an Account of the Restriction laid on the Importation of Slaves into this province, by the Resolution of the people and it is my opinion that the Market will not be open again until April next, and that will depend entirely on the Repeal of certain Acts of Parliament, which we Americans complain of as unjust, oppressive and unconstitutional." Four years later, he was even more emphatic: "I don't like the Complexion of the times, there will be trouble and Confusion in America—Carolina will partake of the Evil. If I was an Owner of African Vessel on this Side I would not trust a Cargo there; if a Merchant there, I would not wish to receive a Cargo."[41]

The Continental Congress, which would become the governing body for thirteen of the original British colonies during the American Revolution, passed the Non-Importation Agreement, as part of its economic boycott of Great Britain, on October 20, 1774. Regarding the slave trade, the delegates stated, "We will neither import nor purchase, any slave imported after the first day of December next; after which time, we will wholly discontinue the slave trade, and will neither be concerned in it ourselves, nor will we hire our vessels, nor sell our commodities or manufactures to those who are concerned in it." Thus, three years before the revolution, America effectively ended the slave trade. It is a shame that they did it for political reasons only: putting a crimp in British trade. It would have been a splendid opportunity to offer a very real liberty and justice to all.[42]

But then, of course, they opened it all up again after the Revolution. Owning slaves was a measure of status, a way of judging worth and power. Ebenezer Hazard sized up the slave-owning class in 1780: "A mixture of vanity and ignorance forms a contemptible character. The country gentlemen are striking instances of this: accustomed to tyrannize from their infancy, they carry with them a disposition to treat all mankind in the same manner they have been used to treat their Negroes. If a man has not as many slaves as they, he is esteemed by them their inferior, even though he vastly exceeds them in every other respect. It is strange that men should value themselves most upon what they ought to be most ashamed of."[43]

Three hundred or more years later, we have forgotten, for the most part, what a huge impact different slave trades had on the economies and cultures of both the Old and New World. West Africa was being mined for slaves, both by its own people and by Europeans. Another slave trade was running from Asia to Central and South America as early as the seventeenth century, according to Charles Mann, with Portuguese slave-ships carrying people from "India, Malaysia, Burma and Sri Lanka," and Chinese junks crammed full of people from Borneo and Vietnam.[44] A third trade mainly serviced Muslim countries around the Mediterranean: these slaves came from North Africa, the Middle East, Eastern Europe, and as a result of North African pirate raids at sea, from as far away as the New World. These pirates were even snatching English people from their coastal villages, and selling them as slaves to fellow Muslims. Slavery was a major driving force in the eighteenth century, yet no traffic was greater than that from West Africa.

Summing up her research on the trade to America during this period, Elizabeth Donnan writes, "At the opening of the eighteenth century the African slave trade was the foundation on which colonial industry and the colonial commerce of European countries rested. It dominated the relations between the countries of Western Europe and their colonies; it was one of the most important factors in the wars of the century; it played a considerable role in the domestic affairs of the nations involved in it." And yet, she notes, its cruelty was eventually to become its downfall: "At the end of the century it saw the development of a humanitarian revolt, which from feeble beginnings grew to power sufficient to convince the world that this traffic was not business but crime, and crime of so intolerable a nature that it must be outlawed by civilization."[45]

The crime of slavery, meanwhile, had created a huge population in South Carolina of the African-born. Not only were they *from* Africa, but they *remembered* Africa, despite thoughts of their white enslavers to the contrary. They remembered their languages, their music, and their stories. They still cooked their favourite dishes, using foods such as okra and eggplant, brought originally from Africa. They passed on to their descendants a distinctively African style of coiled basketry, pottery, and house-styles. (Some of them even remembered elephants. The naturalist Mark Catesby, in Charlestown from 1722 through 1725, had the chance to study several fossil mammoth or mastodon molars found along the Stono River that, he noted, "by the concurring opinion of all the Negroes, all native Africans, that saw them, were the grinders of an Elephant."[46]) They also remembered songs. One of the most beautiful documented survivals of this sort of cultural memory is a Mende funeral song passed down to the present day through the matrilineages of both Mary Moran of Harris Neck, Georgia, and Mariama Suba from Senehun Ngola, Sierra Leone:

> *Ah wakah muh monuh kambay yah lay kwambay*
> *Ah wakah muh monuh kambay yah lay kwan*
> *Hah suh wiligo seeyah yuh bangah lilly*
> *Hah suh wiligo dwellin duh kwan*
> *Hah suh wiligo seeyah yuh kwendieyah*[47]

African-born slaves brought to South Carolina and Georgia were forced to adapt themselves and their cultures to America, and struggle to stay alive and sane. And this importation of Africans did not cease once it was prohibited by law in 1807; it continued long afterwards, through smuggling. Memories of Africa were thus periodically refreshed in the minds of the enslaved. Even though specific family histories might gradually have been forgotten by their descendants, vivid manifestations of African culture still remained to flavour what Carolina and Georgia would become.

Black Loyalists, a mixture of African- and American-born, would bring some of this with them, when they escaped to freedom in Nova Scotia.

Chapter Two

BLACK LIFE IN EIGHTEENTH-CENTURY SOUTH CAROLINA AND GEORGIA

*I*sat beside a dying woman once, at Remley's Point, South Carolina. She liked the sofa in the living room where she could gaze out all night long through her open door. "I lies here," she said, "and dead people come and put their hands on my head." *Dead people come and put their hands on my head:* a really good metaphor for living in the Carolinas. The weight of a past that includes slavery lies heavily upon the landscape, yet there have always been moments of grace and basic goodness. Those who were enslaved here experienced that dichotomy of good and evil. Understanding their lives is possible through autobiographies and oral histories. Other contemporary records—such as correspondence, journals, wills, inventories, and accounts of slave sales—are largely those of enslavers (though some few survive from free blacks), yet they add to our knowledge as well.

Advertisements in South Carolina newspapers for runaway slaves, in particular, have preserved a wealth of information about the origins of enslaved peoples in addition to details about their health, their dress, their trades, their spoken languages, their cultural practices, and their lives as slaves. While by nature brief, these ads are often dense with data. More importantly, they show us *individuals* and their lives at one moment in time.

Here's a typically rich description from one of these ads: "A likely, young, black negro man, named James, and sometimes calls himself James Rivers,

Maryland born, between 22 and 23 years old, 5 feet 7 or 8 inches high, has a high forehead, a pleasant countenance, is very sensible and smart, also very handy about business, his hands and feet are very large, particularly the last, and a little bulging where the hollow part should be, he has a small waist, is remarkable for chewing his tongue when in a hurry about piddling jobs, and wore his beard on his cheek like wiskers, but that and his name he may alter."[1]

And here's a similarly detailed portrait: "Ran away from the Subscriber sometime in July last, a short stout black Wench, named Hannah, known by the Name of Hannah Bullock, well known in Charlestown having followed selling Cakes and other Things in the Market: She had on when she went away, a green Gown, she is pitted with the small Pox, has lost one of her Foreteeth, and walks Pidgeon-toed."[2]

Enslaved people in South Carolina weren't given obituaries in the newspapers, but for those who made a bid for freedom, the runaway-slave advertisements surely serve as their memorials. And as we read eighteenth-century documents like these, including some relating to people who escaped to Nova Scotia, the dead come and share their stories in our minds.

"I AM AN EYE WITNESS TO IT, IT IS NOT WHAT I HAVE HEARD."

Amazingly, three autobiographies—all by Black Loyalist ministers who lived in South Carolina before and during the American Revolution, and who then came to Nova Scotia—as well as an interview recorded with a former South Carolina slave, have survived into the present-day. Boston King's life is the obvious place to start, especially as he alone of the three was actually born into slavery in South Carolina.

"It is by no means an agreeable task to write an account of my life," he begins, "yet my gratitude to Almighty God, who considered my affliction, and looked upon me in my low estate, who delivered me from the hand of the oppressor, and established my goings, impels me to acknowledge his goodness."[3] King was born sometime around 1760 to parents enslaved by a family living on the Ashley River, west of Charlestown. Nowhere in his autobiography does he give the name of his owner, whom he simply calls "my proprietor," but one finds it in the 1783 Book of Negroes: "Boston King, 23, stout fellow. Formerly the property of Richard Waring of Charlestown, South Carolina; left him four years ago."[4]

The Warings had lived in the area for four generations, having bought land at the head of the Ashley River before 1683. There were several Richard Warings living in South Carolina during Boston King's early years. From evidence in his memoir, King seems to have been born on the plantation called Beech Hill, belonging to a Richard Waring who died in 1756 and passed ownership of King's family to his very young son, also named Richard. Examination of Richard Sr.'s inventory suggests that King's parents were named Will and Cate, and that he had a sister named Tenah. The man who inherited them, Richard Waring Jr., was twelve years older than Boston King. He married twice and bought a second property he named Tranquil Hill, where King may also have worked.[5] At sixteen, King was apprenticed to a master carpenter, name unknown, in Charlestown, and it was from this cruel craftsman that he escaped to the British. But listen to the story of his early life in his own words:

> I was born in the Province of South Carolina, 28 miles from Charles-town. My father was stolen away from Africa when he was young....On the Lord's Day he rose very early, and met his family; after which he worked in the field until about three in the afternoon, and then went into the woods and read until sun-set: The slaves being obliged to work on the Lord's Day to procure such things as were not allowed by their masters. He was beloved by his master, and had the charge of the plantation as a driver for many years.
>
> In his old age he was employed as a mill-cutter....To the utmost of his power he endeavoured to make his family happy, and his death was a very great loss to us all. My mother was employed chiefly in attending upon those who were sick, having some knowledge of the virtue of herbs, which she learned from the Indians. She likewise had the care of making the people's clothes, and on these accounts was indulged with many privileges which the rest of the slaves were not.
>
> When I was six years old I waited in the house....In my 9th year I was put to mind the cattle....When 16 years old, I was

*bound apprentice to a trade. After being in the shop about two
years, I had the charge of [the master carpenter's] tools, which
being very good, were often used by the men, if I happened to be
out of the way. When this was the case, or any of them were lost,
or misplaced, [he] beat me severely, striking me upon the head, or
any other part without mercy.*[6]

This is all the detail Boston King gave about his life in South Carolina
before the American Revolution. His father was dead by the time fighting
broke out, and his enslaver, Richard Waring, would die about a year after King
left South Carolina. We will come back to his autobiography again in later
chapters dealing with the war and with the departure of the Black Loyalists
from New York in 1783, for this is one of only four accounts of black life actually recounted by black people themselves, slave or free.

David George, our second autobiographer, was born into slavery about
1743 in Essex County, Virginia. He escaped to South Carolina as a young
man, where he worked for, among others, George Galphin, a deerskin
trader at Silver Bluff on the Savannah River. Eventually, David George and
his wife and children would come to Nova Scotia with a contingent of the
British Army, leaving Charlestown shortly before that city surrendered to the
Americans in 1782. By 1784, the George family had moved from Halifax
to Birchtown, in Shelburne County, Nova Scotia. They emigrated to Sierra
Leone in 1792, where George continued the Baptist ministry he had begun
before the war and then introduced into Nova Scotia's black communities.[7]

David George's early life was painful in the extreme. His parents were
African-born. Renamed John and Judith in slavery, they had eight children:
four boys and four girls. George was put to carding cotton and carrying water
as a child; then he worked in the fields of corn and tobacco. His owner, a
man named James Chappell, flogged his slaves with very little provocation.
George says that his oldest sister, Patty, was whipped until her back was "all
corruption"; his brother Dick was given five hundred lashes for attempting to
escape. He himself was beaten till the blood ran down "over my waistband."
Even his mother, the Chappell's cook, suffered James Chappell's temper. His
greatest grief, David George later wrote, "was to see them whip my mother,
and to hear her, on her knees, begging for mercy."[8]

Mercy was not forthcoming in the Chappell household, so David George determined to run away: "I left the plantation about midnight, walked all night, got into Brunswick county, then over Roanoak river, and soon met with some White traveling people, who helped me on to Pedee river. When I had been at work there two or three weeks, a hue and cry found me out, and the master said to me, there are 30 guineas offered for you, but I will have no hand in it: I would advise you to make your way towards Savannah river."[9] He worked with a white man named John Greene for about two years, but word trickled back to Virginia, and the Chappells came after him.

"Then," he writes, "I ran away up among the Creek Indians. As I travelled from Savannah river, I came to Okemulgee river, near which the Indians observed my track. They can tell the Black people's track from their own, because they are hollow in the midst of their feet, and the Black's feet are flatter than theirs. They followed my track down to the river, where I was making a long raft to cross over with. One of these Indians was a king, called Blue Salt; he could talk a little broken English. He took and carried me away about 17 or 18 miles into the woods to his camp, where they had bear meat, deer meat, turkies, and wild potatoes." All this food must have seemed a feast to David George, used to the standard, sparse cornmeal-and-peas diet of the plantation. "I was his prize," he says, "and lived with him from the Christmas month till April, when he went into his town Augusta, in the Creek nation. I made fences, dug the ground, planted corn, and worked hard; but the people were kind to me."[10] This time, his original owner's son, Samuel Chappell, put in an appearance, reclaiming him from Blue Salt by a payment of trade goods: linen cloth, rum, and a gun. Before he could be taken back to Virginia and beaten half to death, however, George escaped yet again, and went to live with the Natchez Indians, with their "king" Jack.

At this point, fortune smiled upon him, and the Chappells sold him:

> *Mr. Gaulfin, who lived on Savannah river, at Silver Bluff, and who was afterwards my master, traded in these parts among the Indians in deer skins. He had a manager here, whose name was John Miller. Mr. Miller knew king Jack, and agreed with him and S.C. as to the price Mr. Gaulfin was to pay for me. So I came away from king Jack, who gave me into the hands of John Miller.*

Now I mended deer skins, and kept their horses together, that
they might not wander too far and be lost. I used also once a year
to go down with the horses, carrying deer skins, to Mr. Gaulfin's,
at Silver Bluff. The distance, I think, was 400 miles, over five or
six rivers, which we crossed in leather boats. After three years,
when I came down, I told Mr. Gaulfin, that I wished to live with
him at Silver Bluff. He told me I should; so he took me to wait
upon him, and was very kind to me.[11]

George's "Mr. Gaulfin" was George Galphin, a man of Irish descent and sometime Indian Agent, who made his money off the trade in deerskins. Galphin was a bigamist; he had married and left behind a wife in Ireland, then married again in Charlestown, also taking two Native American women as wives, and he had a black mistress. Numerous children resulted, and Galphin had a little school for the white ones at Silver Bluff. These children taught David George to read: "They would give me a lesson, which I tried to learn, and then I would go to them again, and ask them if I was right?"[12]

All his life, David George valued kindness, and Galphin was good to him, but some time later, George found his calling: "I was with him about four years, I think, before I was married. Here I lived a bad life, and had no serious thoughts about my soul; but after my wife was delivered of our first child, a man of my own color, named Cyrus, who came from Charlestown, South Carolina, to Silver Bluff, told me one day in the woods, that if I lived so, I would never see the face of God in Glory." These words worked so on his mind that he came close to a breakdown: "I felt my own plague; and I was so overcome that I could not wait upon my master. I told him I was ill." He wrestled with the spirit, and found, at last, a peace beyond anything he had previously known: "Soon after I heard brother George Liele preach….I knew him ever since he was a boy. I am older than he; I am about fifty. His sermon was very suitable, on 'Come unto me all ye that labour, and are heavy laden, and I will give you rest.' When it was ended, I went to him and told him I was so; that I was weary and heavy laden, and that the grace of God had given me rest."[13]

The Rev. Wait Palmer asked George Galphin's permission to preach to his slaves; Galphin agreed. He baptized David George and others, and formed the little congregation into a church at Silver Bluff. Here, for the first time, George received communion, and was encouraged to preach and exhort: "So I was appointed to the office of an Elder and received instruction from Brother Palmer how to conduct myself. I proceeded in this way till the American war was coming on, when the Ministers were not allowed to come amongst us lest they should furnish us with too much knowledge…[then] I had the whole management, and used to preach among them myself." Grant Gordon, who edited George's narrative, adds in a note, "This gives George the distinction of being the first black Baptist pastor of an all black Baptist congregation in North America."[14]

George's story also (and most importantly) shows that slavery did not always involve stark cruelty——something we now tend to forget. It could encompass, even in one person's lifetime, a range of situations, from vicious masters to kinder ones, who sometimes allowed those enslaved a fair amount of autonomy.

John Marrant, author of our third autobiography, was born free in New York, and his memoir provides a vivid glimpse of life in the free black community in Georgia, where he spent his early childhood; nothing comparable has survived. John Marrant's early life contrasts strongly with David George's in its relative ease. His father died when he was four, and his mother, a strong-minded woman who must have had some money, moved her family from New York to Saint Augustine. Eighteen months later, she took them north to Savannah, Georgia, perhaps to be with her brother, as Marrant speaks of his "uncle's house" in Savannah. He left school at age eleven: he and his married sister then moved to Charlestown, where his mother intended him to apprentice to a trade. Shortly after arriving, Marrant heard music being played for a dance and told his sister that music was what he wanted to learn. His mother actually came to Charlestown to dissuade him, but he was stubborn and she gave the music teacher twenty pounds for eighteen months of lessons; within twelve months, Marrant had taught himself to play both the violin and the French horn and was soon performing for balls and parties. By the time he was thirteen, he writes, he was leading a life of pleasure and dissipation—but all that was to change when he heard the Methodist missionary George Whitefield preach.

"One evening," he recalls, "I was sent for in a very particular manner to go and play for some Gentlemen, which I agreed to do, and was on my way to fulfill my promise; and passing by a large meeting house I saw many lights in it, and crowds of people going in." A friend dared him to go inside and disrupt the meeting by blowing his horn: "I was pushing the people to make room, to get the horn off my shoulder to blow it, just as Mr. Whitefield was naming his text, and looking round, and, as I thought directly upon me, and pointing with his finger, he uttered these words, 'Prepare to meet thy God, O Israel.'" Marrant fainted at this, and was taken to compose himself in the vestry, where Whitefield spoke with him after the service. "Jesus Christ has got thee at last," he said. Marrant managed to stagger home where he collapsed. Days later, a minister visited and prayed with him until something, as with David George, blossomed in his mind: "The Lord was pleased to set my soul at perfect liberty, and being filled with joy I began to praise the Lord immediately; my sorrows were turned into peace, and joy, and love."[15]

John Marrant did nothing but pray and read his Bible after that. The man he worked for came and asked for him; he wouldn't go. His sister asked him to play the violin for her; he refused. Finally, after three weeks, he decided to go back to Savannah. Much consternation ensued when he wept at his mother's dinner table because they did not say the blessing first. Things went from bad to worse with his family. His siblings could not cope with his religious fervour, and finally even his mother had had enough: "I rose one morning very early, to get a little quietness and retirement, I went into the woods, and stayed till eight o'clock in the morning; upon my return I found them all at breakfast; I passed by them, and went upstairs without any interruption; I went upon my knees to the Lord and returned him thanks; then I took up a small pocket Bible and one of Dr. Watt's hymn books, and passing by them went out without one word spoken by any of us."[16]

Now came John Marrant's sojourn in the wilderness of his mind; it took him into the wilderness of Georgia, where he drank water from mud puddles and ate grass, reading the Bible and walking until he collapsed. He was found by a Cherokee hunter, who knew his mother and sisters because he sold skins in Savannah and who told Marrant that he had come some fifty-five miles from home. Many months and adventures later, Marrant finally returned home. His family thought he was an Indian. Who was this odd person? They wanted him to leave. Then his littlest sister came home from school, and recognized him right away: "Thus the dead was brought to life again; thus the lost was found." He concludes the account of his early life by saying, "I remained with my relations till the commencement of the American troubles."[17]

The fourth surviving first-hand account is a very short interview with a former South Carolina slave, conducted in Africa on February 18, 1812, and now part of the Paul Cuffee Papers in the New Bedford Library, Connecticut. It contains a short but shocking depiction of slave punishment in eighteenth-century Carolina. In 1812, Warwick Francis, a Black Loyalist who had emigrated from Nova Scotia to Sierra Leone in 1792, described to Cuffee, a black Quaker ship's captain visiting Sierra Leone, some of his experiences in bondage. He was by then an old man but had lived in South Carolina before the American Revolution afforded him escape with the British Army. According to the Book of Negroes, he had been a slave of Aaron Jellot's, from whom he escaped in 1778; he was listed as twenty-six years old when he left New York for Nova Scotia in 1783.[18]

Francis spoke, in particular, about the suffering undergone by slaves he had known. He once saw his owner, Dr. Aaron Jellot, tie a slave boy "on a wooden spit so near the fire that it Scorch him well and basted with Salt and Water, the same as you would a pigg." Another time, he told Cuffee, he witnessed Jellot take "a pinchers and clap it to a mans tooth the Soundest in his head about one hour and a half and then draw it out, the two persons was his own Slaves"—adding, "I have seen the same A Jelot shoot a man Down the same as You would a Buck. This was about Nine or ten o'clock at night." And that wasn't the end of the cruelty Warwick Francis witnessed in South Carolina:

> I have also seen Joseph Belseford in the same County chain two
> of his slaves and make them Walk on a plank at a mill pond and
> those 2 got drowned and the said Joseph Belseford gave a man
> 360 lashes and then wash him down with Salt and Water and
> after that took brand that he branded his Cattel with & make the
> Brand red hot and put it on his buttocks the same as you would
> brand a creater [creature]. I have seen John Crimshire oversear
> on Barnet Eliot [Barnard Elliott's] estate [give punishment] a
> man whose name is Tom had 300 Lashes and [was] put on the
> pickit with his Left Hand tied to his left toe behind him and his

Right hand to post and his Right foot on the pickets till it worked
through his foot [evidently a form of torture involving an iron
picket fence]. John Draten [Drayton] I have Seen him take his
Slave and put them in a tierce [a barrel] and nailed spikes in the
tierce and Roale down a Steep hill.

The cruelty and punishment of the Slave which I have seen
would not permitt me to make mention but for Lashes 300 or
400 a[nd] to be Washed Down with Salt and Water is but Slite
punishment. Many poor [pregnant] Women which I have Seen
likely to be Deliver the child and oblige to wear a mouth peace [to
prevent them from stealing food and eating it] and Lock out the
Back part of it, the keys the Driver keeps and are obliged to Worke
all Day and at Night put in Clos Houses [confinement cells]. I
have Seen them with a thim [thumb] Screw Screwed till the Blood
gushed out of their Nails. This I have Seen at Isaac MacPersons....
this is what I have said I am an Eye Witness to it, it is not what I
have heard.[19]

I am an Eye Witness to it, it is not what I have heard. This is one of the
very few first-hand testimonies to the darkest side of South Carolina slavery.
Extremes of torture and punishment such as these gruesome particulars that
go way beyond whippings, very few now acknowledge. Testimony by slaves
was not accepted in courts of South Carolina law, but the fact that here we
have an enslaved person speaking about his own experience (and with the
perpetrators *named*), makes it all the more believable—and all the more horrific. It is evidence that power corrupts. And enslaving, as we see in Warwick
Francis's account, can corrupt faster than any other kind of power.

THE RICHARDSON FAMILY

Oral histories—accounts passed down by word of mouth, mother to daughter,
father to son—can shed additional light on black life in eighteenth-century
South Carolina. Robert Weir, writing about slavery in colonial Carolina, dis-
cusses the trauma of the middle passage: "This was survival of the fittest with

a vengeance, and in all probability for every person who lived to become a slave in the New World, there was one who died along the way. That any survived testifies to the resiliency of the human spirit and the physical stamina of these Africans." He then goes on to underline something that I had taken in subconsciously, during my childhood, but which only in the last ten years has come sharply into focus: "That in actuality many survived also suggests that African cultural traditions supported them in the valley of the shadow of death." Weir notes that such traditions, though varied, "were well integrated internally and therefore self-reinforcing, and in all probability, extremely durable. Certainly, later colonial administrators often described Africans as 'this incurably religious people.'"[20]

Oral histories confirm this. The endurance of African culture in the New World was shown me through a friend's memories. Melissha Richardson was born and grew up in a very small, very rural family enclave on Richardson's Corner Lane, near Huger, South Carolina. I interviewed her in 1997 about her family history. Listening to Melissha describe her childhood, I began to have the strangest feeling that, underneath everything she was telling me about her family life in Huger, I was seeing the ghost of a social structure—an African way of life, still strong, still manifesting itself after at least two hundred years of exile. I have included Melissha Richardson's oral history here, with her blessing, as one of the most vivid descriptions I know of what life might have been like for black people in eighteenth and nineteenth-century South Carolina.

Melissha and I were able to trace her ancestors back to Coming Tee Plantation on the Cooper River, where the earliest surviving references to her kin (beginning about 1834) could be found. Her great-great-great-great-great-grandfather, referred to as Old Stephen in plantation records, had a grandson named Brawley; as an older child, Brawley slept in his grandfather's cabin, helping out. A young woman named Binah lived close by. Brawley married Binah, and eventually the two became elders to the Coming Tee community of black people, who stayed on Coming Tee to work for wages after the end of the Civil War in 1865. Brawley became a preacher and, after the war, took the surname Haskell. In old age, he fathered or possibly adopted a son, whom he named Nelson Richardson after a free black minister he admired. Brawley died soon afterwards. This son, Nelson Richardson, born

April 12, 1861, appears on the 1870 census as living with a Thomas and Theresa Manigault. Nelson Richardson's own son, Arthur Ned, later named two of his children Thomas and Theresa (he spelled the latter Teretha), so it is certain that the little boy on the census is their ancestor. Nelson Richardson was Melissha Richardson's great-grandfather: he married Sarah Toomer and died November 12, 1934.

Just as Brawley and Binah Haskell had been the patriarch and matriarch in their community, so too were their grandson, Arthur Ned Richardson, and his wife, Ruth Bryant Richardson. This was an innate social pattern, brought over from Africa and long established in the Carolinas. Henry Laurens noticed this same pattern with Old Cudjo, originally leased from another owner to watch over a group of new Laurens slaves: "I observe he makes larger Crops of Rice and Corn for himself than the most able Young Negroes, which I believe is greatly owing to their Aid for they all Respect and Love him."[21] Arthur Ned and Ruth Richardson were honoured with the same love and respect. "Everybody would call for their advice," Melissha told me. "When somebody was getting married, they knew they had to introduce their fiancé to Arthur Ned and Ruth. If he approved, all would be well with the marriage. Sometime he would pull them aside and say 'better not.' And if they went on and did it anyway, later on they found out 'I should have listened to Bubba Ned.'"[22]

Melissha's grandfather was a minister and preached at the Short Chapel, which his family had helped to build. He was also the community historian. Every Easter Sunday, he would lead the children of Richardson's Corner into the cemetery and tell them about their ancestors. (This tradition is still carried on, and I was invited once to go with them.) These ancestors sometimes came back, reborn as new babies in the family. Arthur Ned and Ruth Richardson's son Thomas died at the age of five; when Melissha's brother Kyle was born, "Granddaddy told us that Thomas's spirit was in Kyle; he could feel it. And Kyle, when he was little, he would just do and say amazing stuff, and my grandfather would say, 'That's Little Thomas come back.'"

Although Arthur Ned Richardson could see spirits, he felt that with the coming of electricity, these had withdrawn somewhat from men's sight. Two of these spirits continued to appear with some regularity, however. The Red Boot Man lived in the swampy pond at the curve of Richardson's Corner

Lane. If one could make it past the curve, he couldn't chase one any farther, but people were afraid of him, especially after dark. There was also a huge tree, covered with moss, just inside the gate of the Richardson property. Melissha's grandfather said that a woman had died and come back to live in that tree. If somebody got sick or had a backache, the Richardsons would take some of moss from that tree and wrap it around the suffering person.

Melissha gave the following portrait of her grandmother, who was known in the community as a weather-prophet:

> *She was a strong woman. Nothing could shake her. She took care of the house and the fields and everybody—the whole neighbourhood. She was the person everybody would ask if it was going to rain, especially if they were planning a wedding. She would go outside, gaze at the sky, and pronounce. And if she said no, it did not rain. She was good with plants and crops, and she just kept everybody in check, even the neighbors. If somebody was getting out of hand, Aunt Ruth was informed. (We called her Mama, but others called her Aunt Ruth.) She would take the person inside and talk to them, and that was the end of any trouble.*

Of her grandparents as a couple, she said,

> *They both just knew how to read people. They could just look at a person, even at first meeting. Especially my grandmother. She could just look at you and know what was needful. If she could help you, I don't care who it was, she would. People from all over would come. My grandfather would go in his closet and give people his clothes, or somebody who wanted to go to church or something and didn't have any, he would just go in his closet. If it was too big, my grandmother would sew it up, if it was too small, she would let it out, they were just giving to people—to everybody, this was how they were. When she'd gather her crops, she'd make sure she sent some to everybody in the neighborhood. Make sure she did that. Generous. Even though they didn't have a lot, what they had was yours if you needed it.*

Ruth Richardson would never eat at a table; she liked to sit in her own chair, and she always ate out of a bowl, not off a plate—a strong African tradition continuing here, confirmed by local archaeology.[23] She went barefoot everywhere, and would sometimes even take off her shoes in church. She liked to do things by herself, working in the fields or fetching wood from the forest and chopping it herself. She could carry huge bundles on her head, straight as an arrow, no hands. And she could *really* cook: "She made the best fried chicken. Everybody on Sunday used to come to our house to eat, the pastor and his wife, other people. Golden fried chicken."

Her husband was very sociable. He rocked the children to sleep and read to them out of the Bible. He loved having people around. Friends and relatives used to come from miles away to sit on his porch at night, with no light except that from the pinestraw burning in an old oil drum, to keep off the mosquitos. If they had a question about local places or people, Arthur Ned Richardson would delve into oral history for an answer. He also had a wide repertoire of tales about Brer Bear and Brer Buzzard, which he used to teach children proper behavior: "He taught us responsibility, how to care for ourselves and other people." His speciality, however, was ghost stories, especially ones in which he himself had seen the ghost. He was so good at these that even the adults would be afraid to go home until daylight.

Both of Melissha's grandparents were recognized as healers in the community. They knew all sorts of cures from locally available plants and animals, even from the very earth itself. When Melissha had an abscessed tooth as a child, her grandparents went into the henhouse, got a fresh-laid egg, scraped the inner lining off the eggshell, and packed it into the cavity, mixed with baking soda. They did that for three days, and the abscess went away. Another time, her grandfather walked several miles to a particular hill to get red clay because she was having terrible pain in her hip joint. He made a poultice of red clay and vinegar for her leg. "The pain was still there," she said, "but I could bear it." Her grandfather told her this was due to the magic of the clay.

When she was eleven, Melissha saw her first spirit: a man smoking a cigarette. Her grandfather told her she had his gift, and when she cried that she didn't want it, he said that people don't need to be afraid of spirits, only of the living. "Spirits will come," he said, "and tell you things, and guide you through your life."

Melissha's grandmother died in 1993, squeezing her daughter Teretha's hand one last time. Melissha's grandfather died in 1996: "The night before he died, we sat up with him all night, singing to him. We did not go to bed all night. Everybody loved Daddy. Everybody....That's all they talk about—Bubba Ned. 'If Bubba Ned was here today,' people would say. I was talking to my cousin yesterday and she was telling me, she said, 'If Bubba Ned was here, he would love my boyfriend,' she was saying. 'I wish he was here to meet my boyfriend.'"[24]

We stopped the interview then, because history had overcome us both.

Chapter Three

PROFILES OF SEVEN
CAROLINIAN BLACK LOYALISTS

*I*t is almost impossible to tell the histories of black persons held in
bondage without consulting their enslavers' personal or business
papers and tracing their family genealogies. Family wills and inventories, as well as newspaper advertisements, were particularly helpful in my
research. Using the resources available, I have assembled profiles of seven
Black Loyalists who escaped from South Carolina to Nova Scotia at the end
of the American Revolution. These profiles include men and women who
came to Nova Scotia as slaves, as persons freed by the war, as indentured servants, and as soldiers in the British Army.

BENJAMIN

Benjamin was still a slave when the ship he boarded in New York, *Friends*,
sailed for Halifax in April 1783. The Book of Negroes describes Benjamin
as a "stout [healthy] fellow," aged twenty-one. He did not provide a surname, and the commissioners did not assign one to him. His owner is listed
in the Book of Negroes as a Mr. William Coulson of Newcastle-upon-Tyne
in Yorkshire, England. All we know about Coulson is that on February 18,
1782, he had been in Charlestown, where he purchased Benjamin from a

widow named Jane Callaghan. From there, the two went to New York, sailing to Nova Scotia at the end of April as part of the first fleet of Loyalists evacuated from the city. Coulson's presence in New York suggests that he was one of the Loyalists or British merchants who left Charlestown prior to or at its surrender to the Americans in December 1782. It is not known whether Coulson intended to settle in Halifax or was merely on his way back to England, though it seems likely that he ultimately took Benjamin with him to England. The Coulson name continues in Yorkshire, but the only evidence for it in the Nova Scotia Archives is a 1795 marriage bond for a Thomas Coulson.[1]

Since I couldn't find any information about Benjamin beyond April 1783, when he was listed in the Book of Negroes, I don't know if he even got to Halifax safely (he may have died en route). My search for him, as a result, had to focus on his early years, using what documentation I could find on his previous owner, Jane Callaghan.

It's always easy to find data on rich men; it's much harder with poor men, and harder still for women of that period. The first name of the "widow Callighan" was not recorded in the Book of Negroes, nor was her surname even entered correctly. Moreover, I didn't know her husband's first name or her maiden name. Her life appeared as though it would be impossible to track, or so I thought, but she was actually the very first person on my list of enslavers about whom I discovered information.

While I was searching the *Royal Gazette* at the South Carolina Historical Society, there she was in an administrator's notice for her husband's estate: "All persons any ways indebted to the estate of John Callaghan, late of Charlestown, saddler, deceased, are desired to pay off their respective accounts....Jane Callaghan, Executrix. Charlestown, May 17, 1781."[2] John Callaghan left all his property to his wife and his two sons, John and George Washington, in a will dated May 5, 1781. He wanted all his estate "justly valued by three lawful good Men in one month, or as soon as possible after my decease, and inventorys thereof recorded in the Secretary's Office of this province," and since he couldn't write his name, he signed with an x. Thus we have not only his will but also an exhaustive inventory, completed on May 15, illuminating the daily life of his slaves.[3]

Callaghan's inventory gives a vivid and detailed look at what it took to run the business on his family property at 167 King Street in Charlestown. Callaghan had a tanyard, a bark mill, a saddlery shop, and a shoemaker's shop. He must have done some of his own blacksmithing because he owned an anvil and tools. The business was profitable, his dwelling was nicely furnished, and he had his own "Compting House" where he did his accounts. His appraisers went through the house, room by room, and then listed his slaves and their valuations.

"In the Shoe makers Shop," the inventory shows 594 pairs of "Negro shoes," together with 33 pairs of "fine shoes," and 9 pairs of "French Shoes." "In the Tanyard" outside were 17 cords of red oak bark, 200 salted hides, 20 calfskins, 4 sides of "white Allum Leather," a cask of tallow, a barrel of salt, and a quantity of wool. At the time of his death, the tanyard vats were filled with 577 hides, 49 calfskins, 253 sheepskins, and 14 deerskins. "A Bark Mill" ground the oak bark used in tanning. "In the Currying Shop" were various currying and carpenters tools. "In the Garden," the appraisers counted 2 iron pots "sett in brick work." The inventory also details the home of the enslavers: dining room, front bedroom, back bedroom upstairs, "back room below," all absolutely crammed with furniture. This, then, was the world Benjamin lived in, before John Callaghan died.

The total value of the Callaghan estate came to £1644.4.2. The enslaved people were listed by name and value in pounds, sometimes with their trade appended.

Jemmy a Cook 15	*Tom, Saddler 50*
Nero a Shoemaker 90	*Will, ditto 45*
Old Prince ditto 20	*Trim, ditto 50*
Cyrus ditto 40	*Lindey, a Wench 7*
Ben 15	*Chloe & her Child*
Hercules, a Tanner 70	*Marian 50*
Thomas, d'o [ditto] 50	*Nancy a House Wench 45*
Jack, ditto 40	*Sarah, a d'o [ditto]*
Lancaster 33	

Jane added to these a tanner named Jack, bought from George Dener on October 24, 1781.[4]

Attached to this inventory is another list: "Amount of Sales of John Callaghan's Estate, which were sold at publick Vendue on February 18th 1782." Almost this whole community of blacks had their lives disrupted. Jane Callaghan kept only Jemmy the cook and Tom the saddler. Lindey's value was so low at the time of inventory that she must have been ill even then; when the inventory was re-certified under American law in 1783, Jane Callaghan noted on it that "Lindey—a Wench, died before the sale." "Hercules, Chloe & Child" went for £56.12.7. Jack and Nancy went for £29.8. Trim sold for £29.8. Will was sold for £49, and Cyrus for £33; Sarah was sold for £42 and Thomas for £46.5.9. Lancaster brought in £35.18.8, Prince brought in £7.12.3, Nero £7.12.3, and James £13.4.4.[5]

Benjamin, or Ben as he is listed in the inventory, was sold to William Coulson for the smallest amount of all: £5.8.9 (or just five pounds, eight shillings, and ninepence). He is not listed in the Book of Negroes as having a particular trade, but the Callaghans would have needed a lot of unskilled labourers, especially in running the tanyard. After her husband died, Jane Callaghan would have begun to consider the sale of her property; she would eventually dispose of the tanyard, and this may have been why she sold her slave Ben, having no further use for him. (Others of her more valuable black people were bought up by a Callaghan family friend or agent, and resold to her later. It was a way for her to gain clear title in her own name.)

So Ben was auctioned off to Coulson, travelled with him to New York, and boarded the *Friends* to Halifax. I have not been able to trace him any further. Ironically, one of the Callaghan slaves *not* sold managed to escape, though he isn't mentioned in the Book of Negroes since he did not go to New York. Tom the saddler, one of Jane's most valuable workers, made a successful run for freedom. On the 9th of September, 1782, Jane Callaghan had bought back from Alexander Barron her four best workmen: Tom, Prince, Nero, and Trim. I suspect, from the low prices she paid, that Barron had purchased them to hold for her.[6] In 1783, when having her husband's inventory re-certified, she noted on it that Tom had fled to the British at Jamaica, and had joined Lord Charles Montagu's regiment there on May 25.

KATY

Katy, a runaway slave employed by the British Army in New York, left for Nova Scotia aboard the ship *Elk* on October 7, 1783. She is recorded in the Book of Negroes as being twenty-two and as having worked in the waggoner's department, perhaps as a cook or laundress. She was just nineteen when she made her escape to the British Army in February 1780, on the eve of the siege of Charlestown. Only a few Black Loyalists sailed on the *Elk*—which was bound not for Halifax but for Port Mouton—and of these, three other young women were also from Charlestown. Isabella, twenty-two, and Molly, twenty-one, had, like Katy, escaped before the siege began; Suky, twenty-one, managed to get away after the city surrendered in May 1780. One imagines that these women knew each other and were friends: they were all about the same age, worked in the same army department, and had similar histories. But because, like Benjamin, they did not give surnames, they have all been impossible to track further.

According to the Book of Negroes, Katy escaped from a "Mr. Lawrence" of Charlestown. I think this was likely Henry Laurens, the wealthy Charlestown planter and slave trader. The Book of Negroes often left out the first names of well-known rebels, and Laurens was certainly one of these—captured at sea by the British while on a diplomatic mission to France, he spent the tail end of the war in the Tower of London, on a charge of treason. His name, moreover, was often spelled Lawrence in documents of the period. The Laurens fonds is the largest known collection of documents belonging to any one person living in eighteenth-century South Carolina. No other slave trader's, no other businessman's, no other colonial Carolinian's surviving papers cover so comprehensively such a long period of time (1747–1792). (An extract I did of his mention of personal slaves alone, as opposed to those he traded, ran to about sixty-eight manuscript pages.) Consequently, his papers, letters, and account books provide a small glimpse into a possible life for Katy, who was very likely his slave.

Henry Laurens made a fortune off the slave trade, brokering slaves from the west coast of Africa and the West Indies in that triangular relationship of English merchants, West African kings and English factors, and New World vendue masters. He inherited slaves and also bought slaves to serve in his house, to work in his business, to labour on his several plantations, and to crew and command his canoes, piraguas, and other boats. In addition, he apprenticed his slaves to various trades and hired them out to other people. Laurens owned slaves all his adult life, and while he could be moved to pity, he could just as easily be moved to rage and irritation. "Chastise them severely but properly & with mercy" was one of his mixed messages to an overseer. In another, he remarks, "She is a sullen Slut but easily kept down if you exert your Authority." He dreamed of one day emancipating all his slaves, yet, in the end, he could never quite bring himself to do it. A single manumission, for a slave named George, son of Old Lucy, is the only one on record. The full inventory of his enslaved people, sadly, has not survived.[7]

As for Katy, she vanishes from history after 1783, either through death or marriage, or perhaps because she left Port Mouton after the fire the next spring destroyed the town. Whatever ensued, she would carry with her the comfort of her Carolina companions, and the knowledge of her own freedom.

JOHN AND PRINCESSA PRINCE

From the Book of Negroes, we know that a man named John boarded the *Clinton* in New York Harbour on July 26, 1783. He is recorded as "John Prime," aged thirty-nine, formerly the property of Valentine Lynn of Ponpon ("Ling, Pond Pond South Carolina"). Either the recorder or a later transcriber of the Book of Negroes list must have misheard or misread his surname. The muster roll of the *Clinton* does not show a John Prime; it does, however, show a John Prince, who disembarked at Annapolis Royal. According to the muster roll, John Prince was accompanied by Princessa Prince. The Book of Negroes lists her merely as "Princessa" (no surname), aged thirty, and also a former slave of Valentine Lynn's ("Lind of Point Pond"). Checking the *Clinton* muster roll against the Book of Negroes list for that same ship, I have found that the muster roll usually spells names more accurately. My money, therefore, would be on John and Princessa Prince—Prince is certainly the name used most consistently in documents in which they are named.[8]

In 1784, the muster roll of Loyalists receiving provisions from the government in Annapolis County listed John Prince and wife as living with other Black Loyalists in Digby, Nova Scotia. They had no children. The Princes probably emigrated to Sierra Leone in 1792, as most of the Annapolis people did; after 1784, I wasn't able to trace them further, so once again I examined their enslaver.[9]

Valentine Lynn or Linn (both spellings are used in surviving documents) was an innkeeper at Jacksonburg, on the Ponpon, as that portion of the South Edisto River was then called. He was not, by any means, a man of inherited wealth or property, and he seems to have started his life modestly, working for other planters. During the 1760s and 1770s, Lynn lived in various places in St. Bartholomew Parish, bounded on the east by the South Edisto River and on the west by the Combahee River, and in St. Paul Parish, which runs east from the South Edisto to the Stono River.[10] On March 25, 1760, Lynn, described at that time as an overseer in St. Bartholomew Parish, wed Mary Monroe. His wife died almost immediately, possibly in childbirth. The very next year, on December 22, he married again, this time to Elizabeth White.[11] Upon his marriage, Lynn bought himself some cloth breeches, a large knife, and a man's saddle and bridle, and he placed several orders for half gallons of rum over the following months. Elizabeth White Lynn ordered some Bohea tea, along with a teakettle and teacups. Valentine had been more accustomed to drinking rum, but his wife obviously had more genteel tastes. Alas, he could not pay off his bill of £147.1.11, and the merchant sued him, thus preserving in the judgment rolls for 1763 some additional insights into the life of John and Princessa Prince's enslaver. This suit was only the beginning of a long series of lawsuits filed against Valentine Lynn for non-payment. Lawsuits, in fact, became the milestones of his life. Records survive from twenty-two of them, and tell us much of what we know of him.[12] Lynn was working as an innkeeper in Jacksonborough by 1769, when he himself sued James Christie for an unpaid tab stretching from 1769 back as far as 1765.[13] Jacksonborough lay on the main "high road" from Charlestown; it crossed the Edisto opposite a four-hundred-acre tract of land granted to John Jackson in 1701, much of it later sold as town lots.[14] Valentine Lynn's slaves at this juncture in his life would have run the ferry service and helped in the inn, cutting and splitting wood, carrying water, doing the cooking and the laundry, killing chickens and plucking them, kneading bread, herding and feeding geese and pigs, raising vegetables, harvesting hay, stuffing mattresses with pinestraw or moss, washing dishes, making beds, bottling beer, serving food and drink, cleaning grates and building fires, or currying horses and mucking out the stables. Perhaps he even let them go fishing and hunt ducks for his table. In return, he or his wife fed and clothed them, doctored them when they were sick, midwifed them in childbirth, buried them when they died, and advertised them when they ran away.

In 1772, a doctor, or apothecary, named Alexander Fitzgerald sued Lynn for £155.10, payment for "Curing the said Valentine his Children, Servants and Attendants of Divers Infirmities." Fitzgerald had paid a visit to the inn in September 1769, "for your man John per your Order, to Emetic for d'o [ditto]," also giving him some paregoric (an opium derivative). This suggests that Valentine Lynn did indeed have a slave named John at Ponpon in 1769.[15]

Eight years later, in 1777, John successfully escaped, followed in 1778 by the woman who was, or would become, his wife, Princessa. They took the last name Prince, and travelled from southern South Carolina or Georgia to New York City. Interestingly, if the Book of Negroes entry is correct, they accomplished this *before* the British Army entered South Carolina in 1779. In other words, the army didn't swing by, sweep them up, and convey them to safety. They freed themselves. One wonders where and how they hid themselves from Valentine Lynn, until reaching some sort of British safety and employment.

One reason John may have chosen September 1777 for his escape is that his enslaver was ill, and could not pursue him. That same month, Joshua Lockwood sued Lynn for £156.17.6, "being for the rent of his house in Jacksonburg," and the writ issued has an addendum which reads, "I have by John Gregg my lawful Deputy Served the within named Defendant…and the said Deputy doth believe that the Said Defendant was very Sick and Could not be brought to Goal [gaol; jail] but with great Danger to his life."[16]

During this time, as evidenced by court records, John and Princessa Prince's owner was still keeping an inn, and a marvelous thumbnail sketch of life there has survived in a record of another sort. In 1778, after the colonies declared their independence from Great Britain and began setting up their own governing infrastructure, Ebenezer Hazard, surveyor of the post roads, made a journey "to investigate and improve postal communications." He kept a journal on this trip—"They have many goats in South Carolina"—and one of his more miserable nights on the road was spent at Valentine Lynn's inn:

13th [February 1778]....Jacksonburgh, which lies upon Pon Pon,
is a small village, the buildings wooden, framed....Lodged at
Linn's, where I had good victuals and drink, but a bad bed. The
sheets were very coarse tow cloth, and the bed full of bugs which
waked me; I laid among them till 12 o'clock, when, finding I could
get no rest, I went down stairs and had another bed made up. Just
as I was going to sleep a sow under my window began to suckle
her pigs; she grunted, they squeeled, and the geese began to cackle,
and I was kept awake till between 1 and 2 o'clock.[17]

One of the ways Valentine Lynn paid off his debts may have been by selling his slaves piecemeal. There is evidence of at least one such transaction.
Jacob Valk was a Charlestown vendue master who often sold black people
at auction. In 1778, he sold a man named Isaac for Lynn, paid off the
sheriff and the debt Lynn owed, took his commission, and then wanted
the balance of the money he had disbursed on Lynn's behalf. Lynn didn't
have it, so Valk sued him for the balance, the interest, and the court costs.
It's possible that John and Princessa Prince fled to avoid being sold away
from each other.[18]

Leaving when they did, they also escaped being sold at his death. By
1781, Valentine Lynn was living in Charlestown under British rule as an "Inn
Keeper." Two weeks after he wrote a will on August 29, he was dead.[19] All his
remaining slaves were auctioned off, and went on to other situations.

It is interesting to note that the very day Ebenezer Hazard left Lynn's
inn, February 14, 1778, he witnessed the recapture of a runaway slave, a scene
that left a deep impression on him:

Saw a Negro man on the road who had run away from his
master: I came up just at the instant that another Negro was
tying him with a hair rope; his young master was sitting by, on
horseback, with a gun in his hand. The poor Negroe's looks, arising
from terrible apprehensions of future punishment, were such as
I think must have affected a savage: his young master appeared
unmoved. Heaven will avenge the cause of the Negroes."[20]

John Prince had run away only the year before Hazard's visit to the inn. He was one of the fortunate few. Heaven had not then avenged the cause of the enslaved, but the war had certainly furthered John Prince's own bid for freedom. Perhaps he was able to return to recover his wife, Princessa, who stated in the Book of Negroes that she escaped Lynn's enslavement in 1778. At any rate, whether he came back for her or whether she managed to run away on her own, they found one another again, and accompanied the British Army (or possibly the navy) out of either South Carolina or Georgia, travelling at some point to New York City, and on to Nova Scotia.

TOM CAIN AND SILLAH BANBURY

Tom Cain is listed in the Book of Negroes as having had a *black* enslaver: John Thomas. When the commissioners were rowed out to register Black Loyalists aboard His Majesty's Armed Transport *L'Abondance*, anchored off New York City in July 1783, Tom told them that he'd been owned by a free black man in Charlestown, and had escaped in 1779. Assuming this was the truth—and there were very good reasons why some people doctored their resumés for the commissioners—he is, according to the Book of Negroes, the only individual from South Carolina listed as enslaved by another black person.[21]

If John Thomas was indeed the real name of Tom Cain's enslaver, he left no paper trail. Who was John Thomas? Here's what I found out about him: nothing. He may have been an artisan, a cooper, a mason, or a blacksmith, with black apprentices as well as slaves. Certainly, a free black population existed in Charlestown well before the American Revolution. The database of the South Carolina Department of Archives and History provides glimpses into the lives of eighteenth-century free blacks, both in Charlestown, where their numbers were comparatively higher, and in the Carolina countryside. These records, however, are analagous to one-line biographies: they show free blacks buying and selling land, or selling their own slaves, but little else. Moreover, no John Thomas appears.[22]

Wills and inventories are another way to search for people. A number of wills of free blacks are registered for Charlestown County—alas, none for John Thomas. A final source I checked was the South Carolina section of the first United States census, conducted after the war's end in 1790, and every ten years since. While many names of free black people appear here, his (at least as "John Thomas") is not among them. Perhaps John Thomas escaped with the British Army or Royal Navy but in such a way that precluded his being included in the Book of Negroes. Or perhaps he died or moved on, changed his name, was entered in the census without a surname, or became re-enslaved—a legal possibility in those days. (For example, a free mulatto man named John McLeach was fined £50 in Charlestown during the war, for harbouring a run-away slave named Silvia, and sentenced to be resold into slavery if he could not pay his debt by a certain date.[23]) Despite the perils and hardships he would undergo emigrating to Nova Scotia and later to Sierra Leone, Tom Cain had at least removed himself from the possibility of legal re-enslavement. In this sense, Tom could have lived out his days in greater security than would his former enslaver, John Thomas, left behind in South Carolina.

Once in Nova Scotia, Tom Cain worked both as a fisherman and a farmer. His wife, Silla Cain, listed as forty in the Book of Negroes and formerly enslaved in Charlestown to a John Ward, had escaped in 1776. On the 1784 Birchtown muster, the names of Silla and her husband follow immediately after a John and Lucy Banbury, also from Charlestown (enslaved by Arthur Middleton), and Silla's name is given as "Sella Banbury." All four had voyaged to Nova Scotia on *L'Abondance*, suggesting that they may have been kin.[24]

In 1791, Tom Cain and wife petitioned to remove to Sierra Leone. He stated at this time that he was fifty, that he had been born in Africa, and that he had served in the army as a pioneer. In the years since 1783, the Cains had acquired a town lot with a house, "improved," as well as a forty-acre lot, "unim-proved." Tom Cain requested to take with them a musket, an axe, two hoes, a saw, and a chest of tools, in addition to two chests of clothes, two barrels of other items, and a bedstead. They were certified as people "of good character."[25]

PATTY SHUBRICK AND HER BABY

Patty Shubrick, aged twenty, came to Nova Scotia neither slave nor free. She was contracted as an indentured servant to Stephen Shakespear. She left New York in April 1783, sailing to Port Roseway (later Shelburne) with another of her employer's servants, Nero McCulloch, twenty-two, who had escaped from a "General Scribbins" (possibly Screven), in Georgia. Whether Stephen Shakespear was aboard is undetermined; he is also shown as having four other indentured black servants (Peter and Judith Johnson and Dinah Edmonds and her small son Thomas) leaving New York on another ship, the *Ann and Elizabeth*, and he may have travelled with them instead.[26]

The Book of Negroes describes Patty (spelling her surname "Shewbrick") as a "likely wench" and as a "mulatto," a term applied to very light-skinned people with some European ancestry, usually either a father or grandfather. She had given birth the previous year, and at time of departure, her unnamed baby boy was ten months old. The name of the baby's father is nowhere recorded; he could have been her fellow servant or her indenturer, or someone else entirely. She had left her enslaver, Thomas Shubrick of Charlestown, five years previously in 1778, when she was fifteen. After boarding the ship in New York harbour, she and the baby vanish from the historical record. She does not appear in the Birchtown muster of the following year, held to determine possible abuses in the distribution of the "King's Provisions," so she hadn't been cast off by her employer and moved to Birchtown. He may have sold her indenture to someone living elsewhere. She may have married, died, or run away.

Thomas Shubrick, Patty's enslaver, himself died at the beginning of the nineteenth century, and the inventory of his estate gives us a glimpse of the enormity of slavery in South Carolina and the huge impersonal business it had become.[27] Shubrick's estate, even after years of war and ruin, was valued at "the Sum of two Million, one hundred three thousand, eight hundreds Pounds Currency." An Englishman by birth, Shubrick had over three hundred people enslaved on his various properties. Patty is the only one of these slaves we know of who managed to escape.

If, as seems likely, she worked at Shubrick's town house, the names of friends, acquaintances, and possible family she left behind when she fled would have included Dye, Will, Moll, Peter, Philander, Ammon, Dick, Attus, Duke, Richmond, Mingo, London, George, Cuff, Bram, Cato, Molly, Castalia, Jemmy, Mary, Phillis, John, Tony, Nancy, Bess, Peter, Statira, Mary, Hannah, William, Sampson, Brewington, and Scipio. The human property, thirty-three souls in all, was appraised at £214,500. This partial inventory, the first of three, appears to be for those serving at the town house, as the remainder of the property inventoried here shows no plantation tools, animals, or much else besides house furnishings, £4000 worth of rum, and a phenomenal £6000 worth of empty bottles ("& sundries") in the storeroom.

Thomas Shubrick's *second* establishment showed on inventory two schooners and three canoes, carpenter's tools and plantation tools, "27 Pictures" valued at £300, and another £350 of books. It included thirty-three more people: Brutus, Peter, Ben, Will, London, July, Simon, Ammon, Billy, Charles, Adam, Bull, Charles Jun'r, Tom, Prince, Dick, Moll, Sue, Kent, Quaco, Bacchus, Nancy, Balthesar, Sally, Sukey, Silvy, Sappho, Charlotte, Nanny, Billey, Billy, Sib, and Quaco. This second group, valued at £231,000, probably lived at Shubrick's country seat on the Cooper River, just outside of what was then the city limits on Charleston Neck.

Shubrick's *third* inventoried establishment, a working rice plantation furnished with eleven rice sieves, two wind fans, cooper's tools, blacksmith's and wheelwright's tools, ten spinning wheels (and fifteen guns valued at £500), was probably his Quenby plantation, further up the Cooper, on its eastern branch. Quenby was a world sufficient unto itself, despite the aftermath of war, and at the time of Shubrick's death, the plantation included 1,200 bushels of potatoes, 1,000 bushels of corn, 1,200 bushels of rough rice, 500 bushels of peas, 15 bushels of white rice, 5 bushels of oats, 18 horses, 64 hogs, 181 head of cattle, 56 sheep, and the people who maintained and ran all this, all of them black, and all of them enslaved. Their only value to their owner was a monetary one, and it was considerable. The 247 humans on Quenby were appraised at £1,976,000. This is almost two million pounds and, even in the local currency of the time, was a fortune. And yet it represented people, real people—so many of them, one wonders if Thomas Shubrick knew even a fraction of their names. Names like Yarrow, Juba, Long Nat, Quash, Quamina, Quaco, Tenah, Siby, Korah, Winter, Epsom, Grog, Israel, Old Dido, Mingo, Monday, Molly, Maryann, and Rose. Hundreds of names, way too many to list completely here.

So many souls are mentioned in the Shubrick inventory that it is almost impossible to grasp the fact that each one of them really lived, got up in the morning, ate rice and peas, collards and cornbread, worked all day, laughed, teased one another, screamed in pain, gave birth, sickened, died, and were buried and mourned by those who shared their world with them. They have all vanished beneath the grass, and except for this one list, their names have vanished with them. Patty Shubrick must have thought of them, missed them, and longed for them at times during her life, however long or short it was—but she would be the only one of this multitude of people to live and die in freedom.

Part
TWO

Chapter Four

PRECURSORS TO WAR AND FREEDOM

hat encouraged the Black Loyalists to escape to the British? The laws of the day gave out severe penalties for running. One of the most shocking yet legal practices found in runaway ads is solicitation for the killing of human beings: murder for money. People of the highest rank in South Carolina society offered rewards for dead slaves. In fact, a colonial governor, Sir Robert Johnson, led the way with this ad in 1734: "Run away from His Excellency the Governor a Negro Man, named Prince, His Excellency's Coachman: Whatever white Man or Negroe shall take him alive or dead shall have five Pounds reward." Of course, taking someone in was easier if he were dead.[1]

Proof of death, of course, was demanded before the reward money would be paid, the usual requirement being to bring in the head of the runaway. Later ads made it more profitable to bring in a runaway slave dead than alive. "Whoever apprehends the said run away, and delivers him to the warden of the work-house, shall have Three Pounds reward, besides all reasonable charges," wrote William Harris in 1752, "but whoever brings his head alone, shall be paid Ten Pounds."[2] The price for murder continued to rise. Three years later, Thomas Smith offered £10 for Frank, alive, but promised £20 for his head. By 1770, William Waight was offering £10 for a man named May, alive, and £100 for his head alone.[3]

Attempts at escapes often proved unsuccessful. Many African-born slaves ran away not knowing where they were or what they ran to; they just wanted out. Usually they were recaptured. After all, they were living in a society that noticed black people out of place almost immediately. And if they tried to flee through the forest, local tribes would often bring them back for reward money. Caesar, who was born in Guinea and spoke little English, tried surviving in the woods with a friend. He lasted two years before stumbling into a Cherokee house, his friend, Jeffrey, having "died in the Woods by eating a Snake" the previous year.[4] In another heroic but doomed escape attempt, four men, newly arrived from Africa and purchased by Governor Sir James Wright, ran from Ogeechee, Georgia, taking a woman with them. A Joseph Weatherly, possibly their overseer, posted the following notice of their doomed attempt to find home: "These people went away with the wench in a small paddling canoe, and put her ashore...she says the other negroes told her they intended to go to look for their own country, and that the boat was not big enough to carry her with them." Weatherly speculated that they would be retaken "either to the southward or northward of Savannah," but they could have also died of hunger or thirst or the workings of the sea long before that happened.[5]

Throughout South Carolina's early history, slaves kept making breaks for freedom but, sadly, with small hope of success. Two developments in the late eighteenth century, however, combined to convince people that they had now had a better chance to escape bondage and journey to a new life. One was the British promise of freedom to slaves during the war that would sweep the American provinces beginning in 1775. The other was the abolitionist movement in Great Britain, with all the attendant publicity and consequent misinterpretation of the 1772 Somersett case. The abolitionist movement laid the groundwork for blacks to believe British promises during the chaos that was to come with war, three years later. Furthermore, with war, chances of successful escape rose exponentially.

THE ABOLITIONIST MOVEMENT IN GREAT BRITAIN

Attitudes toward slavery in Great Britain were polarizing toward the end of the eighteenth century. *London Magazine* published an anonymous letter in

1740 entitled "The African Slave Trade defended: And Corruption the worst of Slaveries." A response to an earlier epistle attacking the trade, it began, "Sir, the Guinea Trade, by the Mistake of some, or Misrepresentation of others, hath been charged with Inhumanity, and a Contradiction to good Morals." Elizabeth Donnan, who reprinted the letter in her 1931 collection of slave-trade materials, says, "This item is scarcely worth preservation for its intrinsic importance, but rather because its appearance is indicative of a changing attitude toward the slave trade."[6]

The arguments of the day are vividly exemplified in the opposing stances taken by Dr. Samuel Johnson and his biographer, James Boswell. In the biography, Boswell records Johnson arguing that slavery could never have been man's natural state. Toward the end of his 1775 pamphlet "Taxation No Tyranny," a response to the demands of the First Continental Congress of America, he asks, "How is it that we hear the loudest yelps for liberty among the drivers of negroes?"[7] Boswell, in an editorial comment refuting Johnson's sentence above, says that he himself, having studied the subject deeply, has determined that slavery is a blessing to the enslaved: "To abolish a *status*, which in all ages GOD has sanctioned, and man has continued, would not only be *robbery* to an innumerable class of our fellow-subjects; but it would be extreme cruelty to the African Savages....To abolish that trade would be to 'shut the gates of mercy on mankind.'"

The slow turn in the tide of opinion against slavery began in Great Britain before the American Revolution. Faint as it was, it still provided hope to slaves in the Old World and the New. In 1772, however, the Somersett case fanned the flames of this hope into a bonfire of determination. Henry Laurens, visiting England shortly before the war, made light of the case in a letter to his brother James in Charlestown: "Westminster, 29th May 1772.... They say Supper is ready, otherwise I was going to tell a long and comical Story, of a Trial between a Mr. Stuart and his Black Man James Somersett, at King's Bench, for Liberty." Laurens had a vested interest in the outcome as he too had brought a slave with him to England, but, as he reassured himself in the same letter, "My man Robert Scipio Laurens says, the Negroes that want to be free here, are Fools."[8]

Yet, as the editors of Laurens's papers note, the Somersett case proved to be "the first victory of the English abolitionist movement led by Granville

Sharp."⁹ It was, in itself, a minor victory. Chief Justice Lord Mansfield weaseled out of answering the question of whether or not slavery was legal or ethical by ruling only on whether Somersett's owner could remove his slave from the country. Slavery was not thereby ended in Britain, but the case was almost instantly mythologized into something that it was not, as F. O. Shyllon points out with this example from a newspaper of the times: "The Middlesex Journal of Tuesday, 23 June, reporting the decision of the Court, told its readers that Lord Mansfield decreed, 'That every slave brought into this country ought to be free, and no master had a right to sell them here.'"¹⁰ The heart believes what it needs to, and this matter was distorted or exaggerated both by its admirers and its detractors.

Attitudes toward slavery were changing in America as well as in Great Britain. The *Nova-Scotia Gazette* of March 24, 1768, reprinted an anonymous letter which had first appeared in the *Boston Chronicle*, advising men never to be to "very zealous in the cause of liberty, till you have in all proper ways, borne testimony against the African slave trade, for it makes us very ridiculous in the eyes of men of just sentiments, to be running a sword into the bowels of our right hand man, and at the same time making a great outcry for being pinched a little on the left." These abolitionist sentiments were not merely an afterthought arising from the struggle to liberate America from Great Britain. As Ellen Gibson Wilson points out, "Before 1750 there had been at least fifteen published attacks in America on black slavery."¹¹

Of course, those on whom these arguments had the greatest effect were the American slaves themselves. Despite the modest outcome of the Somersett case, the news of it seems to have had a real and immediate influence on many enslaved men and women, who acted upon this report—or their understanding of it—by trying for their own freedom. While I did not find direct evidence that enslaved people in South Carolina had read about or been told of the Somersett case, it's likely they knew of it. I did find direct evidence in nearby Virginia. As soon as the news reached North America, knowledge of the case began sweeping through the black communities around Chesapeake Bay.¹²

John Austin Finnie of Surry County, Virginia, advertised two runaways in September 1772 (barely four months after the ruling in the Somersett case), saying, "they will endeavour to get out of the Colony, *particularly to Britain, where they imagine they will be free* (a Notion now too prevalent among the Negroes, greatly to the Vexation and Prejudice of their Masters)"[13] Gabriel Jones of Augusta, Virginia, advertised a man named Bacchus in 1774, saying, "He will probably...attempt to get on Board some Vessel bound for Great Britain, *from the knowledge he has of the late Determination of Somerset's Case*."[14] As war came closer, escapes intensified. Holt's *Virginia Gazette* of August 2, 1775, reported, "This town and neighbourhood have been much disturbed lately with the elopement of their negroes, owning to a mistaken notion which has unhappily spread amongst them, of finding shelter on board the men of war in this harbour."[15]

Black people in South Carolina no doubt would have heard of the British court case in much the same way as did their fellows in Virginia, through reading the newspapers, or by listening to irritated slaveowners complain while passing the port around the dinner table. This was news that demanded to be shared with others, news that would have spread like wildfire. It was news that had a direct bearing on what happened when war began.

THE GATHERING CLOUDS OF WAR

The Seven Years' War (or, as it is called in the United States, the French and Indian War) ended in 1763. Britain had taken Quebec from the French and acquired Florida from the Spanish by treaty. The whole eastern seaboard of North America was now part of the British Empire, but wars are expensive, and the British national debt was enormous. Over the next twelve years, the government's attempts to deal with this debt through taxation of the colonies would lead to yet another war.

On August 24, 1774, from Mount Vernon in Virginia, George Washington put his sentiments and those of his fellow American colonists in writing: "I could wish, I own, that the dispute had been left to posterity to determine, but the crisis is arrived when we must assert our rights, or submit to every imposition, that can be heaped upon us, till custom and use shall make us as tame and abject slaves, as the blacks we rule over with such arbitrary sway." He saw no irony in this juxtaposition at all. White Americans deserved freedom. Black people and Native Americans could continue as their slaves.[16] I often wonder what Washington would have replied had

Thomas Day put this question directly to him: "If there be certain natural and universal rights, as the declarations of your Congress so repeatedly affirm, I wonder how the unfortunate Africans have incurred their forfeiture. Is it the antiquity, or the virtues, or the great qualities of the English Americans, which ... entitle them to rights from which they totally exclude more than a fourth part of the species? Or do you choose to make use of that argument... that they are black, and you white; that you have lank long hair, while their's is short and woolly?"[17]

Despite this contradiction, independence fever continued to rise. "That Americans are intitled to freedom, is incontestible upon every rational principle," Alexander Hamilton stated flatly. "No man in his senses can hesitate in choosing to be free, rather than a slave." He was speaking here of white Americans, although he would later, post-war, extend this view to promote the cause of abolition in New York.[18]

A catalytic event for American independence took place on April 19, 1775. On April 25, the *Essex Gazette* gave the following report: "Last Wednesday, the 19th of April, the Troops of His Britannical Majesty commenced Hostilities upon the People of this Province, attended with Circumstances of Cruelty not less brutal than what our venerable Ancestors received from the vilest Savages of the Wilderness." (Each side would continue to blame the other for starting the conflict.)[19] On May 20, Vice-Admiral Samuel Graves, on board the *Preston*, wrote to the royal governor of Virginia, saying that Boston was now under siege.[20] On June 17, at Breed's Hill (now referred to as the Battle of Bunker Hill), a "bloody Engagement" took place between the Americans and the British. The American insurgents held out against the experienced British Army for about two and a half hours, until their powder was gone and they were fighting with rifle butts and rocks. There was hope, however: George Washington was coming to command the American troops surrounding the city.

At this point, almost all the royal governors were frantically writing the vice-admiral, seeking reinforcements.[21] Lord William Campbell, formerly a lieutenant-governor of Nova Scotia and the man who would be South Carolina's last royal governor, was one of them. After announcing his arrival in Charlestown, he immediately asked the admiral for naval reinforcements, and the next day, wrote General Thomas Gage in Boston as well: "Your

Excellency can hardly conceive a more distress'd & or embarras'd situation than the one I am at present in." Gage replied to him on August 9, saying, "I fear a long and Bloody War between Great Britain and the Colonies, and not unlikely before it finishes some of the Maritime Powers may have possession of some of the Provinces, I wish your Lordship may not at length fall a prey to the Negroes."[22] Sir James Wright of Georgia announced to Lord Dartmouth that he was beginning to feel there was no place in Georgia for a Royal Governor. As tensions mounted, slaves—perceived either as threats or as weapons—were uppermost in the minds of both sides. The North Carolina militia ran Captain John Collett out of Fort Johnston on July 21, saying he had "basely encouraged slaves from their masters, paid and employed them, and declared openly, that he would excite them to an insurrection."[23] Alexander Schaw, sent over to England by Sir James Wright to report on the current situation in Georgia, suggested to Lord Dartmouth that a threat of freedom to slaves would be the most effective device for controlling the rebellious colonists.[24]

The American victory in Boston led to the first evacuation of Loyalists, white and black. On March 17, 1776, George Washington wrote Massachusetts governor Nicholas Cooke, "I have the Pleasure to inform you, that this morning the Ministerial Troops evacuated the Town of Boston, without destroying it, and that we are now in the full possession."[25] The Royal Navy fleet that would transport Bostonian refugees to Nova Scotia also gave passage to a group of free or newly freed people who had done service with the British as pioneers in "the Black Company." Their names have not survived, but they would be the first Black Loyalists to be transported to Nova Scotia. Black slaves were also out on the water. (Captain Francis Hutcheson wrote Major General Frederick Haldiman, "Old Juba is still alive and Embarked with me, between my Man John & I, he does not fare badly.") Not all of these men and women would arrive safely in Nova Scotia, however. The brigantine *Elizabeth* was captured by the Americans en route, and the crew and passengers taken prisoners, "among whom are four Negroes (two men & two women)," wrote Joshua Wentworth, "wch I have Confined in Goal [gaol; jail] here, concluding they may be Esteem'd a part of the prize."[26]

A British officer in the fleet penned the following description of the sea journey from Boston to Halifax Harbour:

My last was from Nantasket Road on our leaving Boston; our voyage hither was the most disagreeable I have ever had, as you may well suppose, when I tell you that we were a month from leaving the Road to our arrival in this harbour, which is one of the finest perhaps in the whole world. The wind was for the most part against us, but the fogs that prevailed on this coast were our greatest hindrance. Sometimes we were just off the Harbour's mouth, when the fogs came on, then immediately about ship and stand to sea, perhaps not able to see the ship's length, so that we were obliged to ring the bell and keep a loud noise, to prevent any of the fleet falling foul of us; at length we got into the Harbour, all except about four sail, who have come in since, and considering every thing, I think it is a miracle we have heard of no loss....I have not yet been ashore, on account of a hurt I received in my leg, when one of the fogs came on, by running foul of one of the guns, for it was so dark, though the middle of the day, that I could hardly see my hand before me. They tell me that the fogs here last two thirds of the year....The people here are glad we are come, and I assure you we are glad as they, having been obliged to keep a good look-out, and row guard every night in Boston Harbour.[27]

The hardships for these Loyalists continued on land. In April, Abigail Adams wrote her husband from Massachusetts, "We have inteligance of the Arrival of some of the Tory Fleet at Halifax that they are much distresst for want of Houses, obliged to give 6 Dollars per month for one Room, provisions scare and dear. Some of them with 6 or 8 children round them sitting upon the Rocks crying, not knowing where to lay their heads."[28] The black people who sailed from Boston to Halifax, whether enslaved, indentured, or free, must have found themselves in even more dire straits. While no list of these first Black Loyalists has been found, we know from city burial records that there were blacks living in Halifax from its founding in 1749 (for example, "Febey [Phoebe] / 5 February 1769 / a mullatto"). Burial records after 1775 most likely include Bostonian blacks, but we can only guess at their histories or what their lives were like in Halifax. Here are some burial records for those who may have been among the first Black Loyalists:[29]

Violet / 16 October 1775 / a negro
Lawlers, William / 1 April 1778 / a negro
Jacobs, M. / 15 November 1778 / negro
Prudence / 10 June 1778 / negro woman
Shaw, Peter / 27 March 1779 / a negro
Pierpont, John / 26 April 1779 / a negro
Unknown / 9 June 1779 / A Negro Woman
Neptune / 26 August 1779 / a negro
Unknown / 10 October 1779 / A negro
Susannah / 14 October 1779 / a negro
Parker, Easter / 8 December 1779 / a negro
Sarah / 20 April 1780 / a negro
Hannah / 2 September 1780 / a negro
Charity / 1 October 1780 / negro
William / 31 October 1780 / a negro

In December 1775, David Hartley rose in the British House of Commons to say goodbye to America: "The fate of America is cast. You may bruise its heel, but you cannot crush its head. It will revive again. The new world is before them. Liberty is theirs."[30] *Liberty is ours as well,* must have thought many people enslaved in North America. Even before the War of American Independence began, a seed had been planted in the minds of black men and women: freedom was obtainable, if one could get to Britain. Of course, once war had been declared, Britain was as close as the nearest Royal Navy vessel, be it a man-of-war of the first rank or merely the tender to one of His Majesty's sloops. Britain was as close as the nearest detachment of British soldiers or the camp of any royal governor. It was as close as Nova Scotia or East Florida, still under British rule. After August 1776, it would become as close as New York, where the British would establish a command that lasted until the signing of the Treaty of Paris in 1783.

"LIBERTY TO SLAVES" IN VIRGINIA

This idea of there being a sanctuary for enslaved people behind British lines was made official in 1775 by John Murray, fourth earl of Dunmore, Virginia's last royal governor. Dunmore, summed up as "a Man who has not one good quality to recommend him,"[31] had previously spent a year as governor of New York, during which time he managed to award himself fifty-one thousand acres of land. When he got to his new post, he still had his eye on the main chance—his royal governorships having given him what might be called some very nice acquisitional opportunities.[32] The earl, for this reason, had a strong vested interest in preserving British rule in North America, but the way he went about it probably drove more Americans into the rebel camp than any other single action in the war: he offered freedom to slaves.

One of the ironies of Dunmore helping to free those who would become the first emancipated Black Loyalists emerges in a letter he wrote to the earl of Hillsborough on May 1, 1772, shortly after taking up his appointment as governor of Virginia. He placed before Hillsborough the fear that the colonists had of their own slaves: "The people of this colony are very anxious for an Act to lay an additional duty upon the importation of slaves in order to restrain the introduction of people, the number of whom already in the colony gives them just cause to apprehend the most dangerous consequences therefrom and therefore makes it necessary that they should fall upon means not only of preventing their increase but also of lessening their number, and the interest of the country would manifestly require the total expulsion of them."[33] In other words, Dunmore was unaffected by the sorrows of those who had first been enslaved, and then demonized; he was concerned only with the "interest of the country" that sought to drive them away in order to make white colonists comfortable and secure. Their plight never really touched him, even during the years of the war when they would become his allies.

This last royal governor of Virginia proceeded to lay out for Hillsborough the dangers to the colony of a slave population whom any enemy might incite to insurrection. The slave population, he noted, was double that of its enslavers; the slaves had no ties of loyalty to their masters and could easily be persuaded, by any foreign power, to rise against them in return for promises of future freedom.

Three years later, faced with rebellion by the same colonists he had, at first, been so eager to protect, Dunmore had already defined the perfect means of retaliation. On November 7, 1775, he declared free any slave or indentured servant who would join the king's standard and fight for Britain. This was the first hard offer of freedom to slaves, and it was an offer in writing. Out of the hundreds of Black Loyalists in Maryland, Delaware, and Virginia who took it in 1775, only some twenty-two are recorded in the Book of Negroes in 1783. A mere eight women, ten men, and four children lived long enough to emigrate. Countless others joined Dunmore, and found their freedom in death.

How had Dunmore, in three short years, come to inciting slave uprisings? In April of 1775, the earl made the fatal mistake of removing the gunpowder from the colony's magazine in Williamsburg and having it carried on board a vessel of the Royal Navy.[34] Dunmore should have remembered his 1772 letter to Hillsborough. The fear of an attack by slaves was very real in the minds of Virginians. Without gunpowder, they were powerless to defend themselves, and the "enemy" was living in their very houses, sleeping only a knife blade away. Never mind that Virginia slaveowners had created this situation themselves, or been born into it. They were afraid, and they acted on their fear, rioting and demanding the return of their gunpowder. Dunmore, fearful, lied to them, saying he had removed the powder to prevent its falling into the hands of black persons. "This did not satisfy them & the fury of the People was still represented to me as uncontroulable & the dreadful consequences of it as not to be averted by any other means than complying with their humour....Two days ago, three gentlemen of principal families in the Country, arrived deputed as they declared, from a body of 2000 armed Men, who were collected in the neighbourhood of Fredericksbourg, about 100 miles, from this place, & who only waited to be informed by these Messengers that I would deliver up the Powder, as they were determined otherwise to proceed to Williamsburg & assault my house, & spare neither me, nor any person adhering to me."[35]

Dunmore told the Virginia magistrates that either they calmed the situation down or he would take steps to see them all destroyed: "That otherwise I shall be forced, & it is my purpose, to arm all my own Negroes, & receive all others that will come to me, whom I shall declare free—That I do enjoin the Magistrates & all others professing to be loyal Subjects, to repair to my assistance, or that I shall consider the whole Country in an actual state of Rebellion, & my self at liberty to annoy it by every possible means, & that I shall not hesitate at reducing their houses to ashes & spreading devastation wherever I can reach."[36] Note how he says he will receive *all* slaves who come to him, not only those enslaved by rebels—a position he would later be forced to qualify. Dunmore and family would end up fleeing to HMS *Fowey*. By August, he was in Norfolk and had commandeered a merchant ship, the *William*, as his floating residence. In addition to his family, servants, and slaves, he brought aboard a company of "Soldiers belong: to the 14th Reg't for the protection of His Excel'cy Ld. Dunmore."[37]

As news about the battles at Lexington and Concord in Massachusetts reached Virginia in late April, the rumors of Dunmore's threat to liberate slaves resulted in an increase in black runaways to the Royal Navy in Chesapeake Bay. Dunmore began staging a series of little raids up the coast, acquiring food and more slaves, before being turned back at Hampton by American militia. Increasingly concerned about matters in Virginia, the earl wrote his now famous proclamation, offering liberty to the slaves of rebels who would join the British cause: "And I do hereby further declare all indented Servants, Negroes, or others, (appertaining to Rebels,) free that are able and willing to bear Arms, they joining His Majesty's Troops as soon as may be, for the more speedily reducing this Colony to a proper Sense of their Duty, to His Majesty's Crown and Dignity."[38]

The American slaveowners' reaction was predictable, as shown by this anonymous letter to a Philadelphia newspaper: "We have just to hand, by express from Virginia, that Dunmore had issued a proclamation, declaring all Negroes and servants free that belonged to men in arms for the defence of their country....Hell itself could not have vomited any thing more black than his design of emancipating our slaves; and unless he is cut off before he is reinforced, we know not how far the contagion may spread."[39] Even some blacks were cynical. "An honest negro (Caesar, the famous barber of York)," reported a local newspaper, "being asked what he thought of lord Dunmore's setting negroes free, said, that he did not know any one foolish enough to believe him, for if he intended to do so, he ought first to set his own free."[40] Nonetheless, black people proceeded to make use of the proclamation for their own ends.

Small raids by Dunmore's collection of loyalists, naval crews, soldiers, and freed blacks continued, enabling more slaves to make their break for freedom. Pinkney's *Virginia Gazette* announced in November, "The tenders which came up to Jamestown the week before last, being hindered by our riflemen from burning the ferryboats at that place, went down the river, and in the night destroyed the boats at Mulberry island, and at Hardy's, on the opposite shore; where there was no notice of their arrival, and consequently no opposition."[41] This night raid on Mulberry Island may have enabled William Wells to escape. He appears in the Book of Negroes as "William Wells, 30, stout fine fellow....Formerly slave to Captain John George Wells, Mulberry Island, Virginia; left him with Lord Dunmore, 1775."

The proclamation, however, did not have the miraculous effect that Dunmore had hoped for. He sent a rather downhearted letter to Dartmouth on December 6, complaining, "Your Lordship may observe that about three thousand have taken the Oath, but of this Number not above three of four hundred at most are in any degree capable of bearing Arms, and the greatest part of these hardly ever [before] made use of the Gun." Despite these limitations, he set to work raising two regiments, "one of White People Called the Queens own Loyal Virginia Regiment, the other of Negroes Called Lord Dunmores Ethiopian Regiment."[42] Dixon and Hunter's *Virginia Gazette* gave the following description of the two new regiments: "Since Lord Dunmore's proclamation made its appearance here, it is said he has recruited his army, in the counties of Princess Anne and Norfolk, to the amount of about 2000 men, including his black regiment, which is thought to be a considerable part, with this inscription on their breasts: 'Liberty to Slaves.'"[43] This inscription echoed, ironically, the wording on the medals worn by their former enslavers: "The Rebels are called Shirtmen from their Uniforms, being a long Shirt down to their Heels, with a Leaden Medal at their Breasts, in the Shape of an old English Shield, on which is inscribed, 'Liberty or Death.'"[44]

This same issue of the *Virginia Gazette* also reported a raid that points to a role being played by Black Loyalists: "Last Wednesday night [28 November] some of Dunmore's bandits, about 12, mostly Negroes, came ashore, and went to the house of Mr. Benjamin Wells, at Mulberry Island; after threatening and abusing him in a most infamous manner, they robbed him of all his most valuable effects, and carried off two Negro women." It is probable that William Wells, the escaped slave mentioned above, had something to do with this raid, as he was from Mulberry Island and had been enslaved there by a Captain John George Wells. It is possible that the two black women taken from Benjamin Wells were, in fact, members of William Wells's family. He may not have been able to take more, due to the small size of the boat he was travelling in. Dunmore and the Royal Navy were using blacks to forage for food, to harass the enemy, and to obtain provisions. They were also making use of intelligence gathered from escaping Black Loyalists: their knowledge of the enemy, the terrain, the waterways, and their familiarity with other black people who, as potential allies, might be encountered at raid sites. The Black Loyalists, however, were equally adept in using the Royal Navy and Dunmore to liberate their families.

Meanwhile, in Halifax, Nova Scotia, a Royal Navy captain who would play an important part in the affairs of Black Loyalists in the Chesapeake Bay and in South Carolina had just arrived from England. After his more adventurous Royal Navy service, Sir Andrew Snape Hamond would become lieutenant-governor of Nova Scotia. (Indeed, the village of Hammonds Plains, Nova Scotia, is named for him, and Lady Hammond Road in Halifax for his wife.) He would also write a memoir about his involvement in the war, which began and ended in Halifax.

> I sailed from England about the Midle of September, and after
> stopping a few days at Guernsey, a week at Fayal (one of the
> Western Islands, which in a great measure recovered me out of a
> dangerous fever), I arrived at Halifax in Nova Scotia, in order
> to land Comodore Arbuthnot (who was appointed commander
> in chief in that Port and Commissioner of the Dock Yard there)
> on the 31st of October. I should from thence have proceeded
> immediately to Boston, but as it was well known that a large body
> of the Rebels had marched into Canada, and a probability that if
> they did not succeed there they might attempt to destroy the Dock
> Yard at Halifax, Mr. Arbuthnot, who had also a Commission to
> command the Ships in the Harbour, thought proper to detain me,
> as well as the Somerset Captain Le cras for the better security of
> the Place; and it was certainly most necessary as at that time there
> were not above 300 Land forces in the Garrison.[45]

Captain Hamond eventually received orders to blockade disaffected provinces from the Delaware River through to Chesapeake Bay. He set sail from Halifax, and on February 9, 1776, he and his ship HMS *Roebuck* sailed into the bay.[46] That same day, the *Roebuck* mustered into the crew seven black men who had made their escape out to her. They were "Dan'l Moore, Negro Slave, Virginia, from the Rebels" and six others who gave no last names: Talbot, Paul, Amos, James, Tom and Sampson. All but Paul were discharged on February 16, to join "Lord Dunmore's Ethiopian Reg't"; Hamond kept Paul on board, rating him an "Ordinary Seaman."[47]

Hamond promptly informed the captains of the *Liverpool*, *Otter*, *Fowey*, and *Kingfisher* that Vice Admiral Graves had put them all under his command. Dunmore came on board the *Roebuck*, and the two men conferred. They were joined a week later by none other than Major General Henry Clinton—a surprise visitor on the *Mercury*, accompanied by his two troop transports, the *Kitty* and the *Glasgow*. Expectations for some sort of action against the Americans must have been high, but Clinton had distressing news for Dunmore. The move against the Americans was to take place in North Carolina, not Virginia. Promising massive support, the North Carolina governor, Josiah Martin, had caught the attention of the British ministries. (The North Carolina Loyalists did rise, but not for long. On February 27, the Americans would destroy that hope in a disastrous "three-minute engagement" at Moore's Creek Bridge.)[48] Clinton thought Dunmore's situation hopeless. Illness, both typhus and smallpox, had begun decimating the earl's followers, with the greatest mortality rate being among the Ethiopian Regiment of escaped slaves.

Toward the end of March, 1776, Hamond left the Chesapeake for his long-postponed duty on the Delaware River. In early May, however, Dunmore, hysterical, begged him to return. He feared an American attack was imminent: "I arrived the next day off Norfolk when I found my Lord Dunmore's expectations of an Attack not the least abated…it was thought most adviseable to move the Fleet immediately."[49] The *Roebuck* and the *Otter*'s logs tell a tale of vessels scuttled and burnt and others run aground, the whole exercise rather like that of a sheepdog attempting to herd chickens. Hamond later wrote, "it was three days before they could all be got down to the road, where they amounted to upwards of 90 Sail."[50] Dunmore's fleet ultimately retreated to Gwynn's Island, where they would be entrenched for several months.

The deposition of American sailor William Barry, whose vessel was captured by one of the *Roebuck*'s tenders, has preserved a moment in June when several escaping Black Loyalists came on board the *Roebuck*, confirming that black people were helping to keep Dunmore's fleet informed and provisioned:

> *On the night there came three Negro men from the shore in a
> canoe, who were shaked hands with, and kindly received and
> entertained by the second Lieutenant and other officers. The
> Lieutenant went into the cabin and informed the Captain. He
> afterwards asked them if there would come more of their people
> on board, that if they did they would be well used. The Negroes
> said there would, he then asked them if there were any shirtmen
> or forces lying nigh. They told him there were none nigher than six
> miles. He then asked them is there were any cattle nigh the shore
> in the main, They said there was plenty; he then asked him if they
> thought there were was danger in landing to get them, they said
> there was no danger. He then asked them if they would get some
> fowls that night for the officers, as they were badly off for some
> on board, they said they could get fowls and sheep. He then told
> them they should be well paid; and, besides, should be free when
> this disturbance was over, which he expected would be very soon,
> and then each of them should have a plantation of the Rebels land.
> After which one of the Negroes went and brought some fowls and
> geese, which this deponent heard making a noise coming up the
> side of the ship; and also brought his wife and two children, and
> another Negro man, of which he had told the Lieutenant before.*[51]

William Barry made his escape that same night or shortly thereafter, slipping through an open gunport into the canoe brought by the black family. He seemed astonished that British officers would actually shake hands with slaves. The *Roebuck*'s muster roll lists him as having "swam away from the ship at Gwins Island" on June 29.[52]

The people with Dunmore on Gwynn's Island may have been experiencing a first taste of freedom, but they were soon in a bad way. Illness spread through the camp, the water was brackish and undrinkable, and many had no other shelter than brush arbors. A few attempts at mass graves were made, but it got to the point where the living were too ill to bury the dead, and the British were reduced to throwing bodies into the water and hoping they would go out on the tide. Then, in a surprise attack at five in the morning on Tuesday, July 9, the Americans drove the British fleet off. Those who were ill were left behind. And so Gwynn's Island, in the verdant month of July, offered up the last act in the tragedy of the Ethiopian Regiment. How proud these people must have been just a few months earlier. They had obtained their freedom. They had their uniforms, and their badges stamped with the words "Liberty to Slaves," so sadly similar to the American badges, "Liberty or Death." For many Black Loyalists, however, Liberty would bring Death, and Gwynn's Island became their last resting place.

Purdie's *Virginia Gazette* gave a graphic account of the scene of desolation the Americans discovered on the island:

> *We found the enemy had evacuated the place with the greatest precipitation, and were struck with horrour at the number of dead bodies, in a state of putrefaction, strewed all the way from their battery to Cherry point, about two miles in length, without a shovelfull of earth upon them; others gasping for life; and some had crawled to the water's edge, who could only make known their distress by beckoning to us. By the small-pox, and other malignant disorders which have raged on board the fleet for many months past, it is clear they have lost, since their arrival at Gwyn's island, near 500 souls. I myself counted 130 graves (or rather holes, loosely covered over with earth) close together, many of them large enough to hold a corporal's guard.*[53]

Abandoned Black Loyalists who survived their typhoid fever or smallpox were re-enslaved, a fate desperately bitter after their brief span of freedom. In a strange twist of fate, the names of some of the slaves who joined the governor are preserved in a parcel of Dunmore's papers that the Americans recovered at Gwynn's Island. On July 20, 1776, Dixon and Hunter's *Virginia Gazette* published a partial muster roll of freed slaves, found among these documents. Very few of these appear, seven years later, in the Book of Negroes.

In later life, Hamond would write calmly about what happened on Gwynn's Island, up to and including the disaster of the American victory.

After the successful American attack, Hamond had been furious. On July 18, he wrote a letter to Dunmore. Hamond was in a temper, and he didn't spare to say what he thought of the whole debacle at Gwynn's Island ("a disgrace"), and the incompetence that he was having to deal with.[54] On July 24, however, just twenty days after the United States published its Declaration of Independence, the master's log of the *Roebuck* has an interesting entry. The vessel had gone up the Potomac River to load up with fresh water when "a Boat Came of[f] with 3 of Genl Washington's Servts." One of these "Servts,'" escaping over the water to the *Roebuck* at five in the morning, may have been Harry, or Henry, who later came to Nova Scotia as "Harry Washington, 43, fine fellow. Formerly the property of General Washington; left him 7 years ago." Perhaps this cheered up Hamond slightly, stealing away one of Washington's slaves.[55]

The Loyalists now divided themselves into those who would go north, and those who would go south. Dunmore and Hamond themselves determined to regroup in New York, convoying there most of their weary band, black or white, on the most seaworthy of the remaining vessels.[56] The captain of the *Roebuck* gave the order to get underway: "Accordingly we set sail from the Capes the 5 day Augt with the *Dunmore*, 5 Sail of Transports, two Vessels laden with Rum sugars & dry goods, and 5 small Tenders & Pilot boats, and arrived off of Sandy Hook the 13th Augt where we joined Sir Peter Parker from the So ward, and saild up to New York in Company."[57] The British retook the city of New York in August 1776, shortly after Dunmore and Hamond arrived, which must have given them both some satisfaction.

Others of the white Loyalists, however, determined to leave Virginia for East Florida; they were largely planters, one supposes, who needed warm climates for the crops they were used to growing. Crammed into fifteen vessels with the slaves that remained to them, these people drifted into St. Augustine weeks later, not knowing that the end of the war would require them to go into exile yet a third time.

In September 1777, an Englishman sailing up the eastern shore of Chesapeake Bay would write, "Scarce a white Person was to be seen, but negroes appeared in great abundance. These live in Huts or Hovels near the Houses of their Owners, and are treated as a better kind of Cattle, being bought or sold, according to Fancy or Interest, having no Property not even in their Wives or Children. Such is the Practice or Sentiment of Americans, while they are bawling about the Rights of *human Nature.*" The Royal Navy ship he travelled with, meanwhile, rescued several of these very people as they attempted to paddle out to the vessel, and carried them off to freedom.[58]

SANCTUARY IN NEW YORK

There have been black people in New York almost from its inception in 1624 as a small Dutch settlement (Nieuw Amsterdam). Both the Dutch and the British began importing Africans early in the history of the colony. Spencer Harrington notes that "in 1664, just before the Dutch ceded Manhattan to the British, enslaved Africans made up about 40 percent of the colony's total population." Moreover, ten years later, "on the eve of the American Revolution, New York City had the largest number of enslaved Africans of any English colonial settlement except Charleston, South Carolina, and it had the highest proportion of slaves to Europeans of any northern settlement."[59] Black people were involved in all aspects of New York's life, and gradually a segment of the population attained freedom and began to prosper.

New York was retaken from the Americans in August 1776, although it required a massive attack by the combined forces of the army and navy to accomplish. In 1775, when the conflict began, the province of New York was still nominally under the control of the British. The last royal governor, William Tryon, arrived on June 25, 1775. His tenure would be extremely short. By October 30, he had withdrawn to the safety of a Royal Navy vessel, HMS *Dutchess of Gordon*, anchored out in the harbour, taking with him the last vestiges of British rule.[60] Three months later, the American army was fully in control of the city. Royal Navy captain Hyde Parker of the *Phoenix* sent word to England that about "Three Thousand" rebel soldiers under General Charles Lee had invaded the city on February 5, unopposed: "Firing upon the Town was judged by the Governor, General Clinton and myself, too Severe a Measure, being Confident that the Majority of the Citizens, particularly those of Property are faithful to the King."[61] The city would be retaken, however, by a combined assault of the British Army and Royal Navy in August of 1776. New York would then remain under British control until the end of November 1783—the longest-lasting British stronghold in independent America, and a sanctuary for Black Loyalists from very early in the war.

All through the war, slaves up and down the east coast of North America escaped to freedom by boarding Royal Navy ships, many of which went up to New York to resupply during the war. Fortunately for history, vessels in the Royal Navy had to account for supplies consumed aboard, and so they kept up-to-date weekly muster rolls of who was on board to eat their barrels of beef and pork and peas. Such muster rolls' final section, "Supernumeraries for Victuals"—the lists of persons carried on board and receiving food supplies but no pay—have, as a result, proved a valuable record for the movements of Black Loyalists. The logbooks of the HMS *Scorpion*, for example, show escapees first coming aboard on March 4, 1776. Under "Negroes borne for Victuals at 2/3 allowance," the *Scorpion*'s muster rolls include the following persons, joining between March 4 and August 20: Abraham, Murphy, Dick (1), Thom (1), John (1), Abberdeen, Gilbert, Goosman, Bobb, Fryday, Quash, Morris, Thom (2), Ben, John (2), Dick (2), Betty, Rose, Claranda, Jacob, James, Arthur, Thom (3), Presence, Cato, Maryann, Peggy (1), Polly, Grace, Dick (3), Queen, Patience, Thomas, Peggy (2), Jeffery, and Joshua.[62]

The *Scorpion* was later joined by Clinton's troop transports, arriving from Boston, New York, and their earlier layover in the Chesapeake. Together, in early 1776, they were lying at anchor in the Cape Fear River, waiting to rendezvous with Sir Peter Parker's naval forces, expected from England and long overdue. Implored by Josiah Martin, royal governor of North Carolina, to put on a show of force to encourage the North Carolina Loyalists to rise and take back the province, the fleet arrived too late. At Moore's Creek on February 27, the Americans defeated the Loyalists in a battle—more of a slaughter—which the National Park Service website of 2006 describes as having "ended British rule in the colony forever."[63]

Late or not, Clinton was, at any rate, aboard the *Mercury* by March 13, and on March 20, he was busy writing to Sir James Wright, royal governor of Georgia: "I had flattered myself from some intelligence I received previous to my arrival at Cape Fear, that I should have found a considerable number of people armed in favor of Government in this Province, but was greatly disappointed to hear that the attempt had been rendered ineffectual by too much precipitation."[64]

While Clinton may not have found the "people armed," he did note the numbers of escaped slaves with the navy, such as the Charlestown pilot Sampson Waldron. In addition to those aboard the *Scorpion*, Black Loyalists had joined other vessels at Cape Fear. On April 20, Clinton informed General William Howe that "Forty or fifty Negroes had also found means to get on board the Shipping in this River previous to my arrival and as I conceived they might be very useful to us for many purposes in these Climates I have determined to form a Company of them with an intention of employing them as Pioneers and on working parties and have given the Command to Lieut. Martin of the Marines with the appointment of Lieutenant to Robt Campbell and the Ensigncy to Thos Oldfield till your pleasure shall be further known."[65]

The full text of Clinton's letter announcing the creation of this pioneer company is as follows:

> *On board the Pallissar Transport, Cape Fear River, ye 10th*
> *May 1776. To George Martin, Esqr. Captain of a Company of*
> *Negroes. Having judged it expedient for His Majestys Service*
> *that the Negroes found on board the Shipping in this River*
> *should be formed into a Company, to be employed upon such*
> *Services as may hereafter be found necessary—You will herewith*
> *receive a Commission bearing date the 2d April appointing you*
> *to the Command of that Company, together with Commissions*
> *for Robert Campbell to be Lieutenant, & Thos. Oldfield Ensign*
> *in the same, and for your instructions and further direction in*
> *the Service committed to your Charge I am to inform you that*
> *previous to the admission of any Negro you are to take care that*
> *the Oath contained in the annexed paper be administered, and*
> *that he be properly attested before a Magistrate—and as an*
> *encouragement to them to demean themselves with diligence &*
> *fidelity in the Service it is my direction that they are acquainted*
> *that they are to be regularly supplied with Provisions and to be*
> *decently clothed, and that they are also to receive such pay as may*
> *be hearafter determined, from which the Expence of Cloathing &*
> *Provision will be deducted—and further that at the expiration*
> *of the present Rebellion that they shall be intitled (as far as*

depends upon me) to their freedom—And from my knowledge
of you I shall rely on you and desire that it may be particularly
recommended to the rest of the Officers to treat these people with
tenderness & humanity. I am &c. H. Clinton.[66]

Clinton's promise of liberty, although qualified by the loophole "as far as depends on me," was the second cornerstone in the emancipation of the Black Loyalists, the first being, of course, Dunmore's Proclamation of November 1775. Until I read the document above, I had never thought of Sir Henry Clinton as a humanitarian or a particularly sensitive person, but the Black Pioneers thought well of him, with good reason. The oath included with this letter was headed "For an an Oath to be administered to the Negroes serving in Capt. Martins Company":

I _____ do swear that I enter freely & voluntarily into
His Majestys Service, and I do enlist myself without the least
compulsion or persuasion into the Negro Company commanded by
Capt. Martin, and that I will demean myself orderly & faithfully,
and will chearfully obey all such directions as I may receive from
my said Captain, or the Officers under his Command, and that I
will continue to serve his Majesty in all such services as I may be
employed in during the present Rebellion in America – so help me
God.[67]

Upon the arrival of Parker's fleet from England, the *Scorpion's* muster roll indicates that the black supernumeraries were, in most cases, discharged. Only five of the thirty-seven people included in the *Scorpion* muster were taken directly on to New York, because these five were useful aboard. Dick, John, Thom #1, Joshua, and Aberdeen were possibly sailors or fishermen; they remained on the *Scorpion* until the ship reached New York months later. Dick was discharged on the day after Christmas in New York, with sixteen shillings and eleven pence worth of clothing ("slop cloaths supplied by Navy"). Thom, John, Joshua, and Aberdeen had received their discharges a month earlier, on November 19. They, too, were supplied with clothing. Eighteen members of the newly formed "Negro Company," male and female, were put to work on the fortifications at Fort Johnson; others accompanied Clinton to South Carolina, and then went with him to New York after the British defeat at Charlestown in June 1776. Fourteen less useful people were dumped on shore and apparently left to fend for themselves. Thus, the muster roll offers a pretty accurate picture of where the vested interests of the British really lay.

Ironically, while it was impossible to track Dick, John, Thom, Joshua, and Aberdeen after they went to New York, I was able to find at least four people who were discharged in North Carolina to work on the fortifications, but who later ended up in New York, probably traveling with Clinton's forces. These were the men mustered as Abraham, Quash, Thom #2, and Murphy. They appear to have stayed together in the same group of pioneers throughout the war, beginning their service in North Carolina in 1776 and going from there to South Carolina and eventually New York, and they can all be identified in the Book of Negroes.

Abraham, mustered March 4 and discharged May 21 to work on the fortifications, is almost certainly "Abraham Lesslie, 31, stout fellow, (B. Pioneers)." Abraham had escaped in 1776 from Richard Quince of Upper Town Creek, North Carolina. He came to New York with other Black Pioneers, and went on to Annapolis Royal, Nova Scotia, on *L'Aigle*. Under "Black Pioneers Settling at Digby," he was mustered again in 1784 as "Ab'm Leslie, Serg't., 1 man, 1 woman, 1 child over ten years, 1 child under ten years."[68]

Quash was owned by Parker Quince, a relative of Abraham Leslie's master, also of Upper Town Creek in North Carolina. Quash almost certainly knew Abraham Leslie. Not only had both of them been enslaved in the same town, to men with the same surname, but Quash reached the *Scorpion* only two days after Abraham was entered on the books. In the Book of Negroes, as on the *Scorpion* muster, Quash lacks a surname: "Quash, 39, ordinary rascal, Black Pioneers. Formerly servant to Parker Quints, Upper Town Creek, North Carolina; left him in 1776." He came to Nova Scotia on the same ship as Abraham Leslie, *L'Aigle*. He is also the Black Pioneer named Quash (no surname), mustered in 1784 at Annapolis with Sergeant Thomas Peters and Sergeant Murphy Steele—and with Abraham Leslie, who had at that time just moved to Digby.[69]

A woman named Polly on board the *Scorpion* is almost certainly in the Book of Negroes as Polly Williams, who escaped in 1776 from "Parker Quince of Cape Fear in North Carolina." This suggests that the Quince people on board may have shared intelligence that led to other Quince slaves being liberated. I think it highly likely that Abraham and Quash and Polly wanted to free relatives left behind in slavery, and either proposed a raid, or gave information about the Quince holdings which convinced the navy that it would be profitable to attempt one. Purdie's *Virginia Gazette* of April 5, 1776, reports that "Capt. Collett, in the *General Gage* armed vessel (some time commander of fort Johnston, and well known to be a pert audacious little scoundrel) has lately committed divers acts of piracy and robbery....The town of Brunswick is totally deserted, and the enemy frequently land in small parties, to pillage and carry off negroes....Mr Quince had 18 slaves lately stolen from him."

The second Thom (Thom #2) entered on *Scorpion*'s muster roll on March 7, and discharged May 21 "on Service No. Carolina, per Order of S P Parker," is almost certainly the famous Sergeant Thomas Peters of the Black Pioneers, who appears in the Book of Negroes as "Thomas Potters [other copies show "Petters"], ordinary fellow, Black Pioneers. Formerly slave to William Campbell, Wilmington, North Carolina; left him in 1776." The year of escape is right, and this Thom was certainly a Black Pioneer from North Carolina. He had been sworn into the "Negro Company" under Captain George Martin of the Queen's Rangers by a New York City alderman named William Waddell on November 14, 1776. He rose to the rank of sergeant.[70] Sergeant Peters eventually got to Nova Scotia along with Murphy Steele, though their ship, the *Joseph*, was caught by a winter storm just as it was entering the Bay of Fundy and blown back out to sea. The storm winds then blew them clear to Bermuda. They overwintered there along with the rest of the ship's company, and the *Joseph* limped into Nova Scotia in the spring. Under "Black Pioneers arrived in the Ship *Joseph*, intend to Settle at Digby," he is listed on the Annapolis Royal muster roll of 1784 as "Serg't Peters, 1 man, 1 woman, 1 child under ten years." Years later, he would travel to England to beseech aid for the Black Loyalists, an appeal that would result in the British offer to resettle people in Sierra Leone.[71]

Murphy, mustered on the *Scorpion* March 4 and discharged May 21 to work as a pioneer, almost certainly appears in the Book of Negroes as "Murphy Steele, 34, ordinary fellow. (Black Pioneers). Formerly slave to Stephen Daniel, Wilmington, North Carolina; left him in 1776." No other man in the Book of Negroes appears with that first name, and the year, place of escape, and occupation also match. Murphy Steele lived in New York for several years before the evacuation of the British in November 1783. He and his wife, Mary, then settled in Nova Scotia, appearing on the 1784 muster of "Black Pioneers living at Annapolis" as "Sergeant Steele," with a wife and a child under ten years of age. Mary Steele was born in 1759, enslaved to Charles Cannon of Portsmouth, Virginia; she escaped in 1778 and worked with the Black Pioneers as well.[72]

While in New York, Murphy and Mary lived in the Pioneer barracks on Water Street, where Murphy experienced a vision from God, a vision so overwhelming that he felt compelled to report it to Clinton. Someone, probably at the desire of Sir Henry, wrote it down. It is a fascinating account, given here in full:

> *August 16th 1781. Murphy Stiel of the Black Pioneers Says, That about a fortnight ago at Noon, when he was in the Barracks of the Company in Water Street, he heard a voice like a Man's (but saw no body) which called him by his name, and desired him to go and tell The Commander in Chief, Sir Henry Clinton, to send word to Genl. Washington That he must Surrender himself and his Troops to the King's Army, and that if he did not the wrath of God would fall upon them. That if General Washington did not Surrender, The Commr in Chief was then to tell him, that he would raise all the Blacks in America to fight against him. The Voice also said that King George must be acquainted with the above. That the same Voice repeated the aforesaid Message to him several times afterwards and three days ago in Queen Street insisted that he should tell it to Sir Henry Clinton, upon which he answered that he was afraid to do it, as he did not see the Person that spoke. That the Voice then said that he must tell it, that he was not to see him for that he was the Lord, and that he must acquaint Sir Henry Clinton that it was the Lord that spoke this; and to tell Sir Henry also, that he and Lord Cornwallis was to put an end to this Rebellion, for that the Lord would be on their side.[73]*

There were other barracks for Black Loyalists working with the army besides the Water Street establishment where Murphy Steele had his vision. Ellen Gibson Wilson notes that "at least four were established in New York, at 18 Great George Street, 8 Skinner Street, 36 St. James Street and 10 Church Street....They were crowded: Sixty-four laborers shared one set of five and a half rooms, seventy-eight others had six and a half rooms, and thirty-seven Black Pioneers lived in three and a half rooms. The ration was one lamp and pint of oil or one pound of candles per room per week."[74]

One such barracks was set up in Brooklyn for the men and women in the waggoners' department. A brief glimpse into life there comes to us through the records of an inquest. On October 20, 1783, Brooklyn jurors were called to view the body of Jenny, wife to a black man named Andrew, a driver in the "Waggon Department." No marks of violence were found on the body "excepting a very slight wound on her head." Diana, a black woman, "wife to Isaac a Black Man & Driver in the Waggon Department at Brooklyn," gave testimony, saying that she had been at the "Negro Barracks" during the morning of October 18. "Sundry Black people were there, and amongst them was Andrew, a Waggon driver & Jenny his wife, an Indian Woman that the said Jenny being much intoxicated with Liquor, a difference arose between the said Jenny & her husband Andrew, that the said Andrew struck his wife over the Head with the Butt end of a whip he then held in his hand, that Jenny's head blead very much, that Andrew immediately went out of the Barrack & did not return untill dinnertime, that in the afternoon Jenny left the Barrack much intoxicated."

John Leith, the assistant surgeon of the hospital, later testified that the cause of Jenny's death was not the blow to her head; she had frozen to death. Diana reported that Andrew "remained in the Barrack from the time he came in about Noon on the Eighteenth Instant till the next morning when he went out to work, that he returned about breakfast time when he was informed of the death of his wife at which he appeared to be much affected & immediately went out of the Barrack to go to the place where his Deceased wife was lying." Through her account, we see that meals were eaten in the barracks, that work began early, even before breakfast time, and that people worked of necessity on Sundays.[75]

A final reference to barrack life can be found in the testimony of Samuel Burke, a Black Loyalist who described under oath in London on September

13, 1784, his services during the war. Burke had been born in Charlestown, South Carolina, and christened in Ireland. In 1779, he worked as a servant to Lieutenant-Colonel Thomas Brown, superintendent for the Creek (Muscogee) and Cherokee. Burke had borne arms in the war and was twice wounded ("Swears that he killed at least ten Men at the Hanging Rock"). He had remained with the army and come to England with the troops, but in all this time had never received a salary. During his army service, he was stationed in New York, where he married a "Dutch Mulatto Woman." His wife owned a small house and garden that she had inherited from her former husband. "This was in Dutch Street No. 5," said Samuel Burke. "This was used as a Barrack House." Whether it was a barracks for Black Loyalists is not specified, but it seems likely.[76]

Throughout the war, the British military brought slaves to New York, either as freed Black Loyalists or as booty. In January 1782, John Peebles, a Scots grenadier, tried to sell Ned, an eleven-year-old child he'd "picked up" on James Island, South Carolina, for use as a regimental fifer. He offered Ned to George Duncan Ludlow, superintendent of police on Long Island, New York. According to the twentieth-century editor of Peebles's diary, "Ludlow refused to buy Ned because he had 'the Itch.'"[77] So Peebles decided to indenture Ned to himself. He had David Colden, assistant superintendent of police, do the paperwork. This document, now in the National Archives of Scotland, is the only record of a Black Loyalist indenture to have survived. It did "put place and bind a Negro Boy called Ned of the age of eleven years lately from the province of South Carolina (whose former master is without the British Lines) as a Servant to Capt. John Peebles late of the 42d Regiment of foot and his assigns (the said Negro Boy consenting and agreeing before the said Superintendent & his assistant to the same) to dwell and serve from the day of the date of these presents until the said Negro Boy shall arrive to the full age of twenty one years." Peebles promised to have Ned taught to read and write, and to provide him with "Meat Drink Washing Lodging and apparal and all other necessaries in sickness and in health," and to give him a new suit of clothes when his indentureship was up.[78]

The depositions of two women, recorded in 1791 in Shelburne, Nova Scotia, shed additional light on what life was like for Black Loyalists in New York. These depositions are the only extant descriptions of exactly how individual Black Loyalists, other than Boston King or David George, made it from slavery to New York. They are also the only recorded reflections of female Black Loyalists, other than Mary Postell's (discussed below). Kate Fortune and Lydia Carey were asked to testify as to the identity of a boy named Thomas George, formerly known as Stephen George, whose parents they both swore had served the British in New York.

Kate Fortune, the first of the two women to testify, came to New York from Virginia in the British transport ship *Peggy*; she was born near Portsmouth, Virginia, and had lived nowhere else before the arrival of a British fleet and army. She was brought in to a British fort at Portsmouth. Samuel and Patience George and their children, whom she had known previously, were taken at the same time. Kate and her husband, John, went on to New York, where he was employed in the Royal Artillery for three dollars a month. She stated that Samuel George, who was working for the army at Lloyd's Neck, often visited them.

After Kate Fortune signed with her mark, the justices swore in Lydia Carey. Lydia was another Portsmouth woman who came to New York in the same British ship as Samuel George, his wife, and two of his children—Isaac and Stephen, now called Thomas. His parents, she stated, lived at Lloyd's Neck. She was there in the room when Patience died, and saw Samuel die two days later, "in the Service of the King of Great Britain under the direction of a Sargent Moore."[79]

The men and women of the Pioneers and other Black Loyalists helped to swell the black population of New York, which by August 1773, according to a "city and county" census, included 1,085 women, 559 girls under sixteen, 42 men over sixty, 890 men under sixty, and 568 boys under sixteen. British Major General Mathew would bring more Black Loyalists to the city when he returned from an expedition to Virginia in the spring of 1779, and the 1781 Chesapeake venture of Generals William Phillips and Benedict Arnold would drive up these numbers even further.[80] Finally, the evacuations of Charlestown and Savannah in 1782 would once again increase the size of the Black Loyalist community.

After retaking New York, Britain once more turned its gaze south. Captain Hamond was instructed to return to the Delaware and the Chesapeake to blockade the coast. Throughout the next two years, *Roebuck* and the other vessels under her command—including the *Camilla*, the *Falcon*, the *Pearl*, and the *Perseus*—would cruise up and down the east coast of North America, capturing American ships, picking up "refugees for protection," and providing the means of escape for still further Black Loyalists.

Captain George Keith Elphinstone of the *Perseus* was particularly meticulous, and records much greater detail about each day of sailing than almost any other captain whose logs I have read. On Saturday, September 7, he notes that he "made sail up the bay, at 11 Tacked to pick up a Canoe with Negroes who had deserted their Masters, at noon Running up the Bay, in company with a Schooner, Tender to the *Roebuck*."[81] Elphinstone spent a great deal of the first years of the war blockading the city of Charlestown, and chasing vessels up and down the coasts to the north and south of the city. (Once, twenty-six leagues from the Charlestown lighthouse, he even had a sort of one-sided gun-battle with a waterspout that was chasing *him*.) Being so careful about his own charting and his logs, he must have also thought long and hard about Clinton's failure to support the Royal Navy in its attack on Charlestown's Fort Sullivan (discussed in the next chapter), due to lack of accurate soundings of the inlet between Sullivan's Island and Long Island.[82]

Although Hamond could not have known this, his decision to send Elphinstone to cruise on and off the Charlestown bar would reap benefits when the time came to lay siege to that city. When that definitive moment finally arrived, the *Perseus* would be there, and so would the *Roebuck*, with Hamond once more in the thick of things, perhaps with some of his Black Loyalist seamen still aboard.

Now, however, we must return to South Carolina and Georgia in 1775, and trace the course of the war in the southernmost provinces through the five years that followed.

Chapter Five

WAR IN SOUTH CAROLINA AND GEORGIA, 1775–1780

*S*outh Carolina not only had the largest slave population of any province in continental North America, but would also suffer the highest number of battles and conflicts during the Revolution—offering this huge slave population, as a result, almost endless possibilities of slipping away. At the war's beginning, Georgia was little more than an adjunct, an outlying suburb, to South Carolina. It was largely still forested and very thinly populated, with the majority of its settlements clustered along the Savannah River. South Carolina lay just across this same river, on its eastern bank. Indeed, many of Georgia's plantations were owned by Carolinians—Henry Laurens, for one—who furnished them with Carolinian slaves. This new phase of the war would bring freedom to many of them as well.

The growing enmity between Loyalists and their Rebel neighbours during the conflict would lead to seven years of civil war in South Carolina and Georgia—a complete breakdown of law in some places, ranging from isolated raids and individual murders to more than two hundred skirmishes and battles fought, and a devastation of land and lives unmatched in any other province. Everyone suffered, and no one more so than slaves—but at the same time, many black people escaped in the chaos. Eight hundred or more of these freed people would settle, eventually, in Nova Scotia. This chapter explores how that happened.

1775

To begin with, for much of 1775, South Carolina and Georgia were busily preparing to defend their liberties *and* keep down their slaves. Their slaves, on the other hand, were dreaming of escape. Joshua Eden posted that his slave Limus had fled, "for though he is my Property, he has the audacity to tell me 'he will be free, that he will serve no Man, and that he will be conquered or governed by no Man.'"[1] The American sons of liberty loved that sort of rhetoric for themselves; they just didn't care for it in the mouths of their slaves.

News of war came from Boston in April. "Last Wednesday, the 19th of April, the Troops of His Britannical Majesty commenced Hostilities upon the People," Alexander Innes wrote to Lord Dartmouth on May 16, 1775. Most disturbing to the Carolina colony, he said, was the news of the British promise "to grant freedom to such Slaves as should desert their Masters and join the King's troops."[2] Many black men and women would take this promise as Gospel.

On July 7, the *South Carolina and American General Gazette* reported that "Tuesday last his Majesty's sloop *Scorpion*, commanded by Hon. Capt. Tollemache, sailed for Boston, now under siege by the Americans." This is the same vessel that John Marrant would sail with after being pressed into service (the naval term for grabbing people, regardless of colour, on land or sea, and forcibly inducting them into the Royal Navy). "I remained with my relations till the commencement of the American troubles," he writes. "In those troublesome times, I was pressed on board the Scorpion sloop of war, as their musician, as they were told all I could play on music. I continued in his majesty's service six years and eleven months."[3]

Captain Tollemache also, according to Henry Laurens, took away "a valuable black Pilot" in July. This may have been the man later mustered into the crew complement of Clinton's ship in North Carolina; on March 15, HMS *Mercury*'s muster shows that it took aboard "For Protection" a black Charlestown ship's pilot, Sampson Waldron. Parker would use him in Charlestown waters in June 1776.[4]

Royal Governor Lord William Campbell, last British governor of South Carolina, was watching both Georgia and South Carolina slide further and further into open rebellion: "I leave it to any person of common sense to conceive what defence they can make in a country where their slaves are five to one, to say nothing of the disaffection of many of the back-country people and of the Indians. There really is an infatuation in all their proceedings."[5] On September 15, he threw up his hands in disgust, resigned his office, and retreated aboard HMS *Tamar* in Charlestown Harbour, ending the era of British imperial rule over the colony. On December 15, the provincial guard stationed on Christopher Gadsden's enormously long wharf captured a canoe sneaking out to the *Cherokee* under cover of darkness, "clandestinely attempting to go through Hog Island creek to the Cherokee armed ship, having on board two of the domestics of Lord William Campbell, three negroes, the property of inhabitants of this town."[6] One of the black people taken at this time may have been a man named Scipio Handley. After the war, he appeared before the Loyalist Claims Commission in London. He and his witness testified that he was freeborn and lived in Charlestown in a little house with his mother, who sold gingerbread. He went on to state that he "was carrying on trade for himself as a fisherman" and had "never carried Arms or took any Oath for the Americans," but that he "was taken by the rebels when he was carrying things to Lord Wm Campbell on board." The rebels confiscated his boat and he was "put in Irons & confined for this [for] six weeks."[7]

The year ended with the slave trader Henry Laurens reassuring his son John, "Some among us have…rushed us forward towards ruin, but I do not despair, I do not believe we Shall be quite destroyed—we shall rise again & although half naked, we Shall rise in the Splendor of Freedom; who would not Submit to temporary Losses & inconveniences, upon a well founded prospect of recovering his Liberty & transmitting that inestimable Blessing to posterity."[8] This sentiment, that the people would rise "in the Splendor of Freedom," was shared as well by those enslaved in South Carolina, who would use the coming war to recover their own liberty by getting themselves behind the British lines.

1776

As 1776 opened, the citizens of Georgia and South Carolina were still keeping one eye on their slaves and one eye on the Native Americans, while preparing for the British attack that they knew was coming soon. Even then, enslaved people were trying to get to the few British ships still in the area. Henry Laurens found a bewildered man caught up in the rush to escape bondage: "Some Time in May last a strange Negro Man came into my Plantation upon Purrysburgh Neck. He does not speak English enough to tell his Master's or Overseer's Name, nor can he give any Account of his Master's Plantation, but that the Negroes from thence, about 16 in Number, all run away to the big Canoe, (Probably meaning Man of War), and whipped him because he refused to go with them."[9]

On March 26, the Provincial Congress of South Carolina dissolved, reconstituting itself as a general assembly and electing John Rutledge president and Henry Laurens vice-president. On March 30, Thomas Pinckney let his family know the latest: "We have an Account here of the Enemys having 1000 Men in the Harbour of Cape Fear but none Landed, and the usual Reports of Numbers of Transports seen off; which are of service as they serve to keep us from sinking into Profound Indolence."[10]

On May 31, people in Christ Church Parish sent word that they had spotted the British fleet off Dewee's Island, possibly twenty miles north of the bar of Charlestown Harbour. The very next day, fifty sails were outside the bar itself. William Moultrie was now in command at the fort on Sullivan's Island, and although it was still not finished, he felt the fort was defensible.

On June 7, Clinton sent ashore a proclamation, urging the "deluded" citizens to return to their duty or "answer the contrary to their peril." The colonists declined to comply.[11] The British then waited twenty-one days for just the right combination of wind and tide necessary to attack the fort on Sullivan's Island, which they did on a hot June 28. Much to everyone's surprise, William Moultrie's men, amateurs for the most part, proceeded to defeat the Royal Navy and hold on to their small fort (which was later renamed Fort Moultrie). It was a day of heat and noise, Moultrie would write later: "it may be very easily conceived what heat and thirst a man must feel in this climate, to be upon a platform on the 28th June, amidst 20 or 30 heavy pieces of cannon, in one continual blaze and roar; and clouds of smoke curling over his head for hours together; it was a very honorable situation, but a very unpleasant one."[12]

The British ships had anchored in a line of battle directly in front of the fort, bringing their broadsides to bear on it and firing with cannons. To their amazement, the cannonade failed to tear down the fort walls, walls built of palmetto logs whose spongy nature absorbed shot without shattering into shrapnel. The British themselves, lacking palmettos, were taking a beating out on the water. By the evening, the captain's log of HMS *Experiment* records ten men dead, forty seriously wounded, three volunteers killed, and others injured, with the ship's sails and rigging slashed to pieces. Even her captain, Alexander Scott, was badly wounded and later died.[13] HMS *Solebay* had many of its sails set on fire by the barrage from the fort, and the springs on both its anchor cables shot away. By 9:30 Parker sent an officer on board all ships to order them to cease firing, cut their anchor cables, and get under sail. The engagement was over.[14] The British ships picked up Clinton and his men from Long Island (modern Isle of Palms, South Carolina) nearby, then limped off to New York. It had been Britain's first attempt to re-establish control, and it had failed spectacularly. (The British Army, due to a failure of intelligence, was unable to assist the Royal Navy throughout this episode. Before hostilities commenced, Sir Henry Clinton had refused to have his soldiers disembark on Sullivan's Island, the location of the fort; he thought Long Island would be better. He had been assured that the Breech Inlet channel between the two islands would be fordable at low tide. It wasn't. His troops, consequently, sat out the whole battle, cursing, swatting mosquitos, and being shot at by riflemen posted across the water.[15])

Nevertheless, after this defeat, a few British ships continued sporadically to cruise along the islands off South Carolina and Georgia. The Royal Navy was welcoming Black Loyalists, or capturing slaves in raids on plantations, and then shipping them off to St. Augustine. HMS *Sphynx*, for example, sent "Forty Negroes" off in September.[16] The governor of East Florida, Patrick Tonyn, noted that by October 30, there had been "a considerable emigration from the rebel Provinces to this Place," including blacks, enslaved and free.[17]

During this time, Boston King was enduring his apprenticeship to a choleric master carpenter in Charlestown, sometimes "beat and tortured most cruelly." His enslaver, Richard Waring, he writes, "hearing of the bad usage I received, came to town, and severely reprimanded my master for beating me in such a manner, threatening him, that if he ever heard the like again, he would take me away and put me to another master to finish my time, and make him pay for it. This had a good effect, and he behaved much better to me the two succeeding years, and I began to acquire a proper knowledge of my trade."[18]

Late in 1776, John Laurens, who would later attempt to raise a regiment of blacks for the Americans, wrote to his father on the topic of manumitting their slaves, a topic they'd been discussing for years: "We have sunk the Africans & their descendants below the Standard of Humanity, and almost render'd them incapable of that Blessing which equal Heaven bestow'd upon us all—by what Shades and Degrees they are to be brought to the happy State which you proposed for them, is not to be determined in a moment."[19] And so the year came to its end, in a Laurens dream of emancipation that would never come to fruition.

1777

In January 1777, Henry Laurens was appointed to the Second Continental Congress, serving as its president from November 1, 1777, to December 9, 1778. In that same year, his brother's slave Ishmael was captured by the Royal Navy: "Ishmael was among 25 Negroes fishing without Charlestown Bar last Sunday taken by a British Cruiser & carried off."[20] The "British Cruiser" was HMS *Daphne*, as an examination of her muster books twice shows "Slaves Taken off So. Carolina." In the entry for May 24, 1777, the names of eight fishermen captured off the Charlestown bar are recorded: William and Tony Legare, Thomas Wright, June Savage, Sancho Campbell, Dick Axtell, Casham Pinckney, and July Flag. Another page gives a second group of fishermen captured the same day, also labelled "Slaves taken off So. Carolina." This muster includes Laurens' slave, Ishmael, entered as "Ishmael Lawrence"; with him were Frank Izard, Benjamin Wish, Glasgow Johnson, Samuel Simpson, Emanuel Hess, Cupid Read, Thomas Hart, Cha's Frazier, Billy Caesar, York Rhine, Michael Righton, Dublin Graham, Abraham Russell, Thomas Hartwell, Swansey Pinckney, and Josiah Townsend. All these men were off-loaded at St. Augustine, East Florida, where they were sold as booty. The muster roll shows a "D" for "Discharged" on June 22.[21] The turning point of the war year 1777 took place in October, when the Americans fought General John Burgoyne and the British Army at Saratoga, New York. Burgoyne was forced to surrender, and this event brought France into the conflict.

1778

By January 1778, the French had allied themselves with the Americans, dreaming about recovering all their Canadian territories. American morale was high, and South Carolina entered the next year of the war a trifle bloody, but unbowed.

1778 was a year fraught with difficulties for the British. After the capture of Burgoyne's army the previous fall, they soon slid into war in Europe: with France and Spain in June 1778, and with the Netherlands the following January. With resources stretched thin, they nevertheless needed to protect the West Indies, where the sugar plantations and the revenues these generated lay open to attack. The eyes of British tacticians turned southwards, away from New York. According to John Buchanan, the plan was to roll up the southern colonies, thus causing the northern provinces to fall. "The British strategy," he writes, "had in common with other well-laid plans a cold, clear logic unencumbered by evidence."[22] Nonetheless, beginning in 1778, they would invade Georgia and South Carolina.

Although the British Army was once more on the offensive, the target was not Charlestown, not immediately anyway. In the final month of 1778, the Loyalists and British troops in East Florida, encouraged by the failure of an American incursion into Florida, stopped raiding and launched a full-scale invasion of Georgia. They were marching to meet 3,500 troops that had been sent down from New York, under Lieutenant Colonel Archibald Campbell of the 71st Regiment. Campbell got to the Savannah River first, landing on December 23. Deciding not to wait for General Augustine Prévost and the Florida contingent, he attacked Savannah.[23]

George Galphin, David George's enslaver, wrote Henry Laurens in December that his little fortified settlement at Silver Bluff, on the South Carolina side of the Savannah River, had now become the front lines: "December 29, 1778....Since I wrote the foregoing georgia is tacken by the kings troops & all the Continentel troops is tacken out of it." Georgia's rebel forces either surrendered or crossed the river to South Carolina. "I am now the frontier" wrote Galphin, "and will hold them off as long as my two wooden forts stand." He told Laurens that he planned to ship his slaves upcountry.[24]

And so 1778 came to a close. The following year would prove even more stressful. War came south from New York, north from East Florida, and east from the West Indies. Both Georgia and South Carolina would be invested, at least for a time.

1779

By January 1 of 1779, Savannah was in British hands, and the army was marching up the river, taking control of the country. By March 3, however, British troops were in retreat, marching right back downriver from Augusta, thus setting a pattern of advance and retreat, chaos, and bitter civil war that would continue throughout the next three years. Augusta itself went in and out of British hands several times. This first time, having lured any local Loyalists to make themselves known, the British north of Savannah said goodbye. The enraged Loyalists felt betrayed. Abandoning the niceties of civilized warfare—an oxymoron in any case—they fell upon their rebel neighbours, one or two at a time, and were themselves attacked, burned out, plundered, and murdered in return.

The Loyalist Stephen De Lancey, posted from New York to Georgia with the 1st and 2nd Battalions, described the city for his wife in January: "The Town of Savannah is situated on the Banks of the River of that Name on a Sand Bank of which your Shoes are full in crossing a Street." He didn't like the looks of the population either: "The People here are sallow and in general disgusting. Pale faces and large swolen Bellies proceeding from the Fever and Ague seem to be the Characteristics of the Georgia Ladies and their Speech is so Negroish that I cannot help imagining that some of them cannot boast of a Number of Ancestors thoroughly White."[25]

Still less could he swallow the way they behaved toward their slaves, even though he didn't fancy *them* much either. Stephen De Lancey thought black people were just as ugly as their enslavers, and he didn't like the way they smelled. He obviously never met any of the prosperous emancipated blacks in Savannah, people such as John Marrant's mother and uncle, who owned their own homes (his mother's house had two storeys), sent their children to school, and could afford hefty apprentice fees for their offspring to learn a trade. He assumed all the blacks he saw to be slaves, though he did make some strong comments about slavery: "These circumstances of Cruelty to these People render the Persons who exercise it disagreable, nay odious to me. When a Set of People can sit down enjoying all the Luxuries of Life without feeling the least Sensation or Compunction for the Sufferings of those poor Wretches whose Lives are render'd Miserable and Constitutions destroyed for those Purposes, I must conclude them Obdurate, Selfish, and Unfeeling to the greatest Degree imaginable. At what an Expence of Life and Happiness do we eat Rice and Sugar!"[26]

David George, who was also in Savannah at this time, may have been poor and enslaved, but he was not simply one of De Lancey's "poor Wretches." "I continued preaching at Silver Bluff, till the church, constituted with eight, increased to thirty or more," he writes, "and till the British came to the city of Savannah and took it. My master was an Antiloyalist; and being afraid, he now retired from home and left the Slaves behind. My wife and I, and the two children we then had, and fifty or more of my Master's people went to Ebenezer, about twenty miles from Savannah, where the King's forces were." He continues his story, explaining, "The General [probably Prévost, who took command from Campbell on January 15] sent us over the big Ogeechee river to Savages' Plantation, where the White people, who were Loyalists, reported that I was planning to carry the black people back again into their slavery; and I was thrown into prison, and laid there about a month, when Colonel Brown, belonging to the British, took me out."[27]

Vignettes for other Georgian Black Loyalists, those who had passes provided to them by the British army, can be seen through a record of their papers, set down in a 1783 orderly book (a log of military orders given) upon their arrival in Nova Scotia. Ned and his wife, Jemimah, for example, received a pass at Savannah in 1779, declaring them both free and friends to His Majesty. (Two years later, they were in Charlestown, getting an addendum on their papers, allowing them to proceed to Nova Scotia or Ontario.) Ned had supplied "Publick Horses" to Colonel John Maitland for eight months. His pass forbade anyone from troubling him or his wife and three sons, Castle, Ned, and Dublin.[28] Another man, Michael Thomas, had joined the King's forces, perhaps as a pioneer, soon after Campbell set foot on shore, and Prévost himself signed his pass a year later, describing Michael Thomas as "a friend and loyalist since the arrival of Col. Campbell into Georgia, and has been since in His Majesty's Employ."[29]

The British invasion of Georgia had scuttled the American general Benjamin Lincoln's design of invading East Florida. He hastily sent his troops in Charlestown to Purrysburg on the South Carolina side of the Savannah, eventually moving the main body of them into north Georgia and occupying British-vacated Augusta on May 11. Meanwhile, Prévost, either trying to draw Lincoln out of Georgia or taking advantage of his absence from South Carolina, launched an unexpected counter-invasion. The Americans withdrew by stages back to Charlestown, leaving a rich swath of rice plantations open to the enemy, and enabling—for the first time in South Carolina—the mass escapes of hundreds of enslaved people.

The British invasion of Georgia and South Carolina under Prévost in 1778–1779 is usually marginalized by historians or conflated with Clinton's successful expedition of 1780, if not outright forgotten.[30] Yet this invasion, and the events that immediately preceded it, are of paramount importance in the history of the South Carolina and Georgia Black Loyalists, for they provided a means of escape for a huge number of slaves. People along the entire line of Prévost's march into South Carolina—Purrysburg, Black Swamp, Coosawhatchie, Salkehatchie, Tullifinny, and Pocotaglio, "Mr. Pinckney's houses," Ashepoo, Jacksonborough, "Mr. Ferguson's plantation called Spring Grove," Bacon's Bridge on the Ashley River—either ran off to the troops or were seized as booty. Even before the army had begun to cross the Savannah River, the British were accommodating those fleeing enslavement in Georgia, and capturing others who had remained on rebel plantations.

South Carolina enslaver Henry Middleton made up a list of eighty-one slaves lost from his Combahee River plantations during the invasion of 1779.[31] None of them appear in the Book of Negroes, except perhaps Bob from "the New Settlement." By 1783, a man named Bob, formerly owned by a "Mr. Middleton," was certainly on a ship in New York Harbor, indentured to a provost master, probably in a Hessian regiment. A possible fellow slave, John, was on a second ship, listed as "John, 25, stout fellow, waggoner, Regiment Knoblauch. Formerly the property of Henry Middleton, Charlestown, South Carolina; left him four years ago." This John may have escaped from a different set of Middleton's plantations, or changed his name. The seventy-nine others are not mentioned in the Book of Negroes.

Eliza Yonge Wilkinson was living on her rebel husband's land on Yonge's Island south of Charlestown when the army under Prévost invaded from Georgia. In a letter written after a series of raids on her home, Eliza recalls, "The whole world appeared to me as a theatre where nothing was acted but cruelty, bloodshed, and oppression; where neither age nor sex escaped the horrors of injustice and violence; where the lives and property of the innocent and inoffensive were in continual danger, and lawless power ranged at large."[32] Yet some black people actually helped their enslavers and protected them as best they could. And some whites, like Eliza, protected those who had gone over to the enemy. Here, she tells of an encounter with a runaway slave that took place soon after she and her family had set out to leave their island:

> Two of Father's Negro men attended us, armed with great clubs; one walked on before, the other behind, placing us in the centre. It was not long before our guard had some use for their clubs; we were crossing a place they call the Sands, when one of the enemy's Negroes came out of the woods…attempting to pass our rear-guard, he was immediately levelled to the earth; he arose, and attempted to run off, when he received another blow, which again brought him down. I could not bear the sight of the poor wretch's blood, which washed his face and neck; it affected me sensibly. 'Enough, Joe! Enough,' cried I; 'don't use the creature ill, take him at once, I wont have him beaten so....' With that he took him, tied his hands behind him, and gave him to the fellow who went before; he himself stayed behind with us; but the poor wretch was sadly frightened. The fellow who had him in custody, walked on very fast, but he kept looking back on us. At last he said to me, 'Do, Mistress, let me walk by you.' 'Don't be afraid,' said I, 'they shan't hurt you again, I wont let them.' But he looked on me so pitifully—his head continually turning round towards me, with such terror in his countenance, that I felt for the poor creature, and, to make him easy, walked, or rather ran, close behind him; for, to keep up with them I was obliged to go in a half run....I would not quit the unhappy wretch as he claimed my protection, and my presence seemed some alleviation to his misery; so on I went, scarce able to support myself.[33]

The British army's officers and men, and their affiliated loyalist militas, did not hesitate to increase their fortunes by pillaging Americans, both rebels *and* loyalists. The army put the Black Loyalists to good use as waggoners, drummers, fifers, guides, spies, couriers, informants, laundresses and nurses, and as pioneers building fortifications and digging trenches. In Charlestown, the newspapers continued to advertise for their return.

The British used numerous Hessian regiments, hired to supplement their forces, during the American Revolution. These regiments, in turn, took on some of the Black Loyalists from South Carolina. George Fenwick Jones, writing about the black Hessians recruited during the war, has identified at least forty-seven from South Carolina. Of these, he writes, "twenty-eight claimed Charleston as their home, while four claimed Johns Island and one each claimed Ponpon, James Island and Stono Ferry."[34] The Book of Negroes lists Regiment Knoblauch as returning to Germany in 1783, with two black regimental drummers: "June" and "July," both escaped from Purrysburg enslaver John Lewis Bourquin in 1779. Another regimental drummer, a Beaufort man, took the name "Cornwallis" after liberating himself that same year. Francis Stewart, a fourth regimental drummer, managed to get his entire family away with him in his flight from John Williamson in the Indian Lands. Stewart and his wife, Hannah, son, Mingo, and daughters, Hannah, Peggy, and Christiane, would emigrate to Germany with Regiment von Knoblauch. A twentieth-century German, Lieutenant Peter Boehm, taught Fenwick Jones an eighteenth-century Hessian song, composed during the campaigns in South Carolina, a song about the arrival of multitudes of blacks within the Hessian regiments—people who had no clothes or bread or joy, people who were satisfied with a small ration of rice.[35] Those multitudes who survived the war, however, would eventually find their happiness, in freedom.

General Prévost's forces finally reached Charlestown, and came to a halt. He sized up the armaments and fortifications of the city, and decided to return to Georgia. With the failure of supply ships to reach him, he was short of ammunition and other necessities, and his soldiers were dying from malaria and typhus to the point where he informed General Clinton that he feared the summer months would see the entire army ill.[36] Prévost began a cautious withdrawal, first to Johns Island, then crossing island after island until he reached Otter Island.

General Prévost's removal from Johns Island to Otter Island was another significant event for Black Loyalists in 1779, background to both triumph and tragedy. After the war, the British were accused by a former rebel soldier and historian, David Ramsay, of abandoning escaped slaves on Otter Island, and of even cutting off the fingers of some who, desperate to escape, ran into the water and clutched at the sides of their boats.[37] This story is worth exploring, as several historians have subsequently retold it, transposing the events, however, to the major evacuation of British and Loyalist personnel from Charlestown on December 14, 1782. Grant Gordon, for example, correctly references Ramsay's 1785 work but sets the story in the wrong time and place, prefacing it by saying, "One contemporary account described the plight of blacks left behind in Charleston." His source, Ellen Gibson Wilson, does the same.[38] Here is David Ramsay's original account of what happened on Otter Island, one he significantly modified in later works:

> The hapless Africans, allured with hopes of freedom, forsook their owners and repaired in great numbers to the royal army. Collected in great crowds near the royal army, they were seized with the camp fever in such numbers that they could not be accommodated either with proper lodgings or attendance….For want of a sufficient number of boats, a considerable part of the negroes were left behind. They had been so thoroughly impressed by the British with the expectation of the severest treatment, even of certain death from their owners, in case of their returning home, that in order to get off with the retreating army they would sometimes fasten themselves to the sides of the boats. To prevent this, the fingers of some of them were chopped off, and soldiers were posted with cutlasses and bayonets to oblige them to keep at a proper distance. Many of them, labouring under diseases, afraid to return home, forsaken by their new masters, and destitute of the necessaries of life, perished in the woods. Those who got off with the army were collected on Otter island, where the camp-fever continued to rage. Without medicine, attendance, or the comforts proper for the sick, some hundreds of them expired. Their dead bodies as they lay exposed in the woods, were devoured by beasts and birds, and to this day the island is strewed with their bones.[39]

Did this actually happen? Perhaps it did, but, interestingly, no other contemporary sources mention the atrocity, beginning with Charlestown newspapers of the period. The *South Carolina and American General Gazette* of July 30 reported only horses being abandoned on Otter Island: "The following horses, left on Otter Island by the British troops, where they must have inevitably perished in a little time for want of water, were taken and brought off by a reconnoitring party from the detachment at the battery at Chipman's bluff on the Ashepoo river, the 13th of July 1779." Those who investigated the island after the British left made no word about the strewn bodies or bones of abandoned slaves, and you can believe they'd have used it as propaganda. Indeed, no other contemporary historian mentions the incident, so this may be merely a case of overly partisan reportage on Ramsay's part. He dropped it in a later revision.[40]

What we do know is that Prévost had abandoned his post at Stono River for Johns Island. He couldn't take his forces down the inland waterway because he simply did not have enough boats. By going overland to the Edisto River, he could rendezvous with Captain Elphinstone and the naval transports waiting for him. The general began marching the army toward the Edisto, and many freed or captured slaves went with him. He remained on Edisto Island for three days, moved to South Edisto, and then on to Otter Island. He quarantined all slaves infected with smallpox and typhus ("camp fever") away from the main body of troops on Otter Island. General Prévost was retreating; he never intended to take sick and dying Black Loyalists on board his transports. This was standard military procedure and a medical practicality, no matter how heartless it seems in retrospect.

As for the mutilation of fingers mentioned in Ramsay's account, closer analysis of the passage shows that Ramsay understood this as happening along the march itself—not on Otter Island. People attempted to "get off" with the army at various points, presumably as the troops crossed the rivers. If mutilation happened, this was the point at which it did. Ramsay says merely, "They would *sometimes* fasten themselves to the sides of the boats."[41] Many of these poor souls were ill, on top of everything else, and later died in the woods. The sick people quarantined on Otter Island, however, were ones who had accompanied the troops all the way to the rendezvous with the transports.

Similarly, the use of cutlasses and bayonets that Ramsay alludes to pre-dates Otter Island. In other words, there was no single concerted rush of blacks to British boats as the troops evacuated Otter Island. There was no one dramatic scene—just the daily cruelties, the ongoing individual tragedies of war. Clarification is necessary here because the conflation of incidents described in Ramsay's account (particularly, the finger-chopping and the abandonment), along with misconstructions of time and space, have combined to create a myth about the evacuation of Charlestown in 1782. Ramsay's story has taken on a life of its own, spreading through "verification by quotation." The worst example of this mythmaking appeared in a 2006 *New Yorker* article by Jill Lepore. Reviewing Simon Schama's revisionist history of slavery, *Rough Crossings*, she writes: "In Charleston, after the ships were full, British soldiers patrolled the wharves to keep back the men, women and children who were frantic to leave the country. A small number managed to duck under the redcoats' raised bayonets, and swim out to the last longboats ferrying passengers to the British fleet....Clinging to the sides of the longboats, they were not allowed on board, but neither would they let go; in the end, their fingers were chopped off."[42] Needless to say, this never happened—at least not when and where and how Lepore says it did. Schama himself transposed Ramsay's account from 1779 to 1782, suggesting (though with less dramatization than Lepore) that "when vessels departed from Charlestown in December 1782, blacks who had not been authorized to sail were so desperate to leave that they clung to the small boats taking refugees out of the harbour."[43] The truth is the British were happy to take black people from Charlestown, either as freed slaves, because this meant lost profit to the Americans, or as those still enslaved (booty), because that meant profit for themselves. The British evacuated 5,327 Black Loyalists from Charlestown in 1782, and contemporary accounts written by both British and Americans clearly state that this evacuation proceeded peacefully. There was no question of a shortage of boats, and blacks were loaded well in advance of the soldiers. No one had to swim for it at Charlestown. Nobody lost a finger.

The triumph for the Black Loyalists who joined forces with the British is that so many of them actually *did* make it to freedom. Many whose names are not recorded would eventually leave Savannah with the troops in 1782, travelling by sea or overland to East Florida. A good number, however, accompanied the army and navy to New York, where their names enter history through the Book of Negroes. Thomas Heyward's slave Harry McGregor, for example, "joined the British troops under the command of General Provost on its march near Charlestown"; he got his wife away as well. Other people, captured and kept as army booty, would later also be freed to go to Nova Scotia, people like Scipio Simmons, probably enslaved on Simmons Island and twenty-two years old in 1779. The Book says he was then "Given to General Provost," who freed him. Two little boys, Bristol Cibbwine, aged ten, and Paul, fifteen, were taken as booty: "Came from Woodbury, Charlestown, South Carolina, with Major [James] Grant of the King's American Regiment about 4 years ago." At some point, Major Grant cut them loose, and they travelled to Nova Scotia, indentured to one Richard Browne.[44]

All this was happening at the very same time that Clinton was issuing a proclamation, confirming liberty to slaves who would desert their rebel masters and come behind the British lines:

> *Whereas the enemy have adopted a practice of enrolling Negroes*
> *among their troops, I hereby give notice that all Negroes taken in*
> *arms or upon any military Duty shall be purchased for the public*
> *service at a stated price; the money to be paid to the captors. But*
> *I most strictly forbid any Person to sell or claim right over any*
> *Negroes the property of a Rebel who may take refuge with any*
> *part of this Army. And I do promise to any Negroe who shall*
> *desert the Rebel Standard full Security to follow within the Lines*
> *any occupation which he may think proper. Given under my Hand*
> *at Headquarters, Phillipsburg, the 30th day of June, 1779."[45]*

John Williams, who escaped in 1779, received a pass in New York from his employer, a brigade major. The date was April 19, 1783, less than a week before he boarded the vessel *Friends*, bound for Halifax. At the base of the paper was appended a note from his indenturer: "This is to Certify that John Williams came into the British Lines in Consequence of the Proclamation by Sir Henry Clinton and that he has remain'd in my Service Ever since. Wm. Fyers, Lieu't of Engineers."[46] Clinton gave John Williams his paper freedom; Prévost's invasion gave him—and many others—his real freedom.

In May of 1779, Captain Elphinstone of the *Perseus* was in Jamaica, refitting his ship, when he received orders to sail to the assistance of General Prévost, who was set to attack Charlestown.[47] Arriving in South Carolina later that month, Elphinstone, who was a stickler for proper charts, at once had boats "exploring the Bars." He noted, "The Tide flows on the different Bars of So. Carolina and Georgia ful and change 7:15 A.M."[48] The tide of war, though, was another matter altogether, and at this point it began to flow against the British Army. On June 3, just a day after he had gone ashore to meet with the general, Elphinstone recorded in his log that he had received a letter from Prévost. By the following day, he was anchored off the North Edisto River and helping to evacuate the British forces. It must have galled him, this second failure to take Charlestown. Then, having gotten the army safely to Savannah, Elphinstone set sail for New York, where Clinton was thinking dark thoughts about South Carolina.

In the meantime, however, something unexpected happened. The French, having come into the war as allies of the Americans, sent a monstrous French fleet from the West Indies under Vice-Admiral d'Estaing (Charles Hector), and—to the horror of the English in Savannah—began unloading troops at Beaulieu Plantation, fourteen miles downriver from the city. What followed was so inept and embarrassing—on the part of *everyone*—that one hesitates even to mention it.[49]

The American and French forces bizarrely delayed attack, giving the British time to receive reinforcements, and to shore up the city's defences. Savannah was still largely and inexplicably unprotected, but army engineer James Moncrief took extraordinary measures, building fortifications from the river on one side of the city to the river on the other. None of this could have been done without his heroic labour force of black people, a unit of Black Pioneers formed almost as soon as the British landed in Georgia. These Pioneers played a large role in the saving of Savannah; they worked until they dropped, raising the walls and the fifteen batteries. Cassandra Pybus has determined that the British payroll included "620 black recruits" during the siege.[50] The combined French and American attack failed dismally. The French withdrew, and the Americans retreated under General Lincoln into South Carolina. However, the noise and chaos of the siege—and perhaps the deaths of enslavers—provided yet more opportunity for slaves to escape.

David George had moved to Savannah after winning his freedom, and was there for some of the fighting: "I and my family went into Savannah, at the beginning of the siege. A [cannon] ball came through the roof of the stable where we lived, and much shattered it, which made us remove to Yamacraw, where we sheltered ourselves under the floor of a house on the ground." The siege was raised after October 9, but by then, David George had other things on his mind. Smallpox had appeared in Charlestown and quickly spread to Georgia. George had been exposed and, in late fall, felt the fever coming on and the pustules breaking out all over his body. He was so desperately ill that even after he recovered, he could barely walk. A document signed by John Wright, dated December 11, 1779, reads, "The subscriber a good Subject to King George do hereby let [rent to] David George a Free Negro Man, my House, Garden, and Field situate two miles from Savannah near the little Ogeechie. Any persons Molesting or disturbing him in the possession of the premises will be prosecuted to the Utmost rigor of the Law." So, for a while, the family had a good place to live and grow crops. Spring, though, found George still weak. His wife, Phillis, was about twenty years old then; her income from doing washing for a British general kept David and her children, Jesse, Ginny, and Little David, alive all through the winter and into the warmer weather.[51] Fearing a second American advance, the enfeebled preacher sent his wife and children deeper into British safety in the core of Savannah, a mile away from where they were then living. He himself was unable to travel.

Far away in New York, Clinton took Prévost's ability to hold on to Savannah as a sign. Prévost had redeemed himself and boosted British morale through his heroic defence of Savannah, made possible by his black pioneers. For the first time in the war, Britain had a good and serviceable harbour in the southern colonies at her disposal. The invasion of South Carolina could proceed.

1780

In 1780, Clinton finally appeared to have gotten his wish: South Carolina was once more occupied by a combination of British Army and Royal Navy forces intent on bringing Charlestown to its knees. The first troops landed in February, and by May 12, the city was in British hands.

Hessian captain Johann Ewald describes in his journal entry for February 11 the finesse with which Elphinstone engineered the fleet into the North Edisto—the mouth of which was "so narrow that only two ships at a time [could] wind through the sandbars." The troops disembarked on Simmons [Seabrook] Island, he said, and began a long slog through marsh and woods. Finally, they struck a road and the Simmons plantation, and at midnight they moved on, to a Mr. Wilson's land, where there was a dock for provisions and baggage to be unloaded. Ewald said this island landing had so fooled the Americans that not a sign of their army was seen. Crossing over to Johns Island, they examined the Chisholm and Fenwick "plantation villages," moving toward Stono ferry: "Since all the country people, especially the males, had run away, spies and guides were very scarce. With the utmost effort we had gotten hold of a Negro boy of eleven or twelve years who knew the way there. To our ill luck, however, this boy spoke such a poor dialect [Gullah] that he was extremely hard to understand, which predicament was worsened because none of us was provided with a map of this area." After marching along a zigzag causeway through the marsh for thirty minutes, Ewald notes, "we asked the boy when we would reach the Stono River, which cuts off this island from the mainland. 'Soon, soon,' the boy replied."[52]

Suddenly, they came upon the river and immediately realized that they were facing riflemen behind a redoubt on the other side of the water. The colonel quietly ordered the troops to turn back, and the Americans did not fire. On the night of February 15, however, the Americans withdrew from this redoubt, and Clinton ordered the Light Infantry to "cross at Waite's [Abraham Waight's] plantation with the aid of several small boats that had been dragged with great effort overland to Stono River from Bohicket Creek."[53]

The plantations in the army's path were the original homes of many future Nova Scotian Black Loyalists. The journals of John Peebles, a Scottish grenadier, are also helpful in showing just where and when these slaves made their escapes to the army. Peebles mentions, for example, the Simmons place, the Rivers plantation, a Doctor Wells's house, the Wilson and Fenwick plantations, and a Mr. Gibbes's place.[54] Black people came into the army in other ways as well. Peebles notes, "On the 19th the jäger detachment had to go out in three parties toward the passes of Cox Swamp to collect information about the enemy and to hunt up Negroes and livestock"; on the 26th, they scouted "the route toward Ponpon to collect Negroes and livestock, if any were still left."[55] Somewhere along the line of march, Peebles himself "acquired" a young black boy. His entry for Saturday, March 4, reveals that he was working near Fort Johnson when he "picked up a little Negro Boy for a fifer." His editor notes, "Somehow Peebles managed to keep young Ned, then about nine, with him for nearly two years."[56]

Clinton's army next crossed the Ashley River and surrounded Charlestown. Their bombardment of the city began the first week in April, soon to be joined by the guns of the Royal Navy. On April 8, having crossed the bar into the harbour, a British fleet sailed triumphantly past Fort Moultrie, led by Hamond in the *Roebuck*. Johann Ewald was touched by awe at the sight: "It was the most majestic and beautiful spectacle that one can imagine. The fort was veiled in fire and smoke, and the roar of forty-three heavy guns resembled a terrible thunderstorm. Despite all dangers threatening the fleet, it sailed quite slowly past the fort with colors flying proudly, one ship behind the other, without firing a shot. As soon as it had passed the enemy fort, each ship made a sudden turn, fired a broadside, and sailed to its designated anchoring place."[57] It was a masterpiece of execution, and, as sheer spectacle, enthralling to both sides. Johann Hinrichs, another Hessian officer, reported that the Americans were so stunned by the sight that they neglected to fire at their besiegers, who had "jumped upon the parapets of the works!"[58]

The city was fired on for more than a month, with British soldiers and Black Pioneers digging trenches closer and ever closer to the town, setting up cannon, loading, firing, taking cover. By the second week in May, a frustrated General Clinton ordered his artillerymen to heat their shot red-hot, setting fires in the city. Charlestown capitulated on May 12. The army's acquisition (by capture) of black people remaining on rebel estates now increased, as almost the whole of the province came under military control. At the same time, the movement of this army up the rivers and into the mountains provided new avenues of escape for those individuals wishing to cross behind the British lines to freedom.

John Marrant, still with the Royal Navy in 1780, had taken part in the attack on the city: "I was at the siege of Charlestown, and passed through many dangers. When the town was taken, my old royal benefactor and convert, the king of the Cherokee Indians, riding into the town with general

Clinton, saw me and knew me: He alighted off his horse and came to me; said he was glad to see me...."[59] That, however, is all he reports of the war in South Carolina.

Boston King was one of those slaves who had been evacuated into the interior of the province as the war heated up in South Carolina. He felt nothing but relief when Charlestown fell to the British on May 12, for by then, he really needed to run away and the British Army offered sanctuary: "They received me readily, and I began to feel the happiness of liberty, of which I knew nothing before, altho' I was most grieved at first, to be obliged to leave my friends, and remain among strangers."[60] He obtained work with a Captain Grey in the British Army and began a new life with his employer's regiment, at some point taking the surname King. In late May or early June, however, King contracted smallpox and was quarantined at a distance from the main forces.

The second invasion and investment of South Carolina had begun well for the British forces. First a clear victory: Charlestown was taken. Lieutenant General Charles Cornwallis, left to command in South Carolina after Clinton departed for New York on June 8, would soundly trounce the Americans under Horatio Gates at Camden on August 16. Outposts were being fortified to keep the backcountry under control.[61] Many of these outposts would become familiar to Boston King in his later travels with his new employer.

For some reason, King left Captain Grey's regiment a year later: "I tarried with Captain Grey about a year, and then left him, and came to Nelson's Ferry." This would bring him up to December 1781, or thereabouts, and place him at a British outpost on the Santee River: "Here I entered into the service of the commanding officer of that place. But our situation was very precarious; and we expected to be made prisoners every day; for the Americans had 1600 men, not far off; whereas our whole number amounted only to 250."[62] His unit needed reinforcements, but the Americans controlled the countryside between the British forces and aid. South Carolina was shaking off British rule, mile by bloody mile, and the province was no longer safe for an escaped slave.

In early 1780, David George, recovering from the smallpox, though slowly, was able to rejoin his family when the American advance slowed before reaching Yamacraw:

I was then about a mile from Savannah, when the Americans were coming towards it a second time. I wished my wife to escape, and to take care of herself and of the children, and let me die there. She went: I had about two quarts of Indian corn, which I boiled; I ate a little, and a dog came in and devoured the rest; but it pleased God [that] some people who came along the road gave me a little rice: I grew better, and as the troops did not come so near as was expected, I went into Savannah, where I met my family, and tarried there about two years [into 1782], in a hut belonging to Lawyer Gibbons, where I kept a butcher's stall.[63]

Again, he got a pass from the British: "Permit the Bearer to pass and repass about his lawful business unmolested. Edw'd Cooper Town Adjt of Savannah, Savannah, 1 January 1780. The within mentioned David George has a Wife Named Phillis and three children (who are also free) Jesse, David, and Ginny who are all recommended to the protection of his Majesty's Subjects." Even Lieutenant Colonel Alured Clarke gave him a pass: "The bearer David George has my leave to pass and repass on his business."[64]

Family and friends helped him out as well:

My wife had a brother, who was half an Indian by his mother's side, and half a Negro. He sent us a steer, which I sold, and had now in all 13 dollars, and about three guineas besides, with which I designed to pay our passage, and set off for Charlestown; but the British light horse came in, and took it all away. However as it was a good time for the sale of meat, I borrowed money from some of the Black people to buy hogs, and soon re-paid them, and agreed for a passage to Charlestown, where Major P. [Major-General James Paterson] the British commander, was very kind to me.[65]

With his defeat of General Horatio Gates at Camden in 1780, Cornwallis seemed firmly on the path of good fortune, yet he was even then launching himself headlong toward defeat. Victory at Camden was to be the high point of Cornwallis's service in South Carolina—indeed, the high point of his service throughout the entire revolution. Controlling the countryside was a task infinitely harder than either Clinton or Cornwallis or any of their junior officers had supposed in the first flush of victory. In the end, it would prove impossible. The Americans won the battle of Kings Mountain in October, and Cornwallis, reconsidering his strategy, moved to station himself halfway between Camden and Ninety-Six.[66]

1781

As the new year dawned, Cornwallis still wasn't seeing his situation clearly. On January 16, even after the Kings Mountain debacle, he was dispatching orders to John Harris Cruger, then commanding at Ninety-Six, saying, "The power is now totally in our hands. You have a formidable body of good Soldiers at Ninety Six. You must now use your utmost execution to prevent a renewal of the same kind of troubles & calamities which have so long oppressed the deserving inhabitants of your district."[67]

The power is now totally in our hands: a fever dream. American General Greene was even then splitting his forces, sending General Daniel Morgan against Ninety-Six. So Cornwallis sent Banastre Tarleton and a third of his army off to catch the Americans under Daniel Morgan, and plowed on toward North Carolina.[68] Morgan chose his ground well, waiting for Tarleton to come up. He then spent the night of January 16 walking through his camp, encouraging his troops, telling them stories and helping them with their equipment. He never slept, and early on the morning of January 17, he woke early, bellowing, "Get up boys, Benny's coming!" Morgan's brilliant use of the American militia—he took their weaknesses and made them his strength—won him the day. It took less than an hour before Tarleton fled the scene.[69] "At the end of those fatal fifty minutes," write Cornwallis's biographers, "the British had lost eight hundred stand of arms, two 3-pound cannon, sixty Negro servants, one hundred horses, thirty-five supply wagons, and the colors of the 7th regiment. They had also lost something approaching eight hundred men."[70] Cornwallis, ignorant of it all, kept marching on, trying to keep his men alive, and to stop them and their Black Loyalist contingent from looting friend and foe alike. It wasn't until January 18 that Tarleton rode into camp and confessed his failure. Fortunately, Major General Alexander

Leslie marched in to reinforce them at almost the same moment. Cornwallis soldiered on, pursuing General Nathanael Greene in the hope of crushing his army or forcing it out of the state.

Charles O'Hara was camped on the banks of the Wateree River near Camden in January. Communication with Charlestown was "so very precarious" that he feared to commit many of his thoughts to writing. The backcountry was stripped down to the bedrock of hell, in his opinion; the kind of hell that only a civil war can engender. O'Hara was seeing things "beyond description wretched, every Misery which the bloodiest cruel War ever produced, we have constantly before Us."[71] Carolinians in the backcountry, he said, were pitched to extremes of rage he had not previously encountered.

Cornwallis, meanwhile, had finally caught up with Nathanael Greene and the Continental Army. On March 15, at Guilford Court House in North Carolina, the British and American troops came together in long and desperate battle; Cornwallis announced a victory but it was a hollow one, according to modern historians such as John Buchanan: "Despite Tarleton's disaster at Cowpens he had pushed on with some 2,550 men. Now his force was reduced to slightly over 1,400 effectives, and they were no longer fit to campaign. Charles, 2nd Earl Cornwallis, had ruined his army."[72] Greene and the surviving Americans shadowed the earl as he mustered his remaining troops and headed for Wilmington; then Greene marched south into the backcountry of South Carolina. Cornwallis turned north at April's end, heading for Virginia, and his appointment with fate.

Nisbet Balfour, left behind in Charlestown, sent his general a thirteen-page report in May, which could be summed up in one sentence: "I had the pleasure of receiving your Lordships Letter of the 3d of this month, and with much concern I am obliged to informe you, that since that period, we have lost a great part of this province, and Georgia."[73] Lord Rawdon wrote him that same month, to say he had withdrawn from the backcountry: "and we brought off not only the militia who had been with us at Camden, but also all the well-affected neighbors on our route, together with the wives, children, negroes and baggage, of almost all of them."[74]

British control of South Carolina was unravelling just as Charles O'Hara had feared. Ferguson's defeat, Tarleton's rout, Cornwallis's departure: they were a match to the tinder, and South Carolina went up in flames. "The most trifling Check to our Arms," said Charles O'Hara, "acts like Electrical Fire, by rouzing at the same moment every Man upon this vast Continent to persevere upon the least and most distant dawn of Hope, in pursuit of their favorite Independency, which like a powerful talisman has charmed every American."[75]

Black people also carried in their hearts that same "most distant dawn of Hope," and freedom, their "powerful talisman," still urged them to take their lives into their hands and run. Charlestown newspapers were full of advertisements by masters of runaway slaves during this time. The British Army and the Royal Navy still appeared as beacons of promise, even as the territory they controlled continued to shrink. Within Charlestown, the presence of the British—as liberators and potential employers, but more importantly as facilitators for slaves bent on getting out of the province before the Americans took it all—drew people like a magnet. David and Phillis George, down the coast in Savannah, had seen the writing on the wall and were determined to get to Charlestown. Georgia had been stripped of most of its British forces when Clinton invaded South Carolina, and the province was in chaos. The Georges wanted to be with the main body of the army; they saw this as their only guarantee of safety. Others had the same idea.

One of the more interesting ads for runaway slaves is the following, posted by Sarah Faesch of Charlestown in May of 1781: "Absented themselves from the subscriber since the surrender of Charlestown, Priam, a lad about 18 years old, very likely and sensible; Adam about 16 years old, has a scar on his cheek, lost half of one of his foreteeth, is artful, and can tell a very plausible story; they are supposed to be at Camden; Jenny 25 years old, much pitted with the small pox, her make short and thick; she is in New-York. A reward of two guineas each, will be given for the boys, and reasonable charges; and ten guineas for the wench upon delivery in Charlestown. Sarah Faesch. Charlestown, May 2, 1781."[76] Sarah Faesch appears in the 1790 census for South Carolina as "Fash, Sarah (Free)." In other words, she herself is a black slaveowner. This is the first advertisement for a runaway slave that I've ever found issued by a free person of colour. In 1790, Sarah's household consisted of herself and one other freed person; she was the head of the household, but also living with her, according to the United States census for that year, was a "free white male, aged sixteen or above," and two slaves.[77] This is an interesting ménage, and I cannot help but wonder about Sarah's story. How did she know that Jenny had made it to New York? How had Jenny managed to get there?

Throughout the chaos of 1781, everyone was snatching slaves. Enslavers lost people to both sides as well as to roving bands of marauders. Many had their people taken away, were recompensed with the slaves of the enemy, and then had *them* taken away, sometimes by the same side that had awarded them in the first place. Throughout the war, black people were used as currency, as had happened so often in the past. Cornwallis ordered Rebel property sequestered and appointed John Cruden, a merchant of Wilmington, as commissioner of sequestered estates, asking him to deal with captured slaves. Cruden put them to work on those plantations of rebels then under British control. His plan was to grow food and produce cash crops of rice and indigo, and naval stores of tar, turpentine, and ships' masts. It sounded good in theory, but South Carolina was too vast, the transportation too risky, and the countryside too unsettled to make this work. Rebel raids, and the snatching and selling of sequestered blacks by white Loyalists, made his task nearly impossible.

Something else was going on in South Carolina and Georgia in 1781. "Strayed from Thomas Farrier two days ago, at No. 62 Queen-street, a Negro Girl, three years old," reported the *Royal Gazette* on September 15. "A guinea reward will be paid on delivery of her." How did this child wander away? Who was looking after her? There appears to have been a plethora of child disappearances during this year. In my research, I began to wonder whether groups of kidnappers were not quietly making a profit by selling black children to the West Indies. Children would have been easy to subdue and hide aboard ship, and in many cases, unable to complain or even to remember where they had been taken from. Some enslavers certainly thought this might be the case. One ad for a runaway slave reads, "Absented himself near 3 months ago, from the subscriber's plantation near Dorchester, a young negro lad named Billy, 13 or 14 years of age...supposed to be decoyed"[77], while another notes that a boy named Scrub "Ran away or was carried off from Savannah in Georgia."[78]

Disappearances of this sort had been going on for quite a while. It was secretive, but it was there. On January 5, Sir James Wright, governor of Georgia, wrote Nisbet Balfour, commandant at Charlestown, regarding the

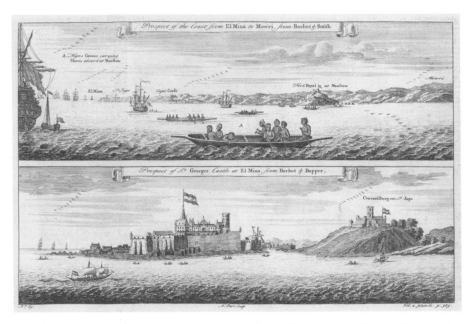

West African slaves being loaded onto European ships. From *A New General Collection of Voyages and Travels*, edited by Thomas Astely, London, 1747: Vol. 2, Plate 61, Special Collections Department, University of Virginia Library, Charlottesville.

CHARLES-TOWN, AUGUST 16, 1770.

RUN AWAY about a Month ago, a Negro Fellow named MAY, he is about five Feet four Inches high, of a very black Complexion, Country born, very sensible, imagined to be about Twenty-fix Years of Age, and well known on *John's-Ifland*. Ten Pounds Reward is offered to whoever will deliver him to Mr. ABRAHAM WAIGHT on *John's-Ifland*, to the Warden of the Work-House, or to Mr. WILLIAM WAIGHT on *St. Helena*, alfo one Hundred Pounds is offered for his Head: and whoever harbours or entertains the said Fellow, may depend on being prosecuted according to Law, by WILLIAM WAIGHT.

Ad for a runaway slave named May, offering the sum of £100 for delivery of his head to his owner. *Continuation to the South-Carolina Gazette*, Charlestown, August 30, 1770. Courtesy of the Charleston Library Society, Charleston, South Carolina. Photo by Terry Richardson.

Memorial to enslaved Africans shipped to the New World and quarantined on Sullivan's Island, near Charleston, South Carolina. Photo by author.

View of Mulberry House and Street, 1805. Illustration by Thomas Coram (American, 1756–1811), oil on paper. © Image Gibbes Museum of Art/Carolina Art Association, Charleston, 1968.018.0001. Mulberry Plantation, on the Cooper River north of Charlestown, was built from 1712 to 1714 by Thomas Broughton, Sr. (d. 1738); it was later the home of Black Loyalist Hagar Broughton's enslaver, another Thomas Broughton (d. 1832). Cabins in the foreground are in the African style. The people on the "street" between the rows of their homes may be actual Broughton slaves, painted from life.

Tranquil Hill, The Seat of Mrs. Ann Waring, near Dorchester, ca. 1800. By anonymous, watercolor on paper. © Image Gibbes Museum of Art / Carolina Art Association, Charleston, 1972.019. Boston King's enslaver, Richard Waring, bought this plantation in 1773, after his marriage to Ann Ball; he died in 1781. Note the slave cabins and the rice-fanner structure in the foreground.

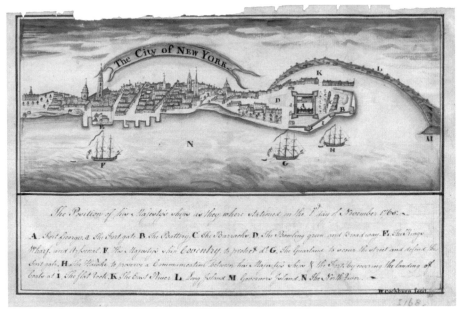

Royal Navy ships off Fort George, New York, in 1765. National Archives of Great Britain, Kew. MPI 1/168. "The City of New York / The Position of his Majesty's Ships as they where [*sic*] stationed on the 1st day of November 1765."

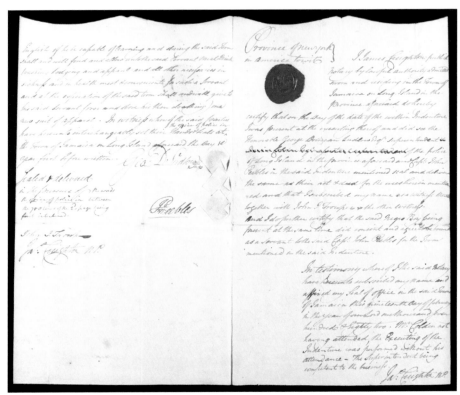

The only surviving indenture of a Black Loyalist, a boy named Ned, taken from James Island, South Carolina, and bound to a British officer in 1782. Courtesy of scotlandsimages.com © 2007. The National Archives of Scotland, Edinburgh GD 21/158; Cunninghame of Thorntoun Papers, "Indenture for Ned, 19 February 1782."

This ferociously secure house on King Street, Charlestown, belonging to wealthy South Carolina slave trader Miles Brewton, served as headquarters for both Clinton and Cornwallis after the city fell to the British in 1780. Photo by author.

Cornwallis's posts at York and Gloucester, 1781. Map by J. F. W. Des Barres, survey by Captain Fage of the Royal Artillery, from the Atlantic Neptune. Nova Scotia Archives, Halifax.

Plantation life at the end of the eighteenth century, probably South Carolina, ca. 1795. "The Old Plantation," watercolor on laid paper. Accession 1935.301.3, Image T1995-1. Abby Aldrich Rockefeller Folk Art Museum, Colonial Williamsburg Foundation, Williamsburg, VA.

Vessels Names and their Commanders	Their Owners	Negroes Names	Age	Description	Claiments Names	Residence	Names of the Persons in whose Possession they now are
				(221)			
Sloop Eliza Peter Stark	Post Millbern	Suky	21	Stout Wench			Morgan & Wells German Loyal...
		Suky	21	Ordinary Wench M.			
		Penny	25	ditto			
		Holly	22	Stout Wench			
		Mary	17	Ordinary do			
		Polly	1	Infant			
		Elijah	7½	ditto			
		Suky	4½	ditto			
11th Octr 1783 Midsummon Morning Wm Rayon	Halifax	Kate	16	Stout Wench			Sr Bignell 33 Regt
		Will Hicks	12	Stout Boy M.			ditto
		Solomon	23	Stout fellow			Capt Stewart 33. Regt
		Dick	21	Able Stout fellow			Lieut Harvey 33. do
		Nancy	37	Stout Wench			Doct Bignell ditto
		Rachel	25	Stout fellow			ditto
Dutchess Gordon James Holmes Mr	ditto	William Simpson	45	ditto			42d Regt
		John Brown	30	ditto			ditto
		Punch	25	ditto			ditto
Fancy Mon James Miller	ditto	Mingo Shiels	24	ditto			ditto
		Sam McLeod	29	ditto			ditto
Rehonoren 11th Octr 83 Sloop Cato	Annapolis Royre	Withdrawn	30	ditto			Stephen Furman
		Joe Freeman	35	ditto			ditto
		Ben Pembroy	35	ordinary fellow			ditto
		Sam Drofe	50	Stout fellow			ditto
		William Freeman	30	Ordinary fellow			ditto
		Arga	30	Stout fellow			Isaac Swaine
		James Brown	21	ditto			Stephen Swaden
		Titus	28	ditto			ditto
		Miquet	20	Stout Wench			Jacob Rose
		Mafsey Acton	31	ditto			Widow Boys
		Nancy King	19	Ordinary ditto			Robin Moore
		Joseph	20	ditto fellow			Jacob Grant
		Timothy	33	ditto			
Sloop Swalcham Wm Nicholson	ditto	Cato	35	Stout fellow			Godfrey Harwood
		Rose Heiwarth	30	ditto Wench with 2 Children	1783 years since		ditto
		Ceasar	51	Ordinary fellow			Mr Grant
		Bill	14	fine Boy			ditto
		Dinah	5	ditto			ditto
		Hannah	30	Stout Wench ditto a child 2 year old	2 Children 1-2 yr old		ditto
		Gofst Person	24	Stout fellow			Ephraim Stanford
		Jenny	20	fine Wench a child 2 year old			William Mill
		Fanny	17	fine Wench			Nathan Haynes
		Margel	15	ditto			James Street
		Rose Jackson	36	Ordinary fellow			John Smith
		Betsey Jackson	16	fine Girl			ditto

ABOVE AND OPPOSITE The first page of a two-page entry in the Book of Negroes, showing a woman named Katie who escaped from Henry Laurens of Charlestown, South Carolina. National Archives of Great Britain, Kew. PRO 30/55/100:107–108.

Formerly Slave to Thomas Smith Charlestown South Carolina left him after the Siege in 1780

Born free in the City of New York

Formerly Slave to John Hope South Hampton Virginia left him in the year of 1779 & came the British

"" to Mr.s Lawrence of Charlestown S Carolina left him before the Siege of Said Town & came the British Troops

"" to Isaac Johnson of Philadelphia left him & came the British Troops in 1778

Born within the British lines

""   ""

""   ""

Inspected by Capt Gilfillan, & armstrong, Lieu.t Col.l Smith, & Samuel Jones Esq.r Secretary

Formerly Slave to Isaac Wade Johns Island South Carolina left them in 1779

Says he was born free at Port Royal South Carolina, stolen from thence by a boat's crew M.r Donald, Master of a Ship

Formerly Slave to Chief Justice Howard of North Carolina, now considered to be the Property of Miss Howard his Daughter

"" free to Edmon Wade Charlestown says he was born free

"" Slave to Isaac Wade Johns Island South Carolina left him in 1779 .... G. B. C

"" "" "" "" ""

"" to Benjamin Singleton Charlestown S. Carolina left him before the Siege in 1780

"" to Peter Porcher "" "" "" ""

"" to Peter Porcher ...... "" "" "" ""

"" to Samuel Steele Portsmouth Virginia left him in the year 1780

"" to Doctor Walter McLood Hampton "" "" ""

"" Near Norfolk Virginia "" ""

"" to Joseph Freeman Little Yorke left him four years agoe .... G. M. C

"" to Samuel Easterby New Port Rhode Island left him Seven years agoe .... ""

"" to Doctor Ross Prince George's County Maryland left him four years agoe .... ""

"" to ?Layton Royal Navy, Says the Captain gave him his freedom .... G. B. C

Free by his former Master as Certifyed by Justus Swanton Middletown Connecticut

Formerly Slave to William Williamson Black Swamp South Carolina left him five years agoe ...... G. B. C

Property of Stephen Snowden as ?p Bill of Sale

"" of "" as "" ""

Formerly Slave to Joseph Dunfree Duches County New York Province left him six years agoe ...... ""

"" to Widow Complete Hampton Virginia left her six years agoe .... ""

John Moores Property

Property of Charles Revere Musquette Cove Long Island

Free

Formerly Slave to Daniel Rusfiel of New Port Rhode Island left him Twenty years agoe

Property of Mrs Ogden by Bill of Sale

Free

Free

Free

Formerly Slave to Samson Benson of Harlem left him Seven years agoe .... G B C

Free

Formerly Slave to Bartholomew Gidney of White Plains, Hogans Property by Bill of Sale

Property of James Brown by Bill of Sale

Formerly Slave to Silas Holly of Stanford Connecticut left him Seven years agoe .... G. B. C

Free Born

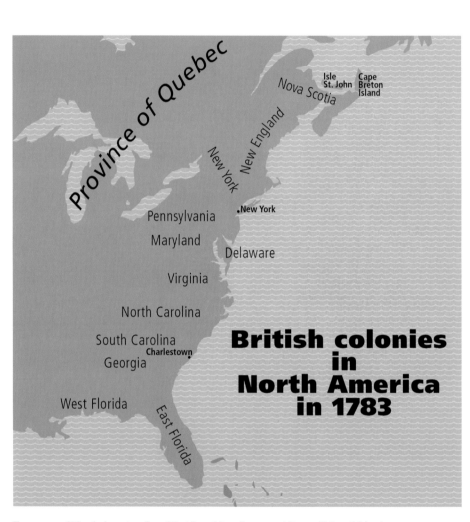

East coast of North America, from Florida to Nova Scotia and Prince Edward Island.

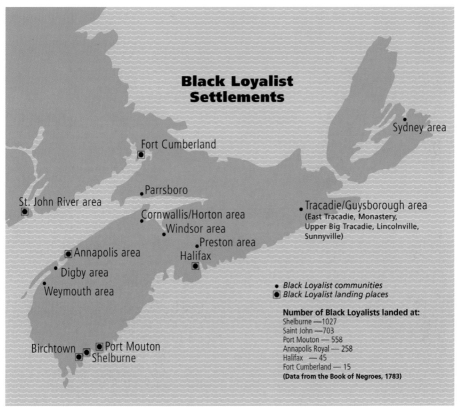

Black Loyalist Settlements

Sydney area

Fort Cumberland

Parrsboro

St. John River area

Cornwallis/Horton area

Tracadie/Guysborough area
(East Tracadie, Monastery,
Upper Big Tracadie, Lincolnville,
Sunnyville)

Windsor area

Preston area

Annapolis area

Halifax

Digby area

Weymouth area

● Black Loyalist communities
◉ Black Loyalist landing places

Number of Black Loyalists landed at:
Shelburne —1027
Saint John —703
Port Mouton — 558
Annapolis Royal — 258
Halifax — 45
Fort Cumberland — 15
(Data from the Book of Negroes, 1783)

Birchtown ◉ Port Mouton
◉● Shelburne

Nova Scotia, showing communities occupied or settled by Black Loyalists.

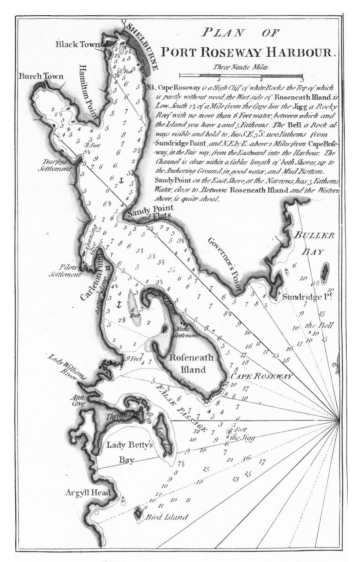

"Plan of Port Roseway Harbour." An insert on "A New Chart of the Coast of Nova Scotia" by Captain Holland, July 12, 1798, showing Birchtown in the upper left–hand corner. Nova Scotia Archives, Halifax. Map Collection: 239–1798.

Logo of the Nova Scotia Museum's travelling exhibit "Remembering Black Loyalists, Black Communities." Design by Allura Communications, from a collage by Ruth Whitehead.

Items from a 1998 archaeological excavation at Birchtown, including a Royal Engineers uniform button featuring a crown and three cannon. A number of other military artifacts were also recovered, including a musket ball, bayonet fragments, a naval boarding-axe head, and buttons from the Second American Regiment. Nova Scotia Museum, Halifax. History Collections, AkDi-23.

Reconstruction in Birchtown of an eighteenth-century pit house, based on the remains of one discovered in 1994 at Birchtown, Shelburne County, Nova Scotia. Photo by author.

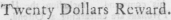

Twenty Dollars Reward.

RAN Away, on Thursday evening, the 18th inst. a Negro Man Servant, the property of the Subscriber, named BELFAST ; but who commonly goes by the name of BILL.————At the time of he elopement he was in the service of William Forsyth, Esq ; and had meditated an attempt to get on board a ship that night which lay in the harbour, bound to Newfoundland ; but was frustrated : It is probable, however, he may still endeavour to escape that way, therefore, the masters of all coasters going along shore, or other vessels bound to sea, are hereby forewarned from carrying him off at their peril, as they will be prosecuted, if discovered, with the utmost rigour of the law.

The above reward will be paid to any person or persons who shall apprehend and secure him, so that I may recover him again.

He is a likely, stout-made fellow, of five feet eight or nine inches high, and about 27 years of age ; of a mild good countenance and features, smooth black skin, with very white teeth ; is a native of South Carolina, speaks good English, and very softly, and has been in this Province ten years.

When he went off, he wore an old Bath-Coating short coat, of a light colour, wore out at the elbows ; brown cloth or duffil trowsers, also much wore at the knees ; a round hat, and an old black silk handkerchief about his neck :—But as he had other cloaths secreted in town, he may have changed his whole apparel.

He will no doubt endeavour to pass for a free man, and possibly by some other name.

MICHAEL WALLACE.

Halifax Weekly Chronicle ad (dated March 15, 1794) for runaway slave and Black Loyalist named Belfast, born in South Carolina. Nova Scotia Archives, Halifax. Newspaper Collection, microfilm: 8165.

Black Loyalist memorial site, Birchtown, Shelburne County, Nova Scotia. Photo by author.

Tracadie Harbour, Antigonish County, Nova Scotia. Photo by author.

Carmelita Robertson, a Black Loyalist descendant, points out the Brownspriggs grant on the east side of Tracadie Harbour, Nova Scotia. Photo by author.

James Desmond investigating a cellar depression at BlCu-3, Birchtown, Guysborough County. Nova Scotia Museum, Halifax. Photo by Stephen Powell.

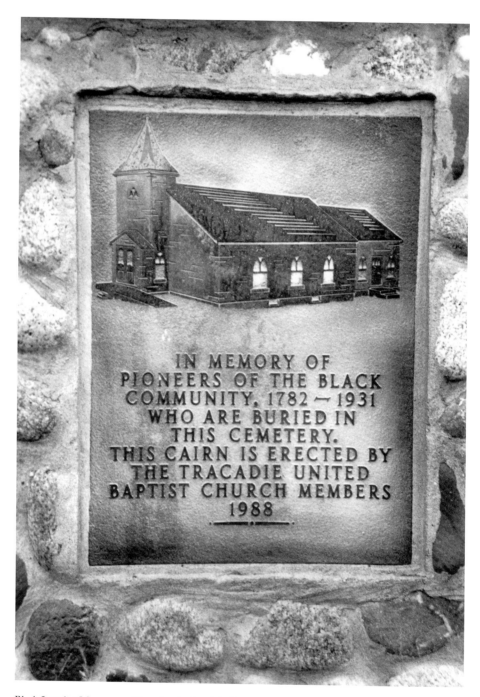

IN MEMORY OF
PIONEERS OF THE BLACK
COMMUNITY, 1782 — 1931
WHO ARE BURIED IN
THIS CEMETERY.
THIS CAIRN IS ERECTED BY
THE TRACADIE UNITED
BAPTIST CHURCH MEMBERS
1988

Black Loyalist Monument, Tracadie, Antigonish County, Nova Scotia. Photo by author.

illicit slave traffic flowing out of South Carolina into Georgia, for resale in East Florida and the West Indies: "I gave Directions, & made all the Inquiry I cou'd about the Negros &c. you mentioned you were apprehensive were brought into this Province with an aim to Sell or Ship off, but could not discover that any were."[79] John Cruden, the commissioner of sequestered estates, also had suspicions. In December 1781, he would publish a proclamation, trying to recover slaves from the sequestered American estates who were being illegally held in Charlestown (or perhaps secretly shipped elsewhere) by those who had no right to them.[80] These blacks belonged, in theory anyway, to King George III. After the evacuation of Charlestown in December 1782, Cruden would discover even more about this traffic in freed Black Loyalists and sequestered slaves, this time through the surviving victims.[81]

At the year's end, two final disappearances were noted in the newspapers. One was a man called Sambo, a shoemaker. Born in Africa, he ran away or was taken off on Christmas Day, 1781.[82] Kate, a professional cook known for her specialty pastries and sweets, "having carried out confectionary," was born in Africa and possibly initiated into a women's society, as she had the marks of ritual scarification on her cheeks. She disappeared from her enslaver, Frederick Smith, at 106 Meeting Street the day before Christmas Eve, and vanished into history wearing a green petticoat and a striped jacket.[83]

Others were in the process of leaving, or had already gone. Thomas and Hannah Williams were shipwrecked sailing from Tybee Island to Savannah. The couple lost everything, including their pass; in July 1781, Alexander Whiley testified for them, and they were given another. Somehow they made it onto a transport and reached Nova Scotia by the coming winter.[84]

Boston King had already departed sometime before July 1781. David George's family would be on their way to Halifax within a year. They shipped out of Charlestown on November 19, 1782, accompanying General James Paterson, who was to take over the Halifax military district.[85] John Marrant was serving aboard HMS *Princess Amelia* in the North Sea by the summer of 1781. He evidently was able to keep in contact with his family throughout the war. At least some of them must have left Georgia with the British because Marrant received word from a brother in Nova Scotia, saying that he hoped for ministers to come to that province. John Marrant determined to go; by 1785, he had been discharged from the Royal Navy, and "ordained in Bath" as a preacher in the tradition of the Countess of Huntingdon's Connexion, an offshoot of Anglican Methodism. On July 18, 1785, he finished up his *Narrative* in London, saying he expected to sail for Halifax in a few days.[86] We will take up his story again in chapter eight.

Chapter Six

WAR'S END, 1781-1783

1781

The war was about to explode into what would prove to be the final major siege for control of America. General Cornwallis left Wilmington, North Carolina, marching north on April 25, followed by countless Black Loyalists from Georgia and the Carolinas. He crossed into Virginia toward the end of May. Well aware of the apparent avenue for escape that the British Army provided, Virginian slaves began fleeing to the British by the thousands. After the war, Thomas Jefferson was to speculate that over thirty thousand black people had run for freedom.[1]

In early April of 1781, Virginian Richard Henry Lee complained to Samuel Adams that the British were making constant forays from ships in Chesapeake Bay, snatching foods, livestock, and slaves from coastal plantations. By mid-month, he was explaining to Thomas Jefferson that Virginia could expect raids on a much larger scale.[2] Little did he know just how bad the situation was to become. By May 20, Cornwallis had reached Petersburg, Virginia, joining General Benedict Arnold's forces. On June 4, Richard Henry Lee was writing to his brother Arthur, "Tis said that 2 or 3000 negroes march in their train, every kind of Stock which they cannot remove they destroy—eating up the green wheat & by destroying of the fences, expose to destruction the other growing grains." By July, he was telling his brother William, "Your neighbors Colo Taliaferro & Colo Travis lost every slave they had in the world, and Mr. Paradise has lost all his but one." Wrote Lee in despair, "Cornwallis is the Scourge."[3]

The British general was using Black Loyalists and captured slaves to swell his baggage train, then sweeping this train across Virginia like a scythe. They were becoming one of his weapons, by virtue of their numbers alone, and the simple fact that they had to eat. Johann Ewald is one of the few eyewitnesses to have recorded a lengthy description of the blacks following Cornwallis:

> Every officer had four to six horses, and three or four Negroes, as well as one or two Negresses for cook and maid. Every soldier's woman was mounted and also had a Negro and Negress on horseback for her servants. Each squad had one or two horses and Negroes, and every non-commissioned officer had two horses and one Negro. Yes, indeed, I can testify that every soldier had his Negro, who carried his provisions and bundles. This multitude always hunted at a gallop, and behind the baggage followed well over four thousand Negroes of both sexes and all ages. Any place this horde approached was eaten clean, like an acre invaded by a swarm of locusts. Where all these people lived was a riddle to me.[4]

Ewald had no illusions about why the British had welcomed Black Loyalists into their fold: "These people were given their freedom by the army because it was actually thought this would punish the rich, rebellious-minded inhabitants of Carolina and Virginia."[5]

Although some of these Black Loyalists had followed the army from Georgia and the Carolinas, their numbers increased exponentially with the addition of the Virginia blacks. Yet, out of this "swarm of locusts" described by Ewald, and out of Jefferson's thirty thousand fled, only fourteen runaways were advertised in Virginia after Cornwallis's surrender. I searched Virginia newspapers for ads going forward in time for over two years, without finding any other mentions. Was it because so many were recaptured? Or was it because so many of them died? Cornwallis purportedly had another use for blacks: as carriers of the deadly smallpox virus, *Variolus major*. "Here," wrote Josiah Atkins in his journal, "I must take notice of some vilany. Within these days past, I have marched by 18 or 20 Negroes that lay dead by the way-side, putrifying with the *small pox*."[6]

Elizabeth Fenn has researched American charges of biological warfare, vis-a-vis the smallpox virus, against the British. "It would be easy to dismiss these accusations as so much American hyperbole," she writes. "Evidence indicates that in fact, the British did exactly what the Americans said they did."[7] And yet, reading his correspondence, Cornwallis comes across as a man whose modus vivendi was denial and moving on, rather than ruthless pragmatism. Far from sending black people out as an army of the nearly dead, at least at this point in time, Cornwallis seems to have dealt with the situation by doing nothing. He was certainly aware of the harm smallpox was wreaking on the people in his train. His brigadier general, Charles O'Hara, not ony informed him but asked what he wanted done with "the Hundreds of wretched Negroes, that are dying by scores every day."[8] Cornwallis replied, two days later, "It is shocking to think of the state of the Negroes, but we cannot bring a number of sick & useless ones to this place; some flour must be left for them & some person of the Country appointed to take charge of them to prevent their perishing."[9]

Charles O'Hara was, as we say in South Carolina, a man with a feelin' heart. On August 9, he wrote again, trying his best to make Cornwallis see the seriousness of the situation. Evidently, he found the general's airy instructions about leaving them some flour totally inadequate. "I shall [continue?] till I receive your positive instructions to the contrary, to victual the **Sick Negroes** [he underlined this phrase twice and wrote it in very black ink] above **1,000** in number, they would inevitably perish, if our support was withdrawn from them—the People of this Country are more inclined to fire upon than receive & protect a Negroe whose complain[t] is the small Pox."[10] Cornwallis replied on August 10, "I leave it to your humanity to do the best you can for the poor Negroes, but on your Arrival here we must adopt some plan to prevent an Evil which not only destroys a great quantity of Provisions, but will certainly produce some fatal distemper in the Army."[11]

Meanwhile, thirty thousand escaped blacks was an enormous loss of labour. Many American enslavers attempted to negotiate the return of those who had fled to the army. Major Alexander Ross, aide-de-camp to Lord Cornwallis, sent instructions on policy to one of his lieutenants as early as June: "I was furnished with your letter relative to the Demand of Negroes. Our onle [only] rule with the Army...is, to give up those that are willing to return & can be conveniently spared from the Publick Service."[12] In other words, the army would retain anyone capable of working, and the "unwilling to return" loophole let out most of the others. These were put to work building fortifications.

Cornwallis, racing the clock, wrote to Clinton on August 22: "I cannot at present say whether I can spare any troops, or, if any, how soon."[13] Neither of them was aware of how soon things would take a fatal turn. The French fleet was sailing towards the Chesapeake. In September, Cornwallis awoke to discover that the West Indian Fleet under Admiral François-Joseph de Grasse had entered the bay, and that he was blockaded. He put the Black Loyalists to work night and day on the fortifications, but this was obviously not going to be enough. On September 8, he sent a desperate message to Clinton: "The French troops landed at James Town are said to be 3800 men. Washington is said to be shortly expected, and his troops are intended to be brought by water from the Head of Elk, under protection of the French ships."[14]

Cornwallis's march through Virginia had come to a full stop. By shutting himself up in Yorktown, he had sealed his fate. Tragically, for most of the Black Loyalists with his army, death or re-enslavement was fast approaching. Cornwallis had doomed them as well. He would, in fact, hasten matters by expelling black people from the city as more of them became infected with smallpox. He also didn't want to have to feed them. His two weapons, starvation and sickness, were returning to haunt him, and so he ordered the Black Loyalists driven out; they were "useless mouths." Johann Ewald recorded what happened next:

> I would just as soon forget to record a cruel happening. On the
> same day of the enemy assault, we drove back to the enemy all
> of our black friends, whom we had taken along to despoil the
> countryside. We had used them to good advantage and set them
> free, and now, with fear and trembling, they had to face the
> reward of their cruel masters. Last night I had to make a sneak

patrol, during which I came across a great number of these
unfortunates. In their hunger, these unhappy people would have
soon devoured what I had; and since they lay between two fires,
they had to be driven on by force. This harsh act had to be carried
out, however, because of the scarcity of provisions; but we should
have thought more about their deliverance at this time.[15]

Ewald's rather mild critique could be shrugged off by the British government, the army, and contemporary historians. But, while a thorough condem-
nation of his actions wouldn't surface for several hundred years, Cornwallis
was sending these people back to slavery and retribution, or to their deaths,
and he knew it.

The general liked to suggest that he surrendered his army to the Americans
and their French allies to save lives: "Under all these circumstances I thought
it would have been wanton and inhuman to the last degree to sacrifice the
lives of this small body of gallant soldiers, who had ever behaved with so
much fidelity and courage."[16] He was speaking, of course, of his white soldiers. That he did not take steps to save his black contingent was a form of
genocide at one remove. These Loyalists were expendable because they were
black—and because so many of them were ill with smallpox, Cornwallis may
have hoped they would injure the enemy by their deaths.

Ewald, though well aware of his general's contradictions, seemed more
upset about the loss of the four hundred army horses Cornwallis had ordered
slaughtered and thrown into the river (so they wouldn't be turned over to
the Americans), and whose "sad corpses" cried out "against their murder."[17]
He never mentions the other sad corpses lying in the mud before Yorktown.
These were the bodies of black persons, dead from smallpox and starvation.

The wife of an American soldier, however, would remember this sight
fifty-six years later, when she made application in 1837 for her husband's
pension. In 1781, Sarah Osborn had embarked with her husband's American
regiment at Baltimore, sailed up the James River "as far as the tide would
carry them, and then landed, and the tide being spent…had a fine time catching sea lobsters." She marched with the army to Williamsburg and then to
"Yorktown, or Little York, as it was then called."[18] Sarah was stationed about
a mile away from the town, "just back of the American tents," where she did

washing, mending, and cooking for the soldiers. She lived with the constant roar of the cannons and the sight of the American entrenchments slowly creeping closer and closer to Yorktown. She also saw "a number of dead Negroes lying round their encampment, whom she understood the British had driven out of the town and left to starve, or were first starved and then thrown out."[19]

Joseph Plumb Martin, quick to see the irony in any situation, encountered vast numbers of blacks in the woods during the campaign and blasted Cornwallis for it in his journal: "During the siege, we saw in the woods herds of Negroes which Lord Cornwallis (after he had inveigled them from their proprietors), in love and pity to them, had turned adrift, with no other recompense for their confidence in his humanity than the smallpox for their bounty and starvation and death for their wages. They might be seen scattered about in every direction, dead and dying, with pieces of ears of burnt Indian corn in the hands and mouths, even of those that were dead."[20] "After the siege was ended," Martin would write later, "many of the owners of these deluded creatures came to our camp and engaged some of our men to take them up, generally offering a guinea a head for them." He appears to have had some sense of compassion for these people in their frightful state—as did some other soldiers, he said, and even a few enslavers.[21]

It was now a mere five days before the British surrender. On October 15, Cornwallis wrote to Clinton from Yorktown: "My situation now becomes very critical....The safety of the place is therefore so precarious that I cannot recommend that the fleet and army should run great risks in endeavoring to save us."[22] On October 17, Cornwallis asked for a ceasefire; the next day he asked for an extension. "Hostilities have ceased ever since five Oclock," wrote St. George Tucker. "A solemn stillness prevaild—the night was remarkably clear & the sky decorated with ten thousand stars—numberless Meteors fleaming thro' the Atmosphere afforded a pleasing resemblance to the Bombs which had exhibited a noble Firework the night before, but happily divested of all their horror. At dawn of day the British gave us a serenade with the Bag pipe."[23]

"They dug entrenchments," Sarah Osborn remembers in her petition, "nearer and nearer to Yorktown every night or two till the last. While digging that, the enemy fired very heavy till about nine o'clock next morning, then stopped, and the drums from the enemy beat excessively." The drums kept up their clamour, and suddenly, on October 19, the American officers began to cheer. "What is the matter now?" asked Sarah of some soldiers. And so they told her the news: "The British have surrendered."[24] Sarah, a pragmatic woman, carried breakfast down to four of the tired and dirty American artillerymen for whom she usually cooked, and watched them eat. On October 20, Cornwallis wrote to his commanding officer, "Sir, I have the mortification to inform your Excellency that I have been forced to give up the posts of York and Gloucester and to surrender the troops under my command by capitulation on the 19th instant as prisoners of war to the combined forces of America and France."[25]

Clinton broke the news to Lord George Germain in a letter nine days later, saying, "Nor will the evil end here, my lord."[26] He could not have known of the bomb so innocently being set off, even then, by Charles Cornwallis, through his unfortunate wording of Article 10 in the Articles of Capitulation: "Natives or inhabitants of different parts of this country at present in York or Gloucester are not to be punished on account of having joined the British army."[27] The implications of Article 10 infuriated Loyalists everywhere, especially Royal Governor William Franklin: "To find, notwithstanding the repeated proclamations and declarations from the highest authority in the country inviting them to manifest their allegiance to their Sovereign and promising them the amplest protection, that they were in fact considered by the capitulation in no better light than as runaway slaves restored to their former master would have been, excited, as was natural, sentiments of the highest indignation."[28]

Sarah Osborn stood on the road out of Yorktown to watch the surrender: "The British officers rode right on before the army, who marched out beating and playing a melancholy tune, their drums covered with black handkerchiefs and their fifes with black ribbands tied around them, into an old field and there grounded their arms and then returned into town again to await their destiny....The British general [Charles O'Hara] at the head of the army was a large portly man, full face, and the tears rolled down his cheeks as he passed along." This man, Sarah avowed, was not Cornwallis. She had seen *him* later, she said, "and noticed his being a man of diminutive appearance and having cross[ed] eyes."[29] Cornwallis refused to make an appearance during the surrender.

The general left behind as his legacy a memorial of black corpses, both outside and inside the shattered city. Ebenezer Denny, a Pennsylvanian, wrote in his journal, "Glad to be relieved from this disagreeable station. Negroes lie about, sick and dying, in every stage of the small pox. Never was in so filthy a place—some handsome houses, but prodigiously shattered."[30] Dunmore's call to slaves to join the royal standard, issued so long ago in Virginia, ended there in that same colony, in betrayal and death. The only good to come out of the situation was that Cornwallis's abandonment of the Black Loyalists within his lines may have strengthened Sir Guy Carleton's determination not to act in the same way. When Carleton evacuated New York in 1783, almost four thousand blacks would accompany him, in the teeth of General Washington and all the furious slaveholders of America.

Johann Ewald gives us a final glimpse into the fate of the few Black Loyalists who, as servants or booty of soldiers in the British Army, escaped with Cornwallis's surrendered army to New York. Leaving Yorktown on the *Andrew*, Ewald saw on board some black men and women: "I could not see their faces because they hid them; they probably were contraband….On the 23d we reached Sandy Hook safely."[31] One of these whose name we know was a man named Michael Beacon, born in 1758 and enslaved by Andrew Thomson of New Kent, Virginia. In the Book of Negroes, his name appears in the list of persons inspected on board the *Sovereign*, bound for Saint John, on September 13, 1783. Michael's entry shows he left his owner about three years before 1783 and "joined Lord Cornwallis's Army." He reported that he subsequently had been indentured to an Ensign Boyle, and that may have been the reason he escaped the aftermath of Yorktown.

The surrender at Yorktown, however, did not put an end to British slave raids in the Chesapeake.[32] Throughout 1782, Black Loyalists continued to flee to freedom from the bay. Black men and women escaped from Sussex County, Delaware, and from Sussex County, Maryland. In Virginia, Blacks left from Accomack, Horntown, Northampton, Northumberland County, and a place called Southern Branch. (This is only counting those who survived to become entries in the Book of Negroes.) Even as late as 1783, at least three people got to New York from Virginia. Robert Bias, from Isle of Wight County, was one, and so was a man named William from Westmoreland. The final person recorded in the Book of Negroes who made it from Virginia to New York in

1783 was a fifteen-year-old girl named Molly, a smallpox survivor. She had escaped from Richard Brooks, and in a strange coincidence, the place she managed to get away from was Gwynn's Island, Virginia—the site of so many Black Loyalist deaths at the beginning of the war.[33]

1782

American soldiers were redeployed after Yorktown, and sent north or south to continue the war on other fronts. "Three regiments of Pennsylvania, a detachment of artillery, and Maryland troops, commence their march for South Carolina," wrote one in his diary. "Easy, regular marching; roads generally good, through sandy country. Pass through Richmond and Guilford, in North Carolina." Wrote another, "We encamped on the heights near Guilford Court House, where the late action was fought between Gen. Greene and Lord Cornwallis. We found on said fields a number of buts [butts] of muskets, &c. Between the ordinary and the court house we see a negro's head sticking on a sapling on one side of the road, and his right hand side to a sapling on the opposite side. He was just hanged, then cut to pieces for killing a white man, &c."[34]

In February 1782, General Burgoyne, a prisoner since the battle of Saratoga, was exchanged for a number of American officers, one of whom was General William Moultrie. In September, Moultrie returned to South Carolina and paid a visit to General Greene outside Charlestown, travelling on horseback. The countryside he rode through was devastated—*nothing* left alive, he notes, not even a bird or a squirrel, with human skeletons here and there in the woods, of men killed in skirmishes and left unburied.[35] Moultrie knew that the British were on the verge of leaving their southern outposts. Savannah was first to be abandoned, on July 11. For Georgia's long-suffering royal governor, Wright, this seemingly hasty and poorly planned evacuation was the last straw: "[We] found ourselves constrained to abandon our valuable estates and crops and to quit the province with such of our moveable property as we could collect almost instantly, not having received the least previous notice."[36] The most "movable" of this property were, of course, their slaves.

According to William Moultrie, about a thousand Loyalists left Georgia in the summer of 1782, taking with them roughly four thousand so-called "slaves." How many of these were actually freed Black Loyalists is not known. At least one freed person is documented in the Book of Negroes as departing from Savannah. His name was James, and he found work as a cook on board the *Two Sisters*, a vessel involved in the evacuation of New York a year later. He was indentured to Captain John Browne, master of the ship. James had belonged to a David Hicks of Georgia, who had died; he "left Savannah when evacuated by the British Troops." Another name from the evacuation is Samuel Wyllie, enslaved in Savannah by an Edward Davis. His entry says that he "left the said place with General [Alured] Clark and the troops."[37]

Governor Patrick Tonyn of East Florida reported the arrival of Loyalist refugees in St. Augustine: "Upon the evacuation of Georgia, and of South Carolina now commenced, two thousand one hundred and sixty-five loyalists have arrived and three thousand three hundred and forty Negroes, their slaves, and more are daily coming."[38] Sylvia Frey notes that many freed Black Loyalists could not be accommodated on the transports and were thus sent to East Florida by inland waterways, in canoes and periaguas. Others even marched south overland.[39]

After Savannah was emptied, it seemed likely that Charlestown's evacuation would shortly follow. William Moultrie wanted to be there, but decided on a detour to his home plantation on his way south. He writes, "On my entering the place, as soon as the negroes discovered that I was of the party, there was immediately a general alarm, and an outcry through the plantation, that 'Massa was come! Massa was come!' and they were running from every part with great joy to see me."[40] He adds that a number of the gentlemen accompanying him were still alive and could corroborate that this really happened. Moultrie seems a decent man; perhaps he was a more lenient enslaver than most. However warm his welcome, though, his estate was in ruins. He was rich now only in slaves—two hundred of them.

Down in Charlestown, the British forces also were considering the great wealth that slaves represented. The army and militia units, faced with imminent defeat and departure, were trying to acquire as many saleable human chattels as possible before leaving South Carolina. Then there were the British forays to collect rebel slaves as reimbursement for Loyalists penalized by new American laws of exile or amercement. General Alexander Leslie, commanding in Charlestown, wrote American general Francis Marion on April 4 that he was deeply concerned about Loyalist property, and had authorized raids to acquire for them slaves to make up their losses.[41] Black people were being treated like cash by both sides, without the slightest regard for the disruption of their lives.

The Americans were demanding the return of *all* freed or captured slaves behind British lines. Sir Guy Carleton, having replaced Clinton as commander-in-chief, ordered Leslie to make an accounting of those black people who had been taken by the army, rather than freed.[42] This accounting, however, applied only to those blacks belonging to rebel estates stripped by the British. The order made no mention of the Black Loyalists who had joined the army by proclamation, and who were now wondering what their fate would be. Would the British abandon them as they had in 1776, in 1779, and in 1781?

Of our three black ministers, only David George was still in the south in 1782. Boston King had evidently seen the direction of the war: "Soon after I went to Charles-Town, and entered on board a man of war. As we were going to Chesepeak-bay, we were at the taking of a rich prize. We stayed in the bay two days, and then sailed for New York, where I went on shore."[43] He left South Carolina at some point in 1781, probably in the spring. John Marrant was gone as well. The Georges stayed almost to the very end, amid what must have a fever of anxious speculation.

In an escalating pattern of disobliging one another, the Americans and the British began to discuss the fate of the freed or sequestered people in Charlestown. These rounds of negotiations would lay the ground for what followed with the Black Loyalists. "When the evacuation of Charleston drew near," Moultrie writes, "it was apprehended that the British army would carry off some thousands of negroes which were within the lines." The American governor, John Mathews, wrote to Leslie in August that if the British were to take the Black Loyalists with them, he would retaliate by seizing the debts owed to British merchants and, not stopping there, would hold the confiscated estates of Loyalists beyond any hope of reclamation—including claims through marriage settlements, which had previously protected the interests of women married to Loyalists.[44]

There was a pause. Leslie then proposed a compromise. South Carolina appointed Benjamin Guerard and Edward Rutledge commissioners to act in this matter, receiving any returned human "property" at Accabee on the Ashley, just outside the city perimeter. Edward Blake and Roger Park Saunders were given permission to reside within the city, funnelling recovered slaves to Guerard and Rutledge. James Johnson and Alexander Wright acted for the British. An agreement was reached on October 10, which must have seemed a death knell for black persons who did not want to go home to their old situations as slaves: "First, that all the slaves of the citizens of South Carolina, now in the power of the honourable Lieutenant General Leslie, shall be restored to their former owners, as far as is practicable, except such slaves as may have rendered themselves particularly obnoxious on account of their attachment and services to the British troops, and such as had *specific promises of freedom*." They added a rider that "no slaves restored to their former owners, by virtue of this agreement, shall be punished by authority of the state for having left their masters and attached themselves to the British troops, and it will be particularly recommended to their respective owners to forgive them for the same."[45]

This was cold comfort to the Black Loyalists, who knew that they had no proof of "specific offers of freedom," and that this category was woefully open to interpretation by either side. Their fate was entirely out of their control. They knew all too well that, if given up, they would have no protection against an owner's anger, regardless of what the agreement might say. Their only hope lay in the continuing enmity between the two white factions, and in the reluctance of the British to give up the profits to be made by removing the sequestered blacks for later sale in the West Indies.

Moultrie was adamant that greed was the main factor in what followed, and it certainly seems a believable argument. "The prospects of gain, from the sale of plundered negroes, were too seducing to be resisted by the officers, privates and followers of the British army." The profit to be had was enormous. "It has been computed by good judges," he noted, "that, between the years 1775 and 1783, the state of South Carolina was deprived of negroes to the amount of twenty-five thousand."[46]

In one court case heard in Nova Scotia, a freed South Carolina Black Loyalist, Mary Postell, testified against a white Loyalist man who had converted her into cash (or, more accurately, potatoes). He had promised to get her to safety in East Florida, so she indentured herself to him. During the evacuation of East Florida, he brought her and her two children to Nova Scotia, but there he claimed her as his slave and then sold her and one of her children, Flora, who was carried back to South Carolina by ship. Fearful that he would do the same to her other daughter, Nelly, Mary Postell managed to bring a suit against him. South Carolina Black Loyalists Scipio and Dinah Waring (their names are spelled "Wearing" in court records) were her witnesses. The Waring and Postell enslavers had been neighbours related by marriage, and Mary Postell had known Scipio and Dinah in South Carolina.[47]

Indeed, it is possible that Mary Postell's re-enslaver, Jesse Gray (or his brother Samuel), may have been the same "Mr. Gray" whom the commissioner of sequestered estates, John Cruden, condemned for taking people out of South Carolina for resale, not only in East Florida but also in Jamaica and the Windward Islands. Being himself in Tortola on March 16, 1783, Cruden wrote the local magistrate, George Nibbs, saying, "A certain Mr. Gray, under pretence of bringing Negroes from Carolina, to prevent them from being punished by their owners, has either sold, or offered them for Sale, on this Island. As my information is only from the Negroes themselves, I submit it to you, Sir, to take such measures as to You may seem proper. I have not the least doubt that Gray is guilty, for my information is pointed with respect to his leaving the Island of Jamaica, in consequence of information lodged against him with General Campbell; he having carried on the same trade at the Evacuation of other Garrisons in America."[48]

Cruden compiled a dossier on Gray from information brought him by Black Loyalists and Sequestered blacks who had suffered this fate and had heard he was on the island. On March 24, he wrote a second letter, this time to the Honorable J. Fahia, Esq., president of the council at Tortola, warning him against Gray "making a property of those poor Unfortunate wretches, who are now in their possession and who have been fraudulently taken away." On March 25, he presented further complaints to a Major C. Nesbit of Barbados.[49]

Evidently, this sort of entrapment and illegal slave-trading, sometimes masked in promises of humanitarian aid, was all too common in the final days before the British evacuated Charlestown. Remember Balfour's orders to Sir James Wright in January 1781, "regarding some sort of illicit slave traffic flowing out of Carolina into Georgia"? Both sides wanted compensation for damages and unpaid debts, and, as always, black people were good local currency. The appointment of commissioners was seen as a way to sort things out, but it all came to nothing, and this traffic continued long after the evacuation of the city. So those blacks who fled behind the British lines on their own initiative would come to owe their escape, ultimately, to the British desire to profit from other black people, still enslaved, and from their very natural desire to disoblige the enemy.[50]

The British at last settled on a date for their evacuation: December 14. Among the vessels they amassed for the removal of troops was HMS *Belisarius*, commanded by Richard Graves. The *Belisarius* sailed from Halifax on October 1, in company with HMS *Emerald* and twenty-seven transports. They anchored off the bar on October 24, with HMS *Perseverance*, *Ceres*, and *Magicienne*. The master's log for *Belisarius* records their arrivals, adding that on November 5, the sloop *Vulture* joined the *Belisarius* and the others. On November 9, a group of transports arrived from St. Augustine; more would follow on the 18th, convoyed up the coast by HM sloop *Hornet*.[51]

A cryptic little entry in the *Belisarius* muster roll notes that on November 9 a black man named June came aboard and was entered as a "Refugee." On November 29, he was discharged. In the muster column indicating "Wither and for What Reason" the discharge took place is a stark one-word explanation: "Slave."[52] June, the unfortunate refugee, was probably not returned to the Americans; his discharge only makes sense if he was to be returned to a white Loyalist.

All the British vessels began taking on water and supplies, enough for the next four months. *Belisarius* sent her boatswain and two hands out "to sling Buoys for Buoying off the channell for the fleet to pass the danger at the evacuation of the Town."[53] They received a cargo of eleven boxes of money, for delivery to St. Augustine. On December 2, they took on a pilot, ran down to Rebellion Road, and anchored below Fort Moultrie, which the British were calling Fort Arbuthnot. On Friday, December 13, the day before the town was completely emptied of the British, the *Belisarius* sent an officer and men to help the pilot lay down the buoys in the channel. The master's log doesn't mention the evacuation on the following day, except to say that the weather was squally. The *Belisarius* was to convoy all those vessels sailing from Charlestown to St. Augustine, at first in company with a convoy to the West Indies under the protection of HMS *Emerald*.

General Leslie, in the meantime, had been shipping material and men out whenever possible, even before the formal evacuation. By November 26, transports under the convoy of the frigates *Perseverance* and *Ceres* had arrived in Halifax from Charlestown, bringing with them all the cannon and ordinance stores of the garrison. The final evacuation, they reported, would take place a few days after their departure on November 2. They were off by about six weeks.[54]

David George and his family were part of this preliminary evacuation, arriving in Halifax before December 25. He gives the following description of the journey:

> When the English were going to evacuate Charlestown, they advised me to go to Halifax, in Nova Scotia, and gave the few black people, and it may be as many as 500 White people, their passage for nothing. We were 22 days on the passage, and used very ill on board. When we came off Halifax, I got leave to go ashore. On shewing my papers to General Patterson [sic], he sent orders, by a Serjeant, for my wife and children to follow me. This was before Christmas, and we staid there till June; but as no way was open for me to preach to my own color, I got leave to go to Shelburne (150 miles or more, I suppose, by sea) in the suit[e] of General Patterson, leaving my wife and children for a while behind.[55]

In July 1784, David George, listed as forty and a farmer; his wife, Phillis, twenty-five; sons Jesse, David, and Harry; daughter Jane; and adopted daughter Lucy; were mustered in Birchtown, outside Shelburne. They had, the muster states, come "by themselves from Charlestown to Halifax. Arrived at Halifax in the fall 1782 with Col'l Hamilton from Charlestown and have drawn provisions from that time to the 24 May 1st Mr. Little's [Muster] Company."[56]

The Georges appear in this muster next to the family of another farmer, Michael Thomas, thirty-nine; wife, Sarah, thirty-eight; and sons, Michael, eighteen, and Thomas, sixteen—people who clearly had come from Charlestown in the same convoy. The Thomases and the Georges are some of the very few Black Loyalists to leave Charlestown with the British in 1782 whose names we know.

Among the accounts of the formal evacuation of Charlestown on December 14, William Moultrie's is most moving. He describes how he put on his best uniform (perhaps his only uniform), mounted his horse, and set out for the city. All went as planned. At three o'clock, the American army, the governor, and the council members rode into town, down to Broad Street. They could see the ships of the Royal Navy and the transports out in the harbour before them, the sails like white butterflies fanning their wings in the breeze: "It was a grand and pleasing sight, to see the enemy's fleet (upwards of three hundred sail) laying at anchor from Fort Johnson to Five-fathom-hole, in a curve line, as the current runs; and what made it more agreeable, they were ready to depart from the port."[57] Anchored out in Rebellion Road, where the war had begun for South Carolina, the freed Black Loyalists must have felt a commensurate joy. What the poor sequestered blacks felt, though, most of whom were being taken away from family and friends, their fates uncertain, was another story.

On December 15, *Belisarius* and the other ships and transports prepared to cross the bar. The muster rolls show that, a week earlier, *Belisarius* had taken on board four black men, again recorded as refugees: Tobias, Bob, Peter, and Toby.[58] On December 16, *Belisarius* and the other vessels in the convoy would cross the bar out to sea.

Captain's Log of the *Belisarius*, December 1782:

> *Monday 16th Mod. & cloudy. Repeated the Signal for Masters of Merchantmen to receive their instructions for St. Augustine.* AM *Came on board the Pilot to carry us over the Bar—unmoored*

> *Tuesday 17th Mod. At 3 PM Weigh'd & crossed Charlestown Bar in Cs [consort] with A number of Transports the Troops haveing all embarqued on board. 6 PM Anchored off the Bar there Joine'g H. M. Ships Assurance, Emerald, Endimion [Endymion], Adamant, & Several others....*

> *Thursday 19th Light airs & Clear—all the Convoy under weigh also Joined us the West Indian fleet under Command on* HM *Ships*

Emerald, Endemion, Naressous [Narcissus], and Hornet Sloop of War. AM Convoy of 120 Sail in Co. Joined the Fleet HM Ship Magicienne.[59]

Together, the British ships sailed south. *Belisarius* made St. John's [Sand] Bar, Florida, by Christmas Day. Little did the troops and the refugees the *Belisarius* was bringing to East Florida realize that within two years they would be forced to leave again, when Britain, by the terms of the peace treaty, was obligated to return East Florida to Spain.

Johann David Schoepf, a Hessian naturalist, would visit St. Augustine three months later, sailing from Charlestown. Schoepf's journal describes the horrors of the bar across the mouth of that harbour: "It has become so common at St. Augustine to see ships aground on this bar and this coast generally, that disasters of the sort have almost ceased to arouse sympathy or wonder. After the surrender of Charleston in 1782, within two days no less than 16 vessels, bearing refugies and their effects, went to pieces here and many persons lost their lives."[60]

Once in the city, Schoepf noticed a brigantine at anchor; this vessel had been trying for five weeks to leave the harbour, bound for Nova Scotia, but the wind and tide conditions and the bar itself had prevented this. In his account, he also observes, "There are several churches at Augustin, but almost all of them in ruins....Not far off an association of negroes have a cabin, in which one of their own countrymen, who has set himself up to be their teacher, holds services. They are of the sect of the Anabaptists....Round about the town stand the hastily built cabins of these poor fugitives, walled and thatched with palmetto leaves."[61]

On March 29, Schoepf set sail to the West Indies in one of the sloops evacuating St. Augustine. "Our small vessel," he writes, "was crammed with people and cattle, luggage and household furniture. Our two seamen were negroes; and we carried a parcel of black women and children, being sent to Providence to market." There were also both freed and indentured blacks taking passage to the Bahamas. Several black musicians constantly entertained the passengers, who sang along and danced to the music of the "Gambee" and the "Banjah," a forerunner of the modern banjo.[62]

Schoepf and his fellow passengers sailed on singing, as their ship dipped and rose on the swell of the sea, accompanied by seabirds, dolphins, and medusae, watching floating seagrass, giant turtles, and thundersqualls on the horizon. Finally they raised the island of Abaco, the northernmost of the Bahama Islands; Schoepf noted that Loyalist refugees were now settling it. Later, just at dusk, they were six miles off the island of New Providence and Nassau, its capital. At daybreak they would enter the harbour, past the black rocks over which were breaking the huge ocean combers.[63] Other Carolina refugees, going into exile yet again, would leave Florida before 1785 for the province of Nova Scotia. Theirs would be a much bleaker, colder landfall.

1783

Charlestown, now free of British control, was incorporated in 1783 and its name changed to Charleston. Finally, the announcement came that all had been waiting for: the Treaty of Paris had been signed. The war was over. Prisoners of war began trickling home. Merchants and planters in Carolina began their latest round of attempts to find and bring home all those enslaved people who had either been freed by the British or sequestered from the estates of rebellious Americans. In May, three commissioners were appointed: George Readhead and John Johnson were to act for South Carolina slave-owners in New York City, and William Livingston for Florida. General Washington instructed them to use the American commissioners appointed to inspect ships leaving New York as intermediaries between themselves and Sir Guy Carleton. Livingston was sent to St. Augustine (Governor Tonyn promptly sent him home). Slaveowners were anxious to get their human chattels back before they vanished beyond reclamation, and they knew that some freed slaves had already left New York, on the so-called "First Fleet," which had departed in April. Hence, the commissioners urged all citizens to send in accounts of their losses at once.[64]

A partial listing made by one slaveowner, Henry Middleton, is the only account to have survived. In 1779, Middleton compiled a list of the people taken from his plantations along the Combahee River, dividing his slaves up by the individual plantations from which they had escaped or were collected. A more comprehensive list of the same plantations' losses was evidently composed at a later date, as the new spelling, "Charleston," is used throughout.

By 1783, Middleton had an idea where some of the people who had escaped him had ended up. His slave Cato, for example, went with Colonel Brown's corps to Florida; Old Cato was also there. Kate went to Jamaica; Wanny went with the Hessians to New York. Seven people fled "to the Indian Nation," while numerous others had died of smallpox in Charlestown, Savannah, and St. Augustine.[65]

Ultimately, the commissioners failed in their attempts to reclaim slaves. As Henry Laurens would be told by John Lewis Gervais in December 1783, thousands of plundered slaves had been carried off with no hope of recompense.[66]

Part
THREE

Chapter Seven

LEAVING NEW YORK
FOR NOVA SCOTIA

On April 29, 1783, Lieutenant Nathaniel Phillips of the Royal Navy was rowed out to his new command, HM Armed Transport *L'Abondance*, anchored in Portsmouth Harbour, one of Great Britain's largest dockyards. After being ceremonially received aboard, Philips had the crew assembled to hear the reading of his commission, dated April 28. He had wasted no time getting on board. His orders were to sail directly to New York, to aid in the evacuation of that city.[1] Meanwhile, at Spithead, the deepwater anchorage across from Portsmouth, another vessel was fitting out. Lieutenant Robert Trounce had received his commission as commander of HM Armed Transport *Clinton* on the same day as Phillips. His orders were similar. Together, these two men would transport the bulk of the Black Loyalists to Nova Scotia.[2]

Boston King and the other Black Loyalists waiting for the transports to arrive in New York were desperate. "About [1783], the horrors and devastation of war happily terminated and peace was restored between America and Great Britain," he writes, "which diffused universal joy among all parties, except us, who had escaped from slavery and taken refuge in the English army; for rumour prevailed at New York, that all the slaves, in number 2000, were to be delivered up to their masters, altho' some of them had been three or four years among the English."[3]

King had come to New York on a Royal Navy vessel at some point between May of 1780, when the British captured Charlestown, and the summer of 1781. Having made his escape from South Carolina, he was then forced to undergo the pain of being returned to slavery when American privateers captured the whaleboat he was employed on:

> Here I endeavoured to follow my trade, but for want of tools was obliged to relinquish it, and enter into service. But the wages were so low that I was not able to keep myself in clothes, so that I was under the necessity of leaving my master and going to another. I stayed with him four months, but he never paid me, and I was obliged to leave him also, and work about the town until I was married....I then went out in a pilot-boat. We were at sea eight days, and had only provisions for five, so that we were in danger of starving. On the 9th day we were taken by an American whale-boat. I went on board then with a cheerful countenance, and asked for bread and water, and made very free with them. They carried me to Brunswick [New Jersey], and used me well. Notwithstanding which, my mind was sorely distressed at the thought of being again reduced to slavery, and separated from my wife and family; and at the same time it was exceeding difficult to escape from my bondage, because the river [unidentified, but possibly a tidal arm of the sea] at [South] Amboy was above a mile over, and likewise, another to cross at Staten Island.[4]

King could not bear the loss of his freedom a second time: "Sometimes I thought, if it was the will of God that I should be a slave, I was ready to resign myself to his will; but at other times I could not find the least desire to content myself in slavery." Consequently, he forded this "river" late one night when the tide was out, walked miles and miles to the waterside opposite Staten Island, crossed in a stolen whaleboat, and was saved: "The commanding officer, when informed of my case, gave me a passport, and I proceeded to New-York."[5]

Under the provisional peace treaty, New York was to be turned over to the Americans, which put Loyalists of all kinds in turmoil. In a letter to Lord

Hardwicke in England, one New Yorker described the situation: "Certain it is that, if the whole Army goes away this Year, very few Refugees or Inhabitants within the British Lines will be able to stay behind. Besides those gone to Europe and Canada, upwards of eleven thousand persons have already removed to Nova Scotia and twelve thousand more have given in their Names to be carried to Nova Scotia and other Places."[6]

Having recently escaped a second bondage, Boston King was horrified to find that the treaty with England included a provision for the return of slaves to their masters: "This dreadful rumour filled us all with inexpressible anguish and terror, especially when we saw our old masters coming from Virginia, North Carolina, and other parts, and seizing upon their slaves in the streets of New York, or even dragging them out of their beds. Many of the slaves had very cruel masters, so that the thoughts of returning home with them embittered life to us. For some days we lost our appetite for food, and sleep departed from our eyes."[7]

Article 7 of the provisional peace treaty did indeed state that King George would "without causing any Destruction, or carrying away any Negroes, or other Property of the American Inhabitants, withdraw all his Armies." The world was indebted to none other than Henry Laurens for this. A British prisoner since 1780, now released from the Tower of London, he had been ordered to Paris by the American Congress to take part in negotiations. According to John Adams, another of the negotiators, Laurens did not arrive until talks were almost done. On his first day there, November 29, 1782, he brought up the subject of the plundering that had been done in South Carolina, and the loss of slaves. On the following day, noted Adams, "Mr. Laurens said there ought to be a stipulation that the British troops should carry off no negroes or other American property. We all agreed. Mr. Oswald consented."[8] Richard Oswald was the single British representative at the negotiations. But he was also a friend of Henry Laurens and the former owner of a slave factory on Bance Island, Sierra Leone; Laurens, in fact, had been his agent in South Carolina, selling Oswald's slave cargoes after their arrival in Charlestown.

Back in New York, Sir Guy Carleton was already receiving numerous letters asking for the return of escaped slaves. George Washington demanded the return of all such people living behind the British lines, including some of his own slaves: Deborah Squash, aged twenty, who escaped in 1779; Henry Washington, forty-three, who left in 1776; and Daniel Payne, twenty-two. (All three managed to reach Nova Scotia). Carleton met with Washington in May 1783, at the DeWint House in Tappan, New York. Carleton was just coming out of a bout of fever. According to Washington, the meeting did not go well, and he was convinced that there would be no return of escaped slaves.[9]

Carleton had told Washington that he was expediting the removal of British forces, but that this matter depended on the arrival of the transports that were to take them away. It was, he said, "his Desire to exceed even our own Wishes in this respect," and he had begun sending off Loyalists already: "Upwards of 6,000 Persons of this Character had embarked and sailed and that in this Embarkation a Number of Negroes were comprised." Washington told Carleton that this contradicted the treaty, and Carleton replied that "it could not have been the intention of the British Government by the Treaty of Peace to reduce themselves to the necessity of violating their Faith to the Negroes who came into the British Lines under the Proclamation of his Predecessors in Command," and that the only way he saw to deal with the situation was compensation by Great Britain to the enslavers. Washington, in turn, argued that compensation would be difficult: it was "impossible to ascertain the Value of the Slaves from any Fact or Circumstance which may appear in the Register," and he worried about people changing their names or having "given in a wrong Name of his former Master." Carleton said if people felt secure, they would have no reason to lie. He insisted that the treaty did not bind him to deliver up these people or other property; it merely bound him not to carry them away. He further pointed out that as these people were not under his control, they would undoubtedly leave anyway, but at least this way, their enslavers had a chance to get their money back.[10]

George Washington sent word to his kinsman Lund Washington the next day that he now saw that there was "little prospect of recovering the Negros....In the meanwhile, it is certain that great numbers of Slaves have been carried off to Nova Scotia." Two days later, he sent word to Congress that he had "appointed Daniel Parker Esqr. Egbert Benson Esqr. and Lieut Colo. Wm. S. Smith, as Commissioners on the Part of the United States, to attend and inspect the Embarkations that in future may be made at N. York, previous to the final Evacuation of that City."[11]

In spite of the contretemps about the Black Loyalists, the Americans liked Carleton. Even General Christopher Gadsden, always choleric and ready to hang anybody at a moment's notice, agreed, calling him an excellent officer with no vested interests except the good of Great Britain.[12] "No man stands higher in the estimation even of the most violent Whigs," a Loyalist named Michaelis wrote from New York in October. "Even what they call his breach of the peace, his sending away those Negroes who came in under the Sanction of Proclamations, is not looked upon as the least bright part of his character."[13]

"The only good Tidings I have to send you," another Loyalist wrote to a friend, "is that Sir G. Carleton is not leaving us. While he stays I think myself safe." This same writer goes on to detail Carleton's actions at this time:

> He has an Altercation with those People [Congress] at present about Negroes. An Article of the wise provisional Treaty obliges us to give up all Negroes and accordingly, the Rebels have claimed all that came within the Lines. But many Negroes came in Consequence of Royal Proclamations promising them Protection and Liberty. Sir G. thinks that no minister can by a Treaty disannull those Proclamations; and indeed it would be inhuman to the last Degree and a base Violation of Public Faith to send those Negroes back to their Masters who would beat them with the utmost Cruelty. Accordingly, such Negroes as came in by Virtue of those Proclamations are permitted to go wherever they please. If they chuse to go to their Masters, it is well; if not, they are transported to Nova Scotia or else where as they desire. Sir Guy Carleton in this, as in every thing else, has acted with Openness and Candor. Before any Negroes went off, he desired Mr. Washington to appoint Commissioners to inspect all Embarkations. The Commissioners accordingly came and take Account of all Negroes that go away. The Rebels bluster about this Matter and declare it a Violation of the Provisional Treaty, but Sir Guy goes on deliberately and steadily and refers the Business to future Discussion, that Compensation may be made to the Masters of the Negroes if judged necessary.[14]

In the end, very few Black Loyalists were returned to their former enslavers, and very little compensation was ever paid to the Americans. According to Ellen Gibson Wilson, "For forty-three years the rancorous argument over compensation for war-liberated slaves rumbled on, snarling the fulfilment of other treaty provisions and contributing to the bad feeling which brought about the War of 1812....In 1790 Washington's administration stopped asking for the return of the slaves in person; monetary compensation would do. Some agreement on claims was made and paid in 1798, but no account of the settlement appears to survive."[15] Certainly, I have found no trace of any lists of runaway slaves presented to any commissioners of claims, except perhaps for Henry Middleton's partial list of losses. It seems impossible that politicians could ask for slaves to be returned or compensation paid without such documents (they exist for Virginian slave losses in the War of 1812, for example), but where are they?

They are not in the United Kingdom's National Archives, the papers of John Jay or William Pitt the Younger, or the papers of John Adams or George Washington. They don't appear to be in any collections in South Carolina. John Vandereedt at the National Archives in Washington, DC, kindly looked through anything he thought might be relevant: "We searched the segment of RG76, Internal Claims, Boundaries and Arbitrations, relating to international claims against Great Britain. The only claims that we located related to vessels. We also searched the index to Papers of the Continental Congress.... We did not see a reference to George Readhead. In the published 'The Emerging Nation: Foreign Relations of the United States, 1780-1789,' we located references to complaints by John Jay regarding fugitive slaves and violations of Article 7 of the Treaty of Versailles, but nothing regarding the commission."[16]

Black Loyalists, in spite of the war of words raging about their status, had put their faith in Carleton, and he did not disappoint them. According to historian Graham Russell Hodges, "Carleton placed the Black Pioneers on the payroll in New York City from August, 1782 until their departure in the fall of 1783. During this time the Black Loyalists received a £125 payroll for the black noncommissioned officers and private soldiers. Carleton in effect granted the Black Loyalists veteran's status....[and recommended] that Pioneers each be awarded twenty acres of land in Nova Scotia....By ruling that only destitute Loyalists would be evacuated on government ships, Carleton insured passage for the Black Loyalists."[17]

Boston King, years later, wrote of his enormous relief at Carleton's decisions. Both he and his wife, Violet, who had escaped from North Carolina, received certificates indicating that they were free, as well as safe passage to Nova Scotia: "The English had compassion upon us in the day of distress, and issued out a Proclamation, importing That all slaves should be free, who had taken refuge in the British lines, and claimed the sanction and privileges of the Proclamation respecting the security and protection of the Negroes. In consequence of this, each of us received a certificate from the commanding officer at New York, which dispelled all our fears, and filled us with joy and gratitude. Soon after, ships were fitted out, and furnished with every necessary for conveying us to Nova Scotia."[18]

Carleton showed his good faith in other ways as well, sending agent Edward Winslow to Nova Scotia to prepare for the evacuation with these words: "Your task is arduous, execute it like a man of honor. The season for fighting is over—bury your animosities and persecute no man. Your ship is ready and God bless you."[19] Moreover, in April 1783 Carleton published orders repeating Article 7 (he wished to make it clear to everyone what was required of them); he then announced the appointment of inspectors who would examine all departing ships, as well as outlining the structure he had put in place to deal with any difficulties which might arise out of American claims for the recovery of property. In addition to commissioners representing British interests, he appointed two others to serve the Americans, until Washington should fill those positions. Carleton's orders were included in the original British "Book of Negroes Registered & certified after having been Inspected by the Commissioners appointed by His Excellency Sr. Guy Carleton K.B. General & Commander in Chief, on Board Sundry Vessels in which they were Embarked Previous to the time of sailing from the Port of New York," or the Book of Negroes, as the document came to be called.

Three of these inspectors, T. Gilfillan and William Armstrong acting for the British, plus Daniel Parker acting for the Americans, would later certify that they had inspected those vessels embarking as part of what would be called "the First Fleet," which left in April *before* Carleton's meeting with Washington. The acting British officers particularly stated that they had performed their inspection "in the presence of Messrs. Parker and Hopkins who attended at the whole of the above Inspection as witnesses on the part of the said United States of America." They went on to say, "We also certify that We with these two persons were on board and examined every Vessel then bound to Nova Scotia excepting one Sloop and one Schooner which went off without being examined altho ordered not to do it but with which orders they would not comply. We however sent a Message to Captain Henry Mowatt of His Majesty's Ship La Sophia conveying the Fleet desiring him to bring back to this Place such Negroes or American Property as should be found in those vessels on their arrival in Nova Scotia."[20]

In the meantime, *L'Abondance*, the Royal Navy transport that would take the largest complement of Black Loyalists to Nova Scotia, had crossed the Atlantic and reached New York safely. It picked up a pilot in the East River on July 24 in an easterly wind. On Friday the 25th, *L'Abondance* moored in the North River and discharged the pilot. Immediately the ship's launch was sent to wash out and refill the water barrels. The breeze was fresh, the weather clear. The crew watched as HMS *Perseverance* set sail. On Saturday, the 26th, they saw HMS *Cyclops* depart New York. *L'Abondance* began receiving on board "Negroes Baggage." At some point during these two days, the Black Loyalists themselves came aboard, a boatload at a time, and were mustered into the ship's company as supernumeraries for a passage to Port Roseway. Each man was to receive the "whole allowance of specie without spirits, per order of Rear Admiral Digby, 26 July 1783." Women and children over ten received two-thirds of the allowance of rations usually made to a crew member. Children under ten got half allowances. The master's log shows that provisions were disbursed to the Black Loyalists on July 28.[21] Royal Navy victuals were traditionally monotonous: salt beef one day, salt pork the next, then peas, followed by more salt beef. Fortunately for the Black Loyalists, the voyage would be short, and *L'Abondance* had taken some fresh beef aboard as well as fresh water.

On July 29, the final allowance of the Black Loyalists' baggage was brought on board. *L'Abondance* now picked up a pilot on the North River, to be discharged at sea off Sandy Hook on August 3. By 10 A.M. they had made sail downriver, coming to anchor alongside the *Emerald*, the *Cyclops*, and some other transports. The convoy was forming. The *Nancy* (commanded by Robert Bruce) was bound for Halifax; the *Sally* (William Bell), the *Spencer* (A. Valentine), the *Hesperus* (Samuel Clark), the *Fishburn* (Joseph Gill), the *Mary* (Francis Rowbottom), and the *Peggy* (Jacob Wilson) were all bound for Saint John. The brig *Kingston* (John Atkinson), and the *Stafford* (Robert Watson) were sailing to Port Roseway. The *Grand Dutchess of Russia* (Stephen Holman) was bound for Annapolis Royal. By 11 A.M., a northeast gale had struck: strong winds with heavy rain. The Black Loyalists, down below decks, must have suffered badly from seasickness and apprehension. For tomorrow the commissioners were to come aboard and inspect the ship, listing all black people aboard in what was to form part of the Book of Negroes.[22]

There were 382 men, 230 women, and 48 children recorded by the inspectors in this first ("No. 1" in the Book of Negroes) phase of the evacuation, on ships leaving between the "23d April and 31st July 1783." Many of these black people were either still enslaved, or had contracted indentures with white Loyalist refugees to accompany them as servants. The inspectors assigned to *L'Abondance* were Captain Wilbar Cook of the 37th Regiment, Lieutenant Colonel W. S. Smith, and Deputy Quartermaster General P. Armstrong. They brought a secretary, Samuel Jones, to write down the names of all those Black Loyalists who would be allowed to leave. The inspection, as with an ordinary muster, probably took place on deck, with Jones set up at a small table to write down names and particulars.

Mary Williams was the first South Carolinian to be recorded on board *L'Abondance*. Described as a "feeble wench, aged 40," she had made her escape from Rawlins Lowndes ("Rollins Lawrence") of Charlestown. A former provost marshal, he had served as president of South Carolina in 1778 and 1779. Mary left him in 1777 and managed to survive on her own during the next six years—though she must have wondered how she would live, with no family to help her, in an unknown land and with the uncertain future which awaited.

Binah Jackson, twenty-eight, stepping up next, declared herself free of Thomas Waring of Charlestown; she had left him five years before making it on board *L'Abondance*. Binah was married to Thomas Jackson, thirty, who had been enslaved in Charlestown as well, to Stephen Shrewsbury. Boston King presented himself, aged twenty-three, together with his wife, Violet, aged thirty-five. Binah Jackson may have been familiar to him, as her enslaver was a cousin of Richard Waring, King's owner, and their country estates adjoined.

Flora and Pompey Rutledge, both in their forties, had gotten away from John Rutledge, president of the South Carolina Congress and governor of South Carolina, a wealthy man with a house on Broad Street in Charlestown. The inspectors noted only that Flora and Pompey had escaped from "Gov. Rutledge." They managed to get to the British in 1776, perhaps by means of Sullivan's Island and the Royal Navy. Charlotte Hammond, twenty-two, fled in 1776 as well; she had come from John Hammond's plantation on the Ashley River. Still others escaped in that year: Harry Fruen, thirty-five, left Thomas Sheppard of Charlestown; Abraham Cry, forty, left John Ward; Thomas Evans, forty, fled Andrew Evans; Dublin Gordon, thirty-one, gave the name "Patrick Haynes of South Carolina" as that of his former master (probably a misspelling of Patrick Hinds, a cordwainer in Charlestown).

John Banbury, thirty-eight, had been "the property of Arthur Middleton of Charlestown, South Carolina; left him 7 years ago." His wife, Lucy Banbury, forty, made her escape from the same master a year later. Their enslaver, Arthur Middleton (1742–1787), was one of the signers of the Declaration of Independence. Henry Middleton, sixteen, whose name is given as "Minton" in the Book of Negroes, had been previously "the property of Henry Middleton, Senior, Charlestown," for whom he may have been named. This slaveowner (1717–1784) was elected president of the Provincial Congress in 1775, and was a delegate from South Carolina to the First Continental Congress. Arthur Middleton was his son.

Savinah Miles, twenty-five, ran from John Miles's plantation in the Indian Lands of South Carolina, taking her daughter, Venus, with her. Venus was only nine years old when she escaped with her mother, who kept her free for the next five years, before boarding *L'Abondance*. Hagar Miles, twenty-two, fled John Miles's plantation on the Ashepoo River. Toney Wilkins, forty, escaped with his wife, Sarah, twenty-three, from John Wilkinson in the Indian Lands.

Harry and Sally Harrington, forty and thirty-five, respectively, were approaching middle age. Harry was from Charlestown, and his wife came from Savannah, Georgia. Sikes Rivers, forty, was also from Savannah. Like Sally Harrington, he had escaped in 1777; his wife, Susannah, was thirty and had run from Thomas Fitt in the Indian Lands. Juno Thomas, forty, described as "worn out," was from Savannah as well.

Venus and James Legare of Charlestown brought their seven-year-old son with them. His name isn't given in the Book of Negroes, but *L'Abondance*'s muster shows it to have been William, as does the 1784 muster for Birchtown.[23] James was a chair-maker, formerly enslaved by Thomas Legare; Venus had escaped from Malory Rivers. Hector Peters, twenty, and Kate Mason, twenty-one, both said that they had been born free in Charlestown.

Jane Milligan, twenty, had run from James Johnson of Savannah, Georgia, in 1781. In 1782, she gave birth behind the British lines to a daughter, Maria Milligan, described in the Book of Negroes as being nine months old and a healthy child. Another woman, listed simply as Grace, thirty-six, brought a ten-month-old daughter aboard. Formerly the property of Charles Dawson of Charlestown, Grace does not appear in *L'Abondance* muster, so we don't know her last name, or the name of her child. She either mustered under another name, another gender (see below), or not at all.[24]

Life on board ship would have presented special problems for the mothers with young infants. Did they have to wash diapers in salt water, or were they given fresh water for this? Were they given enough drinking water to keep their milk supply abundant? And what about those whose children were ill? Duskey York, twenty-four, escaped from Nathan Legare of Charlestown, marrying Betsey, a runaway from Virginia, in New York. Their daughter, Sally, only eighteen months old, was "sickly." However, the presence of so many South Carolinians on board must have helped to make *L'Abondance* seem less frightening. These included:

> Sarah Jones, thirty-three; escaped from Richard Stevens,
>   Port Royal.
> Becky Seabrook, twenty-seven; escaped from John Seabrook
>   of Charlestown.
> Nancy Peters, fifty; escaped from Thomas Phipps of Charlestown.
> Jane Roberts, twenty-three; escaped from John Cottarge,
>   Charlestown.
> Silvia Gordon, thirty; escaped from Malory Rivers, James Island.
> William Smith, forty; escaped from Jacob Hemmings, Charlestown.
> Rob Robinson, twenty-three; escaped from John Hearne,
>   James Island.

James Campbell, forty; escaped from Malory Rivers, Savannah.
Francis Jones, forty-six; escaped from William Logan,
    Charlestown.
Caesar McKenzie, thirty-two; escaped from John McKenzie,
    Charlestown.

Going through the muster roll of *L'Abondance*, comparing it with the various copies of the Book of Negroes, one does notice transcription errors. One of the most puzzling mysteries of the muster, however, is that of "Sillah Cain," described in the Book of Negroes as "40, stout wench. Formerly the property of John Ward of Charlestown, South Carolina; left him 7 years ago." Looking at the muster for *L'Abondance*, we find that the only Cain on this ship, other than Tom Cain, is listed with the men as "Shelan Cain, entered 26 July 1783, New York; D [discharged] 2 September Port Roseway, per order Capt. Brabazon Christian." Yet the 1784 Nova Scotia muster (Captain Jones's company) shows a "Thomas Kane, 31; Fisherman" living with "Sella Banbury, 41." This is presumably Silla Cain. Why is she in the men's muster for *L'Abondance*?[25]

It would appear that someone, almost certainly for larcenous reasons, included some of the women's names in the muster of "Men." Savinah Miles, mentioned above, also appears in the men's muster of *L'Abondance*, as "Severn Miles." And besides "Shelan Cain" and "Severn Miles," we find "Edward Gordon" for the female Edie Gordon (as her name appears in the Book of Negroes); "Pat Brown" for Patty Brown; "Dor. Cromwell" for Dorcas Crumwell; "Mat. Brown" for Mary Brow; "Mar. Cromwell" for Peggy Crumwell. Most of these names are given in a way that does not make it immediately obvious that they are women. By contrast, almost all the names in the women's column are written out in their entirety (and anywhere the name Margaret is abbreviated, it appears as "Marg't," not "Mar"). It is also curious that boys above the age of ten are not included in the women's column, even though the heading would lead one to believe this to be the case; instead, they are listed with the men. Even some infants and children younger than ten years are listed with the men. Since women were allowed only two-thirds the food allowance as a man (and children under ten, one-half the food allowance), somebody in the crew was clearly making off with the extra rations.

Three unfortunate women were not allowed to join the evacuation and were removed from *L'Abondance* on July 31, "per order of the Inspectors." Their names were Betty Trewin, Esther Wilkinson, and Celia Richards. Their fates are unknown. As they do not appear in the Book of Negroes, we don't know where they were from, and cannot trace their former owners, to see if they were returned to them.[26]

L'Abondance was also carrying a Black Loyalist from Virginia, blind Moses Wilkinson, who would make a name for himself in Nova Scotia as a preacher of the Gospel. General George Washington's slave Henry Washington shipped on *L'Abondance* as well. In fact, among her "List of 179 Men 147 Women & 84 Children Refugee Negroes, borne as Supernumeraries for Victuals only," the majority were from the combined Chesapeake Bay area: Virginia, Maryland, and Delaware. South Carolina had been home to many. A further handful each came from Georgia, North Carolina, Pennsylvania, New Jersey, New York, Connecticut, Rhode Island, and "New England," including one from Boston and one from Buttermilk Bay, Massachusetts. Two others were from Jamaica and elsewhere in the West Indies.

The second transport to take on a large number of Black Loyalist passengers, the *Clinton*, reached New York by July 16. By July 26, *Clinton*'s master's log noted that Loyalist baggage was coming on board, and that HMS *Cyclops* had sailed for Nova Scotia. More Loyalists came aboard on the 27th, including a large number of blacks headed for Saint John and Annapolis Royal, Nova Scotia. There was a problem on the 29th, when five seamen deserted, taking the ship's cutter and setting the smaller ship's boat adrift. After recovering the cutter from Long Island, *Clinton* weighed anchor and sailed down to Staten Island. The logbooks do not mention commissioners or inspectors coming on board, but the Book of Negroes suggests that the *Clinton* was boarded at some point after *L'Abondance* was inspected, on July 31.[27]

At last, this phase of the evacuation was underway. On Friday, August 1, Captain Brabazon Christian on HMS *Cyclops* made a signal for all the lieutenants to come aboard for orders. *L'Abondance* took on a final load of fresh water, and on Saturday, August 2, at 1:00 P.M., weighed anchor and made sail, in company with the *Cyclops* and the *Clinton*, to convoy the other nine vessels transporting Loyalists, black and white, to Nova Scotia. The master's log records clear weather and strong breezes. The ships sailed out the harbour to Sandy Hook and anchored. Sunday the 3rd was squally, with rain. At 4:00 A.M., *Cyclops* signalled to make sail; by 7:00 A.M., *L'Abondance* had discharged her pilot, was over the bar, and finally out to sea.

By August 17, according to the master's log, *L'Abondance* was nearing Cape Negro, Nova Scotia, had taken on a pilot, and finally had come to rest below Port Roseway (later Shelburne). Since it was a Sunday, Captain Phillips read the Articles of War to the assembled crew and passengers. Despite the fairly decent weather and the short passage, many Black Loyalists aboard *L'Abondance* had become ill. Phillips ordered the ship's longboat hoisted out on Monday the 18th, and in the morning, the crew were "employed making a Tent on Shore for the Sick Negroes," from the spritsail and the main-deck awning. By Wednesday, he'd sent fifty-three sick blacks to this temporary tent hospital.[28]

The master's log for *L'Abondance* says that on August 24, the crew rowed eight Black Loyalists, who had been left behind in Port Roseway by the *Clinton*, over to the transport vessel *Venus* for passage on to Saint John: "Light airs & calms, sent a Boat to Assist the *Venus* Transp't going out & Sent 8 Negroes with 8 days Provisions for them to St. Johns, they being left [here] by the *Clinton*."[29]

L'Abondance's muster roll, on the other hand, says that these eight people—"John Holland, Henry Beaverhoudt, Billy Bush, Sam'l Hutchins, Prince Johnson, Tho's Byng, Henry Floyd, and James Jackson"—came over from the *Clinton* "per Order Capt. Wm Affleck [the commandant of the convoy], being Negro Refugees," on August 28, four days *after* they were supposed to have been sent to the departing *Venus*.[30] The *Clinton* wasn't in Port Roseway on either of those dates, judging by the evidence of its own log and muster rolls; *Clinton* must have discharged these men before August 21, the day her crew complement was mustered "at sea."[31]

The *Clinton*'s muster rolls show other discrepancies for this voyage. First, they state that *Clinton* discharged these men, not to *L'Abondance*, but as follows:

> *Henry Floyd, discharged 2 September at Annapolis Royal*
> *Thomas Bing [sic], discharged 2 September at Annapolis Royal*
> *John Holland, discharged 1 September at Saint John*

James Jackson, discharged 1 September at Saint John
Samuel Hutchins, discharged 1 September at Saint John

The muster shows a "Benjamin Bush, discharged 1 September" at Saint John, but no Billy Bush. The name "Prince Johnson" does not appear at all. Someone on the *Clinton* perhaps wrote up the discharges at a later time: *Clinton*, logically, went from Port Roseway to Annapolis Royal, and then across the Bay of Fundy to Saint John and on to New York, yet the muster shows Black Loyalists were discharged first in Saint John on September 1, and second, in Annapolis Royal on September 2.[32] Perhaps the person keeping the *Clinton* muster simplified matters by writing blanket dates beside the names, regardless of when the discharges really happened—again possibly to make a profit on undistributed rations.

The *Clinton*'s muster roll has, however, cleared up some confusion generated by the Book of Negroes list for this voyage. The *Clinton* was reported heading for Annapolis Royal and Saint John, but the Book of Negroes does not tell us who disembarked at each of these ports. This muster roll (allowing for some discrepancies, discussed above) thus is an invaluable aid to genealogists and historians, identifying which Black Loyalists settled at Annapolis Royal and which at Saint John.

Meanwhile, back at Port Roseway, *L'Abondance* took on a pilot at 10:30 A.M. on Thursday, August 28, "to carry the Ship into the NW Harbour [shortly to be named Birchtown]; weighed and came to Sail." On Friday, up in Birchtown, all the Black Loyalist men were sent ashore to set up tents for their families; on Saturday, the baggage was off-loaded, and on Sunday, August 31, the sick and their baggage were brought up to Birchtown by longboat from Port Roseway. They were quartered on the ship for four days. *L'Abondance*'s crew dismantled the sick tent down in Shelburne, and brought the sails back aboard. On Monday the ship took on water, and on Tuesday they hosed down below decks and "fumigated the Ship with Gunpowder and vinegar." Finally, on Wednesday, September 3, all the remaining passengers were discharged. Thursday they sailed for New York.[33]

On September 12, back in New York, the *Clinton* noted their arrival in the master's log: "Arived his Majesty's Transport Le abundance from Port roseway AM." The *Clinton* had reached New York a few days earlier, on September 8, and was readying for sea; it loaded refugees on the 21st. By September 22, *L'Abondance* had taken on board 208 people and their baggage, and was also loading supplies. Unfortunately, on Wednesday, September 24, the *Clinton* ran afoul of *L'Abondance*. Perhaps both crews were a little under the weather, because the day before they had celebrated the anniversary of the King's coronation. By Thursday the 25th, however, *L'Abondance* was ready for sea and anchored off Staten Island, in company with HMS *Amphion*, under the command of Rear Admiral Robert Digby, and several other transports, including the *Clinton*. On the Friday, the master's log notes, "Came on Board Commissioners & Examined the Negroe Serv'ts."[34] Thirteen Black Loyalists were recorded as aboard *L'Abondance*, but none were from South Carolina or Georgia.

The *Clinton* delayed sailing to take on more refugees on September 27, as well as "a part of the 17th light Dragoons and part of the 7 & 37 Reagments." Her muster of supernumeraries reads, "Sept. 20th/ New York P[er] Order: List of Men, Women and Children above Ten Years Old, Victualled of whole Allowance of all Species except Spirits P[er] Order/MUSTER-TABLE of His Majesty's Ship the *Clinton* between the *1st of September* and the *29th of October following*." This list of names appears to include soldiers, plus some white Loyalists (white women and children, above ten years of age, were given the full allowance of food, whereas Black Loyalist women and older children had only a two-thirds allowance). The *Clinton* was carrying only a few blacks, and these were either indentured or enslaved. All would be discharged from the *Clinton* at Port Roseway on October 26, 1783. The Black Loyalists from South Carolina consisted of three married couples: Samuel Croaker and his wife, Peggy; Samuel Atkinson and his wife, "Minty" (Book of Negroes), or "Miley" (*Clinton* muster); and Samuel White with his wife, Peggy—all indentured to Hugh Walker. The *Clinton* did not put out to sea until October 4.[35]

L'Abondance was once again bound for Port Roseway, recently renamed Shelburne. It had arrived by October 14, when it took on a pilot and anchored below the fort. This second voyage took slightly over two weeks; the first took only fourteen days. HMS *Cyclops* and some transports were at anchor in the harbour. On the 17th, the *Clinton* came in with more transports. On October 20, the refugees' baggage was off-loaded, and through Thursday, the 23rd, the passengers were discharged. This load was mostly white Loyalists and soldiers. As with the *Clinton*, *L'Abondance* was carrying a much smaller number of black people, most either still enslaved or indentured as servants. By the 25th, *L'Abondance* was back at sea. It made New York by November 14 and began preparing for its final run to Nova Scotia, before returning to England. The *Clinton* left Port Roseway the following day, October 26.[36]

Back in New York, Johann Ewald was bored, irritated, and mildly worried about staying further in America. He wanted to go home. Already, according to his diary, his comrades were embarking. New York in November, according to Ewald, had become a chaotic place: "*The 18th*. Fortunate is he who has nothing further to do in New York! As lively as the city was formerly because of its trade, it is now just as dead, since all commerce is at a standstill. The remainder of the loyalists are occupied with nothing but packing up and leaving, and those who would dare to remain in New York look desperate with fear of dark prospects. On the other hand, the rebel sympathizers arrive in the city from all directions by land and water."[37]

Between August 21st and 25th, the regiments embarked and Ewald saw the city delivered up to the Americans: "On all corners one saw the flag of thirteen stripes flying, cannon salutes were fired, and all the bells rang. The shores were crowded with people who threw their hats in the air, screaming and boisterous with joy, and wished us a pleasant voyage with white handkerchiefs. While on the ships, which lay at anchor with the troops, a deep stillness prevailed as if everyone were mourning the loss of the thirteen beautiful provinces. It was on this same day, at four o'clock in the afternoon, that we set sail with a favourable wind. In the twilight, the fleet of perhaps sixty sail passed Sandy Hook, and on the morning of the 26th we had lost sight of the coast of America."[38]

Ewald shipped out on the *Mars*. Johan Seume, another Hessian conscript who had spent his war-service years in Halifax, also went home on a British transport: "A tremendous number of vessels of all kinds and all nations had collected immediately after the peace declaration; and we ran into the English Channel some 200 at one time. Among this gathering were two American frigates with the new flag of the free states—perhaps for an old Englishman the bitterest sight since British fleets sailed the seas."[39]

The *Clinton* got into New York's East River on November 6. It loaded refugees between the 15th and the 19th and, about a week later, was nearly ready to leave. On this third voyage, the *Clinton* must not have been carrying any Black Loyalists, as the ship does not appear in the Book of Negroes after its second voyage in October 1783. The master's logs also do not record the coming aboard of the commissioners to list any Black Loyalists. The *Clinton* sailed to Port Roseway, on to Halifax, and back to England, where the ship was sold out of service in 1784.

The final remaining Black Loyalists still trapped in New York must have felt tension so extreme it resembled a state of shock. At least 142 men, 90 women, and 54 children had not yet gotten out of the city by the time the Americans were to take complete control. Finally, on November 30, this number was mustered and inspected on board the *Peggy*, commanded by James Beasley; the *Danger* (James Duncan); the brig *Concord* (George Robinson); the *Diannah* (Will Browne); and *L'Abondance* (Nathaniel Phillips).[40]

The November run of *L'Abondance* would transport the Black Brigade out of New York. By the 22nd, it was "Employed in geting refugees baggage on Board." On Monday the 24th, it was ready to take on passengers: 233 "refugees for Nova Scotia, P[er]order Rear Admir'l Digby." This, in the minds of those who were boarding, was none too soon. They were just a day ahead of the Americans. And still they had to wait to sail:

> *Master's Log, His Majesty's Armed Transport L'Abondance*
> *Tuesday 25...Emp'd getting Baggage on Board...Sailed Several*
>   *Tranports & a Vast number of Ships Hauled off from the Warfs.*
> *Wednesday 26...The American Troops Enter'd the [city] with*
>   *great Triumph...Sailed H.M. Armed Transp'ts Camel, Clinton*
>   *& Ranger, with several Transports.*[41]

On November 26, just ahead of the American entry into New York, the British commander in chief, Carleton, took leave of the city and had himself rowed out to board HMS *Ceres*, the ship that would carry him to England. One wonders if the boat carrying him across the harbour would have been pointed out to the Black Loyalists on *L'Abondance*, and if they gave him a cheer as they watched him pass. (The *Ceres* muster shows that a man known only as "Buck," possibly black, had come aboard on November 15, but there is no mention of him in the inspection rolls that would become the Book of Negroes. He was discharged in England in January 1784.)[42]

Master's Log, His Majesty's Armed Transport L'Abondance
Friday 28 Wind ENE. *Strong Gales with a heavy fall of Snow.*
  P.M. At 1 came too [anchored] in 8 Fathoms with the Best
  Bower off Staten Island. Riding here H.M.S. *Ceres & a great*
  number of Transports.
Sunday 30 Winds Wes'ly…Received refugees Baggage… Came on
  Board commissioners & examined the Negro Servants.[43]

At last the waiting was over. "On Board His Majesty's Ship L'Abondance," bound for Port Mouton, the following Black Loyalists from South Carolina and Georgia were going to freedom, some of the last people passed by the commissioners at New York:

Thomas Russall, 24 years, stout fellow, Black Brigade. Former
  slave to Doctor Wast of Charlestown, South Carolina; left him
  about 5 years ago. GMC.
Sam Wedder, 30 years, stout fellow, Black Brigade. Formerly slave
  to Doctor Wedder of Goose Creek, South Carolina; left him
  about 5 ½ years ago. GBC.
Morris Seaman, 21 years, stout fellow, Black Brigade. Formerly
  slave to Paul Traper [Trapier] of Georgetown, South
  Carolina; left him about 4 years ago. GBC.
Latice Young, 20 years, stout wench, Black Brigade. Formerly
  slave to William Young of Welltown [Willtown], South
  Carolina; left him about 5 years ago. GMC.
Jack Williams, 24 years, stout fellow, Black Brigade. Formerly
  slave to William Williamson, Horse Savannah, South
  Carolina; left him about 5 years ago. GMC.
Judith Dewitt, 22 years, stout wench, Black Brigade. Formerly
  slave to John Dewitt of Charlestown, South Carolina; left him
  about 4 years ago. GMC.
Dublin Moore, 31 years, ordinary fellow, Black Brigade.
  Formerly slave to John Moore of James Island, South Carolina;
  left him about 5 years ago. GBC.

Thomas Holmes, 22 years, stout fellow, Black Brigade. Formerly
   slave to Cairnes of Charlestown, South Carolina; left him
   about 7 ½ years ago.

Daniel Elliott, 29 years, stout fellow, Black Brigade. Formerly
   slave to Gen. Sumpter [General Thomas Sumter] of Santee
   river, South Carolina; left him about 6 years ago. GBC.

Plante [Plenty] Platt, 29 years, stout fellow, Black Brigade.
   Formerly slave to Peter Thom Platt, Charlestown, South
   Carolina; left him about 5 years ago. GMC.

Betsey Robinson, aged 40 years, ordinary wench, Black Brigade.
   Formerly slave to John Robinson of Charlestown, South
   Carolina, who gave her freedom.

Mingo Leslie, 34 years, ordinary fellow, Black Brigade. Formerly
   slave to John Leslie, Charlestown, South Carolina; left him
   about 3 ½ years ago. GMC.

Dianah Johnson, 18 years, likely wench. Formerly slave to
   William Johnson of Goose Creek, South Carolina; left him
   about 3 ½ years ago. GMC.

Lymus Pandorrus, 52 years, nearly worn out, Black Brigade.
   Formerly slave to Richard Pandorrus [Pendarvis], New river,
   South Carolina; left him about 4 years ago. GBC.

Morria [Maria] Pandorrus, 32 years, ordinary wench, Black
   Brigade. Formerly slave to William Jones of Savannah in
   Georgia; left him about 4 years ago. GBC.

Hager Kennady, 29 years, ordinary wench, Black Brigade.
   Formerly slave to Mathew Hardey, Augusta County, Georgia;
   left him about 4 years ago. GBC.

Sam her son, 1 year, Black Brigade. Born free within the British lines.

Pompy Colt, 27 years, ordinary fellow, Black Brigade. Formerly
   slave to Mr. Colt, Santee river, South Carolina; left him about
   3 ½ years ago. GMC.[44]

The final "GMC" or "GBC" at the end of these entries indicates that the person has a certificate of freedom from General Thomas Musgrave or General
Samuel Birch, commandants at New York.

Worthy of note on board *L'Abondance* on this last exodus from New York were two Virginians who had escaped in 1775 under Dunmore's Proclamation. Both had served in the Black Brigade. Toby Castington was now thirty-three years old; the Book of Negroes says he was "formerly slave to John Conner, Kent County, Virginia; left him about 7 years ago, with Dunmore." Chloe Mann, thirty-four, left her enslaver at that time as well. Two years later, she gave birth to a daughter, "Bettsey Mann, 5 years, Black Brigade. Born free within the British lines."

By Sunday, December 7, *L'Abondance* had raised Nova Scotia for the third and last time, and Phillips had a cask of white wine broached. By Monday afternoon, the vessel was working into Port Mouton, a name that the master, updating his log, spelled both as "Port Matoon" and "Port Mutton." By 3:00 P.M., they were moored, had hoisted out the longboat, and were drying their sails.

On Wednesday December 10, *L'Abondance* offloaded the Black Loyalists' baggage, "sending the men on shore to Build Huts for their Families." On Thursday the 18th, the weather changed for the worse, with a "heavy fall of snow." Regardless of the snow, on the 19th or 20th, *L'Abondance* landed "219 refugees" at Birchtown, with provisions to last four days, "until the 23rd." They wouldn't be re-provisioned until January of the new year. The ship then raised anchor and sailed away.[45] This had been the last trip ferrying Loyalists that *L'Abondance* was to make. After leaving Port Mouton, the ship continued on to Halifax, and then returned to England, where it was sold out of the service the following year.

The Black Loyalists, cold and weary, disembarked upon a new land and a new life. Regardless of how perilous that life was to prove, their descendants would be able to tell the world that they were—like Bettsey Mann, the last black passenger on *L'Abondance* to appear in the Book of Negroes—"born free within the British lines."

Chapter Eight

LIFE IN NOVA SCOTIA, 1783–1792

BIRCHTOWN, SHELBURNE COUNTY

oston King disembarked at Birchtown in late summer: "Every family had a lot of land, and we exerted all our strength in order to build comfortable huts before the cold weather set in. That winter, the work of religion began to revive among us; and many were convinced of the sinfulness of sin, and turned from the error of their ways." He was one of them, saying, "Every thing appeared to me in a different light to what they did before; and I loved every living creature upon the face of the earth. I could truly say, I was now become a new creature."[1] His delight now was to pray.

That winter, the Black Loyalists would need prayers. They were living off provisions doled out by the government, and these were scant. They were shivering in tents, in crude huts, and in structures now referred to as pit houses—basically holes dug into the ground, with a roof thrown over. In the 1930s, Clara Dennis interviewed a grandson of settler Jupiter Farmer, who described the construction of these pit houses as she walked over the land with him:

> *"Surely human beings could never have lived in these places,"*
> *I said. "They are only holes in the ground!" "That's all they*

ever were," said the previous owner of the land. "I've heard
grandfather tell about them. The government gave the negroes
land here, but they had no houses, not even log cabins. They just
dug a hole in the ground and put a little peaked roof over it. They
chose a hill for their purpose because the ground was drier....And
that was the black man's home—a hole in the ground with a roof
over the hole."[2]

The only heat for these makeshift homes came from green wood the black settlers cut and split. Some built crude chimneys out of mud and field-stones; others simply lived with the smoke.

On January 8, 1784, provisions were given out to the free Black Loyalists—630 men and 475 women. White Loyalists were also resupplied. A third category in this muster, "Servants" (whether indentured or enslaved blacks, or even white servants, is not indicated), amounted to 823 men, 289 women, 87 children over the age of ten, and 70 younger ones. In the coming months, individual whites in Shelburne would often withhold provisions or pay from their black employees (as noted in the Birchtown muster of July).[3]

Begun on July 3 and carried on through the first of August, the Birchtown muster gives the occupation of most of the community's free black settlers as labourers; also listed, however, were carpenters, seamen, sailors, ship's carpenters, cooks, coopers, weavers, seamstresses, tailors, bakers, farmers, millers, sawyers, and caulkers, as well as a mason, a bricklayer, a sail-maker, a blacksmith, an anchor-smith, a chimney sweep, a peddler, a painter, and a shoemaker. There was even a skinner, and one "apprentice," trade unspecified.

The muster also records some "Late [former] Indentured Servants to the Inhabitants of Shelburne who are located on Lotts at Birchtown by Order of Mr. Marsdon." (Benjamin Marsdon was the surveyor laying out the lots of land.) From the muster of Captain Cuthbert's company, in particular, come the following sad accounts: Henry MacGregor, a labourer from South Carolina, formerly owned by Thomas Heyward of Charlestown, was twenty-eight. He said he'd been indentured to Alpheas Palmer's family in Shelburne for a year and was to be paid fifty dollars. After coming to Nova Scotia with Palmer, and living and working with the Palmer family for eight months, the two men had a falling out, and Henry was cast off without pay.

He was supporting his wife Dinah, twenty-eight, formerly enslaved by John Dale of James Island, South Carolina, and their daughter Jane, aged seven, at the time.[4]

Jacob Wigfall's story is even sadder. He was twenty-six, a carpenter from South Carolina, indentured to a Richard Wheaton for two years at £40. After he got to Nova Scotia in May, he became sick, and so Wheaton turned him out on August 1, "& never gave him any provision, neither has he received any." Jacob was still alive in July, however, living with his wife, Silvia or Celia, aged thirty. Both had been slaves in Charlestown of Joseph Wigfall, a descendent of one of Carolina's first slave traders.[5]

On July 28, 1784, shortly after the Birchtown muster was compiled, disbanded soldiers and local labourers in Shelburne rioted, beating blacks whom they saw as working for less and thus taking away their jobs and driving many of them out of town. The rioters destroyed a number of the small homes of those Black Loyalists living on the northern edge of Shelburne, including a small church building.[6]

Another fear faced by Black Loyalists in those early years was abduction for resale into slavery. In the Birchtown muster of July 1784, Binah Frost, twenty-five, is listed as having lived with the family of a Mr. Gough in Shelburne that first winter, having come from New York with him on the first fleet. Her husband Benjamin, twenty-four, had been carried to Jamaica and sold by a Mr. Miller who lived with Gough.[7] In 1787, Richard Hill was dragged on board Joshua Wise's schooner in Shelburne Harbour. A justice of the peace, who had Hill's certificate of freedom from General Birch, sent out to the ship to have him returned, but it was too late. Captain MacDonald had already set sail for the West Indies and was nearly out of the harbour. Similar re-enslavements of free people were going on as late as 1791, as the cases of South Carolinian Mary Postell and her daughters, Flora and Nelly, sold back into slavery (by the Jesse Gray discussed in chapter 6) demonstrate.[8] Falsified indentures were yet another effective method of re-enslavement, and indenture contracts could be sold on. Lydia Jackson of Manchester (Guysborough County) couldn't read, and was told her contract was for one year. Her indenture was then sold to someone else, she was taken away to Lunenberg, and there told that she'd signed to serve for thirty-nine years. Lydia found herself a slave again, with an extremely abusive "owner."[9]

Everyone, both black and white, was starting to realize by the end of the decade that the grandiose plans for Shelburne were not working out: the soil was poor, the farm lots miles away, and work for the poorest people scant. Black Loyalists, as revealed by court cases, had marginal existences. Silvia White lived in a house rented from a mulatto woman named Truelove, a "person who had left the settlement," and made a living by picking huckleberries. She shared this house with Betty Johnson, who made her half of the rent by stealing; she had already been "burnt in the hand" by the court for a previous offense. In the same case, neighbour Lydia Newton said that she and her mother, Abby, laundresses when they could get the work, lived nearby in a house belonging to a "Mr. Gable" (probably another property-owner who had left Shelburne). Silvia later rented a room to Phillip Gordon; he was charged with stealing ducks and geese to sell to the barracks. Silvia had plucked them, and had gotten Dinah Ely, a neighbour who owed her for laundering, to sell the resultant pillow in Annapolis for six coppers.[10]

Famine made life an even worse horror for Black Loyalists in the latter half of the 1780s. Prices for what little food was available rose higher and higher. This famine, described by both Boston King and John Marrant, appears to have begun somewhere between 1787 and 1789, simply because that's when court cases for the theft of food begin. People previously stole things they could swap for money or goods, but now they were stealing food directly and eating it themselves. They were hungry.

On March 19, 1787, in the first such case recorded, John Fours broke into Alexander McAuslen's store and took flour, butter, and cheese, telling an accomplice that he had previously stolen pork and cornmeal from the same merchant.[11] Others, such as Samuel and Nanny Legare, and Bosun Vaughan, formerly of South Carolina, were also desperate enough to break the law. In January 1789, these three killed a hog belonging to Thomas Fortune, a black farmer, and tried to eat as much of it as possible before being discovered. When charged, Bosun Vaughan said Samuel Legare killed the pig; he merely helped. Legare said exactly the opposite. Their subsequent testimony is fascinating for the light it sheds on the lives and material culture of Black Loyalists of Birchtown in 1789.

Vaughan lived near Thomas Fortune and stated that, on New Year's Day, Samuel Legare came by his house in the evening, saying he thought there wasn't anybody home at the Fortunes' house. The sow wasn't in Fortune's cellar, but they found her in "a store or shed in the yard of Tho's Fortune house where was some Hay." The sow was struck with an axe, but escaped the two of them.[12] On the evening of January 5th, Legare came to Vaughan's house for a second attempt on this pig, "& stayed till the Moon was down." Fortuitously, the sow showed up near a "Cow house" outside. Vaughan and Legare chased her "into the room" of Vaughan's house; Bosun Vaughan held a torch and Samuel killed the sow with an axe. To hide the blood, they wrapped her head in an old coat, put her in a bag and carried her to the Legare home: "Legrees wife Nanny had 2 or 3 potts of water on, Nanny said to her husband, old man have you got any thing to night, o yes says he Nanny I have got something to night we should have no occasion to go to Shelburne so often as I has done." The three of them butchered the pig and began cooking; they ate chunks of pork and hot fat dripping until well after midnight, and then ate more for breakfast. Legare hid what they hadn't eaten in a bag in the woods.[13]

One tends to believe Vaughan's account because this wasn't the first arrest for Samuel Legare. In June 1788, Phillip Gordon testified in court that in December he'd been at Friday Snipe's house, and "he saw a shoulder blade of mutton & a flank of mutton & a sheep head in it in a stew with potatoes & dumplings there was two sheeps head hanging up in the room." Sukey Marshall swore she'd heard Friday and Samuel Legare planning to steal the sheep: "Fridays wife went to a part of a room divided by a blanket & brought out the 2 pieces of mutton, fresh killed, it was badly butchered, & bloody, this mutton was cut up & put in the stew."[14]

Clearly, some Birchtown residents had cows, pigs, and sheep. Moreover, the testimony offers descriptions of Birchtown structures: houses with cellars, storage sheds, and cow houses, along with single-room huts, some with a room divided by a blanket for privacy. In 1791, Samuel Legare's wife described their "own house" as being on three acres formerly belonging to a Dr. Bodie.[15] Here, also, we have a picture of both Birchtown's poverty and its punishments. On April 15, 1789, Bosun Vaughan and Samuel Legare were each given a hundred cuts with a cat-o'-nine-tails whip, the equivalent of nine hundred lashes. There is no record of whether Vaughan survived it, but Samuel was charged again as an accessory to counterfeiting, in 1791.[16]

Boston King later described those hungry years: "About this time, the country was visited with a dreadful famine, which not only prevailed at Burch Town, but likewise at Chebucto, Annapolis, Digby, and other places. Many of the poor people were compelled to sell their best gowns for five pounds of flour, in order to support life. When they had parted with all their clothes, even to their blankets, several of them fell down dead in the streets, thro' hunger. Some killed and eat their dogs and cats, and poverty and distress prevailed on every side, so that to my great grief I was obliged to leave Burch Town, because I could get no employment." He sought work in vain, here and there; finally, he got an order for a wooden chest from a man in Shelburne: "I worked all night. And by eight o'clock next morning, finished the chest, which I carried to the Captain's house, thro' the snow which was three feet deep. But to my great disappointment he rejected it. However he gave me directions to make another. On my way home, being pinched with hunger and cold, I fell down several times, thro' weakness, and expected to die upon the spot....I had but one pint of Indian meal left for the support of myself and wife."[17]

John Marrant was walking the same road on March 31 (he doesn't give the year but I believe it may have been 1788, after the famine had made itself felt the previous summer): "and when we had got about half way, we came up with two women in the road, one was lying down and just expiring, and the other stood over her weeping; they had both been over to Shelbourn to beg something to eat and were then returning to Birch Town, and had got a little Indian meal, but had not the strength to reach home with it."[18] John helped one back to town and buried the other.

Boston King managed to get home, and then to sell the first chest he'd made. He sold his saw. The second chest was approved, and paid for in corn-meal. Saved from starvation, he got an order for three small boats. Many of his neighbours, desperate for food, were forced to indenture themselves, which King viewed as little better than re-entering slavery. He got another boat order the next winter, and then contracted to go to Chebucto, to build a house for £2 a month along with a barrel of mackerel and one of herring. Once there, he was persuaded to join his employer's fishery instead.

King fished at Bay Chaleur and up the local rivers, taking salmon with nets, before going to Pope's Harbour for herring: "October 24, we left Pope's

Harbour, and came to Halifax, where we were paid off, each man receiving 15 £ for his wages; and my master gave me two barrels of fish agreeable to his promise. When I returned home, I was enabled to clothe my wife and myself, and my winter's store consisted of one barrel of flour, three bushels of corn, nine gallons of treacle, 20 bushels of potatoes which my wife had set in my absence, and the two barrels of fish; so that this was the best winter I ever saw in Burch Town."[19] At some point, Boston King joined the exodus from Shelburne County; he moved to the new black settlement at Preston, east of Halifax, where he continued his work of preaching. He would have found South Carolina people there, with names like Stobo or Cantey.[20] "For blacks as well as for whites, the migration into Nova Scotia meant a struggle for survival, frequently in pioneering conditions and sometimes in a different climate," wrote C. Bruce Fergusson almost two hundred years later. "There was an urgent need for shelter, for provisions, for livelihood, and for land, and delays all too often might be the cause of distress."[21] Or death.

On August 21, 1784, Thomas Peters and Murphy Steele, living down in Annapolis County, petitioned Governor John Parr for aid because they had been given no land, summer was almost over, and their rations, the only food they had to eat, had been terminated. Seven years later, they still had no farmland grants, only small plots in town. Thomas Peters determined to go to England and petition the king. In London, he somehow met abolitionist Granville Sharp of the Sierra Leone Company. "Originally an association to relieve distressed freed Blacks in England who had escaped their masters in America and had found their way to England during the Revolutionary War," Marion Robertson states in a history of Shelburne, "the newly incorporated Sierra Leone Company was looking for likely settlers, both black and white, to found a Christian settlement in Sierra Leone and to promote trade in the natural products of Africa."[22]

With Granville Sharp advising, the British government made Thomas Peters an offer: Black Loyalists could have free passage to Sierra Leone; or they could have immediate redress of the land-grant mess in Nova Scotia; or they could enlist as soldiers in a West Indian regiment, taking their families, with pay and a guinea's bounty. Peters determined to emigrate. He chose Africa; the West Indies were full of white slaveowners, and life there would be too dangerous for free blacks.

How to arrange all this? Royal Navy lieutenant John Clarkson, an abolitionist and brother to Thomas Clarkson, a director of the Sierra Leone Company, was asked to go to Halifax to oversee the removal of any Black Loyalist who wished to return to Africa. This man did a phenomenally good job *and* he kept a journal. Arriving in Halifax on October 17, he had everything and everybody ready to depart by January 1792. He secretly paid off Black Loyalist debts, redeemed adults and children from indentureship, and tried to buy slaves so all these unfortunates could go with their families. He advised one father to hide his indentured son in the woods until time to leave, so that his employer couldn't take him back to the States. While he was not supposed to enlist people without any ability to support themselves, he allowed a woman born in Africa, aged 104, to make the journey. She said she wanted to go home to die; Clarkson took her in.[23] He wrote to the company directors, "It is not in my power to describe the scandalous and shameful conduct shewn to the free Blacks by many of the White people in both provinces, and although Government allowed to many of them from 60 to 100 acres of land, the greatest part have never been in possession of more than 1 or 2 acres, and they have so completely worked the land up that it will not yield half crops."[24]

David George was so fed up with life in Birchtown that he was standing on the Shelburne docks, waiting, when John Clarkson arrived to sign up those who wanted to go back to Africa. On the "List of the blacks in Birch Town who gave in Their Names for Sierra Leone in November 1791," George is the very first person recorded, saying that he was forty-eight, born in Virginia, with a wife, four boys, two girls. His oldest child was seventeen. He gave his occupation as preacher and sawyer, and said he'd been a soldier. He wished to take his four spades, a hoe, and a saw; his wife had a spinning wheel. They had packed two barrels and two bedsteads. He owned five town lots, a fifty-acre lot by Birchtown, as well as "2 houses of Worship in Vicinity of Shelburne, Part Gov't [Grant] & part purchas'd." His character was deemed good, and he and Clarkson became friends.[25]

Boston King summed up the whole Sierra Leone proposal in this way: "The advantages held out to the Blacks were considered by them as valuable. Every married man was promised 30 acres of land and every male child under 15 years of age, was entitled to 5 acres. We were likewise to have a free passage to Africa, and upon our arrival, to be furnished with provisions till we could clear a sufficient portion of land necessary for our subsistence. The Company likewise engaged to furnish us with all necessaries and to take in return the produce of the new plantations. Their intention being, as far as possible in their power, to put a stop to the abominable slave-trade."[26]

King had just found employment as a gentleman's servant, a job that paid two shillings a day, plus room and board. However, he felt God had called him to preach the Gospel in Africa, so he requested passage to Sierra Leone, and it was granted. On January 16, he wrote in his memoir, he and his wife sailed away from Nova Scotia, accompanied by slightly over a thousand other Black Loyalists. Of course, those still indentured or enslaved remained behind, along with others more well-to-do who wished to stay. Together, they became ancestors to contemporary black Nova Scotians.

PORT MOUTON, QUEEN'S COUNTY

The Loyalist settlement at Port Mouton was a disaster from start to finish. On October 10, 1783, members of Tarleton's Legion, a large number of whom had come from North and South Carolina, were, one can only say, dumped there by governmental stupidity. Thomas Raddall, who researched this failed attempt at settlement in 1947, uses the same verb: "On October 5th and 6th, the government surveyors, Marston and Morris, dined together aboard HMS Cyclops in Shelburne harbour, and on the 7th Morris set out in a boat for Port Mouton, 40 miles to the eastward. They or some higher authority had made a wild decision. Tarleton's Legion was to be allotted lands at Port Mouton and to be dumped ashore there forthwith, men, women and children, to get themselves housed as best they could."[27] Morris, the government surveyor, had only three days to lay out plots for them. Raddall describes the place as "totally unfit to shelter or support a host of strangers."

Port Mouton's beaches are scenic on a warm day in summer, but the land itself is hilly, with a mere few inches of acidic soil over a plethora of great big boulders, overlying a granite bedrock. Moreover, winters were colder then, and this one was fast approaching. Daylight diminished with each passing day. Firewood and lumber to build with was whatever the settlers could manage to cut and saw. The few fishermen and Mi'kmaq already living in Port Mouton weren't happy to be invaded by strangers.

A week after their arrival, according to Raddall, HMS *Sophie* appeared in the harbour to off-load "70 negroes—who were put ashore to settle themselves." He seems to think this was the total of Black Loyalists in the settlement.[28] The Book of Negroes, on the other hand, records that 558 Black Loyalists sailed from New York to Port Mouton. Of these, 68 came from South Carolina alone. The sloop *Elk*, inspected on October 7, would bring 13 Black Loyalists to Port Mouton. The brigs *Joseph* and *Elijah*, inspected October 31, were carrying 5 and 87, respectively; the brig *Jenney*, inspected November 9, had 5 aboard. The ship *Nisbett*, inspected November 19, carried a whopping 162. On November 30, the ship *Peggy* had 11 Black Loyalists aboard; the ship *Danger*, 131; the brig *Concord*, 23; *L'Abondance* had 82; and the brig *Diannah*, 38.[29]

Conversely, the Book of Negroes has absolutely no entries for HMS *Sophie*. Perhaps the ship was merely transferring people from Shelburne, once the fleet had arrived, on its way home to England, but I doubt it. The *Sophie* is mentioned in the Book of Negroes only in passing: in April the commissioners note they have sent a message to "Captain Mowatt of His Majesty's Ship La Sophia conveying the Fleet."[30] If any Black Loyalists sailed with the *Sophie* out of New York, they were never recorded in the Book of Negroes. (One wishes Raddall were given to footnoting his references.)

The *Sophie*, on her October 17 visit, supposedly also informed the Port Mouton settlers that they could expect to be joined by "practically the entire base personnel of the British fleet and army operating out of New York since 1776, together with sundry discharged sailors from the dispatch boat Miranda, the transport Neptune, and a few soldiers of the King's Own Maryland Loyalists and the 71st Highlanders, many accompanied by wives and children."[31] Raddall calculated that in those last months of 1783 the population at Port Mouton rose to 2,500 people—a motley crew who would christen their attempt at settlement Guysborough.

Tensions ran high through the winter, as people died of the cold and of disease due to the poor living conditions. Members of Tarleton's Legion despised the commissariat people, who had sat out the war in comfort, and who arrived much better provisioned. The sailors and soldiers of other regiments didn't like either of these factions. Nobody at all cared at all about the Black Loyalists. "The squabbles went on," writes Raddall, "and when the spring court opened in Liverpool April 12th, 1784, there was a rush of litigants from Port Mouton with cases to press or to defend."[32] Many of the commissariat personnel, meanwhile, began packing to leave for more fertile fields.

In late spring, however, a furious fire completely destroyed the settlement. Thomas Raddall explains that it had rained all through April and May, and then on May 14, "the wind swung to the south-west and there followed a succession of hot days. It was the dangerous time that every forest ranger knows."[33] He puts the date of the conflagration at May 19. A few boats survived, and someone went by sea to Halifax with the news. The government sent a naval transport with supplies, and it took some of the homeless refugees of the fire, with any slaves or servants they owned, to what is now St. Stephen, New Brunswick, and to Digby, Nova Scotia. Raddall writes that, in June, three shiploads of refugees were taken up to Chedabucto Bay: "Finally, in July, five government transports carried the rest of Molleson's people to [what would be] the new Guysborough, and the ruins of the old were left to Tarleton's Legion and the seventy poor negroes. Most of the negroes drifted into Liverpool."[34] Perhaps some did, but many went to Birchtown, and even more were sent up the eastern shore to this second Guysborough town.

A number of black refugees taken to Shelburne appear on the Birchtown muster for July 1784 as having come from Port Mouton after April 30. The first of the refugee companies is listed in the muster as "Captain Scott Murray's Company who have drawn provisions (at Port Mattoon with Colonel Mollison to the 1st May &) in this company from 2 May to 24 July 1784."[35] The muster companies of George Wise, Captain Read, Captain George Fraction, and Captain Jacob With were likewise recorded as provisioned until April 30 at Port Mouton, and then at Birchtown from May 1 to July 24, 1784. Does this mean they were removed to Shelburne before the fire? Or that the fire happened earlier? Or is the muster record skewed as to dates? There is no way now to tell.

CHEDABUCTO BAY, ANTIGONISH (LATER GUYSBOROUGH) COUNTY

In the seventeenth century, Chedabucto Bay was home to several Mi'kmaw bands and European fishermen. By the 1780s, there were still Mi'kmaw people there, as well as the fishing community and a few merchants and farmers. At war's end, land began to be granted in the Chedabucto region to disbanded soldiers of the King's Carolina Rangers, the Royal North Carolina Regiment, and the South Carolina Royalists, among others. After the burning of Port Mouton's Guysborough, some of its settlers, both black and white, would join the other inhabitants of the bay, creating a second Guysborough township in this most easterly section of mainland Nova Scotia.

Port Mouton refugees going to Chedabucto were shipped up in June and July 1784. At first, they lived in tents ("marquees") on Little Island out in the harbour, gradually building log houses on the mainland. They spent the winter clearing their lots and cutting firewood. Many perished from cold and hunger and disease; come spring, some of the survivors "gave up and went elsewhere."[36]

The Black Loyalists transported to the new Guysborough were, as was the case elsewhere in Nova Scotia, mostly marginalized to the edges of the settlement and its satellite communities. These people, according to county historian Harriet Hart, "had their quarters on the hill near where the upper road now crosses Mr. Hartshorne's mill brook. It was called 'Niggertown Hill.' They suffered severely from famine and many died from want."[37] Others lived as servants with their employers' families, and may have had slightly better circumstances. Still others continued to work for the army, such as Plenty Platt, mustered in June 1784 as "Belonging to the Department."[38] Plenty was a South Carolina Black Loyalist, formerly a slave of Peter Thom Platt of Charlestown, whom he left in 1778.[39] His "Department" was probably the wagonmaster-general's department.

Black Loyalists living in Antigonish and Guysborough Counties were never informed about the offer to transport interested folk to Sierra Leone.

TRACADIE, BROWNSPRIGGS GRANT, AND THE TRACADIE BACKLANDS, ANTIGONISH COUNTY

In 1787, a man named Thomas Brownspriggs petitioned the Nova Scotia government for a grant of land for local Black Loyalists. Three thousand acres of Crown land were surveyed and granted to seventy-four people, including

Brownspriggs, in an area of Antigonish County where now lie East Tracadie, Rear Monastery, and unnamed areas adjacent to a part of Highway 16. Thomas Brownspriggs, as he is named on the grant, may have come originally from Jamaica at the war's end, as servant "Henry Thomas" to Captain Richard F. Brownrigg of the Duke of Cumberland's Regiment. This regiment consisted "almost entirely of Carolina Loyalists." Brownrigg and his regiment came north to Halifax in two transports, the *Industry* and the *Argo*, in the autumn of 1783. In May of the following year, they were taken up the Atlantic coast in the transport *Content* to what is now Guysborough County, but which was then included as part of Antigonish County. Captain Brownrigg was granted land in the new settlement of Manchester; he died there on February 6, 1786. Perhaps his servant Henry Thomas, out of work, and possibly taking the name Brownrigg (misspelled on the grant as Brownspriggs?), spearheaded the petition for land grants to the Black Loyalists the year after Brownrigg died.[40]

Carmelita Robertson notes, "Although both the warrant and the grant are clear about the dimensions of the land and the names of the grantees, the land was not settled accordingly." Some people receiving land—such as Dinah Lining—were too old or perhaps too impoverished to develop it according to the stringent terms laid down by the government to grantees. They chose to stay in Guysborough town. To confuse matters further, Thomas Brownspriggs evidently gave some lots of land to people *not* named on the original 1787 grant. Next, according to archaeologist Stephen Powell, "The government also subsequently regranted large portions of land to other settlers, on the pretense that the land had been granted previous to the Black Loyalist petition, but that they had not noticed their error until after the fact." Land was then granted to some of these Black Loyalists in the less favourable interior, an area designated for years as the Tracadie Backlands.[41]

A number of South Carolina people, who initially landed in Port Mouton in southern Nova Scotia, had removed up the Atlantic shore of Nova Scotia to Chedabucto Bay, and there helped build Guysborough anew. They included Andrew Izard, Joseph Wingood, Benjamin Gero, and Dinah Lining. Each later received a lot on the Brownspriggs grant. Charles Wingood, a fellow slave of Joseph Wingood in South Carolina, had come to Guysborough slightly later; he'd been evacuated from Charlestown to Florida or the West Indies in 1782, and then removed with other Loyalists or Jamaican regiments to Nova Scotia. His name is also on the grant. Here's what we know about some of these Carolina settlers of what are now Antigonish and Guysborough Counties.

Andrew made his escape from Ralph (pronounced "Rafe") Izard of Charlestown in 1778, and either chose Izard as a surname or was assigned it in the Book of Negroes.[42] Two possible Ralph Izards were alive during the war years. They were second cousins; both had houses in Charlestown and multiple plantations in the countryside. Andrew seems to have been connected to the younger cousin: Ralph Izard of Saint George, Dorchester. Dorchester Ralph's father died in 1761. The inventory of slaves at one of his rice plantations on the tidal section of the Combahee River was done family by family, and shows he owned a boy called Andrew, whose age range indicates that he's probably our Andrew.[43] Andrew's father, living at Combahee in 1761, was named Joe, according to the inventory, and was appraised at £350; his wife, Catharina, was valued at £100 (perhaps she was ill or infirm). One son, George, was obviously quite young because his value is just £30. Andrew, Joe's other son, older than George, but not yet grown, was valued at £100. Andrew would have been about six when this older Ralph Izard died and his slaves were appraised. He likely grew up on Combahee, before the British invaded and swept him off into freedom and another life. We know that a number of Izard people escaped during the American Revolution. The *Charlestown Royal Gazette* for March 1–14, 1781, published the names of Izard slaves employed, as of February 23, by the army.

Andrew Izard spent the war in the wagonmaster-general's department. He was on one of the final ships to leave New York in 1783, boarding the *Nisbett* sometime in November; the vessel was inspected on the 19th, and then set sail for Port Mouton. The *Nisbett*'s muster rolls have not survived. After the little settlement at Port Mouton burned to the ground in the spring of 1784, Andrew boarded a governmental rescue vessel to be transported to his new life up the eastern shore at the second Guysborough, newly under construction. There he married and raised a family, appearing on the 1784 muster as "And'w Isard."[44] Some of his descendants still live in the area.

Before arriving in Port Mouton, Joseph Wingood had lived on a South Carolina farm slightly northeast of Charlestown in an area bordered on its northern edge by the intricate labyrinth of marsh and tidal creeks of the Wando River, and on the east by the ocean. Life there was ruled by the changing tides, the ebb and flow of water, the rise and set of sun and moon. The marsh—green in summer, gold in autumn—and the creeks provided sea bass, trout and flounder, baby shrimp, oysters, and large clams, to supplement a slave's diet. There were birds and bird eggs, and one could snare rabbit, possum, racoons, and squirrels in the forest, while keeping an eye out for alligators and poisonous snakes. Nova Scotia would prove vastly different.[45]

By the time of the American Revolution, several generations of Wingood enslavers had lived and died along the coast of South Carolina, starting in 1697, when they began clearing forest to form small farms. In 1706, the South Carolina Assembly passed the Church Act, creating ten parishes from the lands now settled in the colony. The eighteenth-century Wingoods we are concerned with, and the enslaved people on their farms, became part of Christ Church Parish, "South-east of Wandoe River."

Joseph's enslaver was Charvil Wingood, a name also written Cheverel, Chevel, Cherrel, Charrel, and Charril. Perhaps Charvil was merely a phonetic spelling of Charles, pronounced in the French manner as Sharl or Sharrel, by his mother, who was French Huguenot (Charles was a family name of the Wingood clan). Why the Book of Negroes listed Charvil Wingood as "Gilbert Wingwood, Wandoe" is anybody's guess. We know this reference is to Charvil Wingood, as he was the only rebel Wingood living on the Wando River during the relevant time period. It is easier to understand how the surname Wingood became Wingwood in the Book of Negroes, as this spelling also creeps into South Carolina documents of the period.[46]

Our Charvil's father, Charvil Sr., was a man of small property because he was a younger son, but he proceeded to prosper in the South Carolina manner by marrying Mary Sauseau, who inherited land on the Wando River and slaves Cuffy, Robin, Scipio, Dick, Tom, Boson, Adam, Sam, Ned, Grace, Judith, Blackboy, Quash, Peggy, Amyll, Jupiter, Esther, Nanny, Sabina, and Flora. Charvil Sr. was a house-carpenter. He and his wife attended Christ Church, an Anglican establishment. He died in 1741, and his wife later married Charles Barksdale.[47] Once he came of age, Charvil Jr., Mary and Charvil's son, took over the land his parents had farmed, described in his will as 250 acres, as well as the slaves left to him by his father.

A second Charvil lived in Christ Church Parish, but this man is not a candidate for Joseph's enslaver, as he was a Loyalist. Charvil Jr. left him some money in his will, written in 1786. Obviously he was a relation, singled out by our Charvil as his namesake. This Charvil might have been in need of some behind-the-scenes assistance after the war; he had been a private in the Loyalist Craven and Berkeley County Regional Militia. Its "Pay Abstract Nr 52" for the period July 3, 1780, through March 19, 1781, shows, among other Christ Church Parish neighbours, Colonel Elias Ball; Lieutenant Colonel Elias Ball; Major Gabriel Capers; Captains John Coming Ball, Thomas Dearington, and John Gaillard; Sergeant Daniel Sinkler, a whole bunch of Ansons, Bennetts, Bulloughs [Bullocks], Doars, Dorrells, Duprees, and Murrells—and one "Cherrill Wingood," who had served 135 days. This man, still a private, appears on the pay abstract for March 7th, 1782, with Elias Ball given as his witness. Under the "Return of Distressed Refugees, Charlestown, 11 August 1782," is the entry "Wingood, Chevel, sick," attested by Isaac Allen, lieutenant colonel commandant of Charlestown.[48]

The fall of Charlestown to the British in 1780 enabled Joseph Wingood, who turned twenty-one that same year, to leave a life of slavery. From New York, he took the ship *Nisbett* to Port Mouton; he was listed in the Book of Negroes on November 19, though it may have been December before he got to Nova Scotia. He survived that winter and the fire which wiped out the town, and was taken by government-provided transport up to the new Guysborough.

Joseph married Sarah, called Sally, and both were baptized in Guysborough at Christ Church Anglican on July 30, 1786, as "Joseph Ringwood, 25" and "Sarah Ringwood, 23." Later records show some of Joseph and Sarah Ringwood's children being baptized in the same church: "Sally, daughter of Joseph & Sally Ringwood, b. 25 July 1799 / Eva & Rosa, daughters of Joseph & Sally Ringwood, b. 23 July 1803."[49] Their descendants are still living in Nova Scotia.

Several other Wingood slaves escaped to Nova Scotia during the American Revolution—William, Charles, and possibly young Rose—but they may have come from other Wingood farms in Christ Church Parish. In Nova Scotia musters, their surnames appear as "Ringwood," as does that of Joseph Wingood, Charvil's slave. Almost certainly these people went to St.

Augustine at the evacuation of Charlestown in 1782, and when the province of East Florida was returned to the Spanish after the war's end, were brought up to the Chedabucto Bay area. They joined Joseph Wingood there, and their surnames (transmogrified first to Wingwood, then to Ringwood) appear on the 1784 muster for Guysborough. They do not, of course, appear in the Book of Negroes.[50]

Rose Ringwood, sixteen at the time, was christened on the same day as Joseph and Sally. Charles Ringwood waited until August 31 of that year before he, too, was baptized by Reverend Peter de la Roche, a missionary residing in Guysborough on "private business." William Ringwood doesn't seem to have taken the plunge; perhaps he had already received the sacrament of baptism elsewhere.[51]

It is interesting to note that a former slave of Timothy Crosbie's also settled with these Wingoods in Guysborough. He had taken the name Prince Crosbie as a free man. Their enslavers had been friends, and at least two Wingood servants had married Crosbie servants before the war.[52] It must have been good to see familiar faces in a strange land, to have someone to talk with about old times over a pint of spruce beer, sitting around the fire during the long Nova Scotian winter nights. A number of South Carolina people were in Guysborough, but the Wingoods and the Crosbies were close. They were family. They alone remembered that other, older, Christ Church Parish.

Benjamin, whose surname appears as "Gero" on the Brownspriggs grant, as "Garrow" on his baptismal record, and as "Gerrow" in the Book of Negroes, had been enslaved in Charlestown by Peter Giraud, a stocking-weaver of French Protestant descent. This man also had a surname with varied spellings: Giroud, Giraud, and Guiraud (all pronounced Gero). Christened Pierre, he used the anglicized form, Peter, in doing business, but wrote his name as Pierre when making his will. He first appears in the historical record in the *South Carolina Gazette*, for September 1–8, 1759, as having recently lived in Charlestown. Ten years later, he was working as a weaver on King Street, "making, as good Breeches Patterns, Stockings, Gloves, Caps, &c. of our own Wool, Silk, Cotton, and Thread, as ever were." In this advertisement, his name is given as "P. Giroud." A year later, he advertised "P. Giroud, Stocking-weaver in King Street, Will take two Negro-girls, Apprentices, for two Years, to be taught Carding, Spinning and Knitting."[53]

Although Peter Giraud was a poor man, he was advanced enough in his business affairs to own a slave, a man named Charles who spoke both French and English. All we know about Charles is that he had been born in Guinea and had ritual scarification on his cheeks, in the form of four cuts on either side. Peter Giraud trained him as a stocking-weaver, but he very likely had to work hard at multiple other tasks, as the slaves of poor men often did.

Disaster for an impoverished enslaver struck in October 1776: Charles ran away. Peter Giraud advertised his loss.[54] Apparently, Charles was recaptured, or he returned of his own accord the following summer. Giraud was still angry with him and threatened to sell him. He offered him to Henry Laurens, to whom he owed money, but later changed his mind, because Charles was really good at his work, knew how to do everything just so, and finding and training another like him would have cost Giraud time and money.[55] Nothing further is known of either Charles or Peter Giraud until after the British under Clinton captured the city of Charlestown in May of 1780. In 1781, Giraud, along with a number of other Charlestown rebels, was taken from his home and locked up in the British prison ship *Torbay*, anchored in Charlestown Harbor.

A male slave of his made a successful escape during this time, going to New York, and thence to Nova Scotia.[56] Was this Charles, the African-born weaver, who made an attempt to gain his freedom in 1776? Did he change his name, as many did, becoming Benjamin, and is he the man who appears in the Book of Negroes as Peter Giraud's escaped slave? The entry in the Book of Negroes reads, "Benjamin Gerrow, 25, stout fellow. Formerly slave to Peter Gerrow, Charlestown, South Carolina." (Nova Scotian descendants of Benjamin and his wife, Hagar, a South Carolina woman formerly enslaved by Thomas Broughton, now spell this surname Gero, as it was written on the Brownspriggs grant of 1787.)

On July 30, 1786, Benjamin Gero and his Hagar were baptized by the Reverend Peter de la Roche, at Christ Church, Guysborough, as "Benjamin Gerow, 28," and "Harga Gerow, 21." A later entry in the church records shows their children: "Hannah, daughter of Hagar & Benjamin Garrow, b. August 25, 1799 / John, son of Hagar & Benjamin Garrow, b. July 24, 1802."[57] Benjamin Giraud may have spoken French, as did Giraud's slave Charles. This would have proved a boon when, years later, he received his land grant in

Tracadie, which bordered on land owned by French-speaking Acadians. So, in a very small way, Peter Giraud may have given Benjamin Giraud something that would prove to be of use to him in his new life, in another country. He is thought to have taken up his Tracadie grant, only to be removed to the Tracadie Backlands, where his descendants still live.

James Lennox and his mother-in-law, Dinah, as head of her own household, each received grants in Tracadie as well. We know little about Lennox. The story, however, of his wife, Hannah Lining, is particularly poignant. Hannah Lining was a survivor. At thirty-four and blind in one eye, she helped her elderly mother escape, first to New York and then to Nova Scotia, where, twice widowed, she kept the two of them alive into a ripe old age in Guysborough.

These two women came from a South Carolina indigo plantation called Hillsborough. Dr. John Lining, their enslaver, acquired the place through his marriage in 1739 to Sarah Hill, who inherited it from her mother in 1756. Hillsborough was situated on what is now Old Town Creek, which emptied into the Ashley River above the city of Charlestown; during the American Revolution this creek was called Lining's. Lining was a Scot from Lanarkshire (his name in records of the period is often spelled Linning), a physician known for his meticulous meteorological observations, some of the earliest made in the province. He died September 21, 1760.[58]

Hillsborough's cash crop, over the years of Lining ownership, was indigo, a legume from which a blue dye can be obtained. Growing it is quite labour-intensive, involving plowing, planting, weeding, watering, harvesting, and the complicated stages of processing. March through October was devoted to indigo at Hillsborough. In winter, there would have been other chores. Perhaps Hannah and Diana wove, sewed clothes for the plantation workers, and made sweetgrass baskets in the West African manner. At some point in her life, Hannah was blinded in one eye, almost certainly through trauma. Whether or not it was accidental or because someone hit her is unknown. One Lining slave named Hannah made a run for freedom in 1761; this may have been Dinah's Hannah.[59] Since Dinah was born around 1721 and Hannah about 1749, it is almost certain that they were mother and daughter. Their ancestors had probably been slaves on this same property, as there are Dinahs and Hannahs recorded in the death inventories of the family of their enslaver for generations.

These women's moment of opportunity came in 1780, when the British general Sir Henry Clinton landed troops on the coast south of Charlestown. The British army soon occupied Hillsborough. Different regiments cycled through, camping and then moving on toward the city. Officers were quartered in the Lining house, which temporarily became Major General Leslie's headquarters.[60] This British presence on and around Hillsborough naturally suggests a scenario for the escape of Lining slaves. And, indeed, Hannah and Dinah made it behind the British lines to freedom in this same year, 1780. The women must have come from strong stock because they lived through incredible upheavals: they survived the war in South Carolina, travelled to New York and worked there for a while, emigrated to Nova Scotia, and then less than a year later sustained the loss of everything in the fire which destroyed Port Mouton, their first home in the province.

The Nova Scotia government moved them to Guysborough in 1784, after the fire. At long last, they could settle permanently. Hannah evidently took good care of her mother, who lived to be very old. Both received Anglican baptism at Christ Church in Guysborough on July 30, 1786. Hannah Lining married James Lennox, and in 1787 both he (as "James Lenox") and Dinah Lining ("Dinnah Lumian") were given grants of land at Tracadie. They did not remove there, however. James Lennox died, and Hannah married a second time, only to lose that husband as well. Hannah and Dinah seemed to have spent the rest of their lives in the town of Guysborough, where there were work opportunities, a church, and a wider social life. Eventually, the day arrived when Hannah had to close her mother's eyes and wash her body for burial. She had no children to do this for her when her own turn came, but surely the neighbour women came to lay her out. Hannah and Dinah had come a long hard way from South Carolina to lie at last in peace in Nova Scotian earth. Whatever kind of life their escape had given them, at least it ensured that no one, and nothing but death, would ever part them. If they lie in the Anglican graveyard which surrounds Christ Church there, their graves are marked only by ancient ornamental trees and summer wildflowers.[61]

On April 2, 2002, I was driving through what had once been the Lining plantation. It is now the black community of Marysville, where only one street preserves the Hillsborough name. At the northwest end of Main Street, I met Mr. John Wesley Carr, a retired school principal, very knowledgeable about history. He was a descendant, he told me, of the famous Charlestown cabinetmaker, John Elfe, who had emancipated the black woman who bore his child, and given her land. His family had lived on that land ever since. When I told him about my project, Mr. Carr said, "I'm going to show you something! You see this bush?" He broke a pod off of it. "You know what this is? This is indigo! They all grow wild along the fence line. I had it identified over at Old Charlestown Landing, where they still grow it to show the school classes."

I was stunned. An *indigo bush*, descended from all that indigo Hannah and Dinah Lining once had to plant and tend. It was like seeing a ghost. Those eighteenth-century plants had seeded and their descendants had survived wild on what remained of Hillsborough. Lines of these plants, green and graceful, were growing on the verge of Mr. Carr's long beautiful lawn, right at the marsh's edge. I said hello and goodbye to them, from Hannah and Dinah Lining.

HALIFAX, HALIFAX COUNTY

Halifax, the capital of the province of Nova Scotia, also became home to a number of Black Loyalists, beginning with those who were evacuated from Boston in 1776. Because it was the province's largest town and port, Halifax received a percentage of the wealthier white Loyalists, with slaves or indentured servants in tow. Benjamin (Coulson), profiled in chapter 3, was one such slave. Many people today seemed surprised to find that slavery was going on in Nova Scotia back then, but remember, it was merely one of many British provinces on the Atlantic seaboard before the American Revolution, and slavery was not legally abolished in the British Empire until 1834. It is only *after* that date that what we now know as Canada became a haven for escaped slaves from the United States. As a result, Halifax had a mixed group of Black Loyalists, including slaves, indentured servants, free-born people, and those who had obtained freedom through British proclamation during the war. Some were granted land outside the city, in what became the village of Preston. Both the Halifax and Preston communities grew as the post-war economy declined and Loyalists such as Boston King abandoned Shelburne and smaller settlements for the greater opportunites of Halifax County.

The 1783 Treaty of Paris, as noted, returned the colony of East Florida to Spain, with its British settlers given two years to evacuate. In 1784, these people began shipping out to other venues; those who came to Nova Scotia, attracted by offers of land, often came straight to Halifax, bringing their slaves with them. A number of the American Loyalist militia regiments, who were in Jamaica at the war's end, also chose to be mustered out in Nova Scotia and waited in Halifax to receive their land grants. Poorly paid, many used the currency of the time to pay their bills: they sold their slaves and re-indentured their servants to others.

A runaway-slave advertisement in the *Halifax Weekly Chronicle* on March 15, 1794, tells a bit about one South Carolina person so sold. Belfast, who preferred to be called Bob, came to Nova Scotia in 1784, as a slave, age seventeen. He was sold by his former owner at least once and ended up in the house of politician and judge Michael Wallace, who advertised him as his "property." After ten years in the province, Belfast made a bid for freedom, and tried to get on board a ship bound for Newfoundland. "He is a likely, stout-made fellow, of five feet eight or nine inches high, and about 27 years of age," said his enslaver, "of a mild good countenance and features, smooth black skin, with very white teeth; is a native of South Carolina, speaks good English, and very softly, and has been in this province ten years."

Michael Wallace, a Loyalist from Norfolk, Virginia, could not have acquired Belfast prior to his arrival in Nova Scotia, as Wallace left Virginia for Halifax in 1779 and Belfast arrived five years later, almost certainly in the ships carrying Loyalists from Florida or Jamaica.[62] At some point, Wallace hired him out to serve William Forsyth, Esq., and perhaps poor treatment was why he decided to run—the clothes he was wearing the day he left were described as worn out at elbows and knees. Wallace, however, said he had other garments, "secreted in town" to change into; he was obviously being helped by people in the tight little society of Halifax's Black Loyalists. Perhaps, with their help, he got safely to a new life.

Chapter Nine

CONTEMPORARY BLACK LOYALIST HERITAGE INITIATIVES

*I*n 1991, the Nova Scotia Museum, where I have worked since 1972, made a commitment to create a much-needed and long-overdue databank, the Black Heritage Resource Files, for an under-represented portion of our population. We wanted to understand the history of the people of African descent who have lived in Nova Scotia—some from the time of the first European settlements in the 1600s—as individuals, or groups like the Louisbourg Blacks, the Black Loyalists, the Jamaica Maroons, or the War of 1812 Refugees.

One of the earliest initiatives, a search for content about black people in early Nova Scotian newspapers, led me to a fortuitous meeting with another person with roots in South Carolina. Carmelita Robertson, who took on the newspaper project, has multiple Black Loyalist ancestors who escaped from South Carolina during the American Revolution. I, born in South Carolina, now living in Nova Scotia, have eighteenth-century South Carolina kin who were slaveowners, and some of their slaves also escaped to Nova Scotia at the war's end. We began, in the summer of 1995, to share perspectives. It was my first introduction to the Black Loyalists. Previously I had no idea that South Carolina blacks had emigrated en masse to Nova Scotia, coming to Nova Scotia during the War of 1812, as well as during the American Revolution.

As Carmelita began to educate me, I was able, in turn, to tell her something about the people who had enslaved her family.

We made a number of trips to South Carolina, to walk on land where her ancestors or mine had been born, had worked, and had died—their lives entwined like old wisteria vines. My six-times-great-grandfather, George Smith, for example, married a woman named Rebecca Blake. Her niece, also named Rebecca Blake, married Ralph Izard, whose slave inventory reveals that Andrew Izard, one of Carmelita's ancestors, was living in 1761 on an Izard plantation along the Combahee River.

By 1997, we had created a slide presentation about the Black Loyalists of South Carolina, and in Black History Month, we travelled around the province with it, meeting and talking to people descended from some of these original founders of black communities in Nova Scotia. Carmelita reported that, as she began a project of interviewing Black Loyalist descendants, they would often tell her, "We know we came here in a ship. But that's all we know." I was once told, "We don't know about life in the before-times, the Carolina times, the slavery times." They were intensely curious; they really wished to know and to understand, and so we began, for them, the years of research that ultimately led to the creation of a video, *Escape to Nova Scotia*, and to this book. As Carmelita said in 2012, "Everything just kind of took off from there, just going in all different directions."[1]

The book was originally Carmelita's idea. We chose the Black Loyalists from South Carolina to write about, as that province, when the war began, included the largest black population of any North American colony. Both of us had roots there, and wished to explore them. We hoped that such a book would address stereotypes, presenting people with hard data in a way that would illumine this dark period in history. Unfortunately, after four years of research, Carmelita did not wish to continue, due to other commitments. Because it was initially her idea, and because she contributed four years of work toward the initial research, she forever has my deepest gratitude, and I hope that she will eventually present the broader story of her own ancestors among the Black Loyalists—research she has been working on for many years.

In 2012, I asked her for her thoughts on how the story of the Black Loyalists was unfolding in Nova Scotia. We talked about the creation of the Black Loyalist Heritage Society and its work in the southern part of the province; about the Brownspriggs Heritage Society in the northern counties; and about the Mersey Heritage Society, investigating the Port Mouton site. I decided to interview a few of the people most directly involved. As Carmelita pointed out, "The oral history collected [in 1998]—now almost *all* those people have passed on. So thank goodness we have their voices, their record, their memories."[2]

BIRCHTOWN, SHELBURNE COUNTY

Elizabeth Cromwell is a retired social worker, born in Shelburne, living in Birchtown. She is presently president of the Black Loyalist Heritage Society, which has its headquarters there. A natural leader, she has a beautiful speaking voice and an ability to present information in a clear, focused way—especially when discussing the society, and its beginnings.

A group of neighbours got together, she says, to discuss the difficulties that children of the community were having pulling together their family trees for a school project. There just wasn't enough information available; students didn't know the research process or where to begin: "So it was a combined effort from a few people to assist them, and in doing that, to talk about the actual history of the people who came to Birchtown—the Black Loyalists." After that first effort by a small group—"women, mostly, and a couple of men"—things began to happen really quickly; almost, says Cromwell, as if this larger initiative was meant to happen.[3]

Someone called a group member to say that a piece of property in Birchtown was under consideration for development, adding, "We understand that it is part of the Black Burial Ground, and we thought you should know about it." Immediately, the group moved to investigate. No one wanted to lose the cemetery. First, they found a lawyer. Research in the registry of deeds never turned up a grant of land for this burial site, but they were able to determine its boundaries by examining other grants which bordered on it and which mentioned it as a cemetery for the black people of Birchtown. They began searches through the old Anglican church records as well.

"So one thing sort of led to another," Elizabeth Cromwell explains, "and we did a lot of sitting around each other's kitchens, drinking coffee in the late hours of the night, talking about our own history, how we were brought up, what sort of things happened to us. There was a lot of emotion—it was a very emotional time." The consensus was, "Well, maybe we need to be doing something to mark the passing of our people."

She remembers that this was just about the time that Dr. Pearleen Oliver's video was released. Oliver had tried to do research in Shelburne and mentioned in her video that the Shelburne County Museum could not, at that time, provide her with much information. "That kind of sparked us into thinking, 'That's not right; that shouldn't happen. And what are we going to do about it?' All these things came together at the same time, and we decided to form an organization that would look at [all] cultures in Shelburne County, and out of *that*, came the Black Loyalist Heritage Society, since the only people who joined that group were mostly people of African ancestry." Elizabeth Cromwell repeats that it was a very intense time: "I know we had at least two years of just getting together and talking about the way of life—what happened in your family, how were they treated in Shelburne? That kind of thing." As people let their memories out into the light, they had to deal with a lot of pain, "a lot of concern that we had to work through emotionally. It took a while. It really did take a while."[4]

That was the birth of the Black Loyalist Heritage Society in Shelburne County, and it went from strength to strength, creating a small park with a Black Loyalist memorial on the shore of Birchtown together with commemorative highway signage and a small museum in an old schoolhouse there. The society also encouraged archaeological work over the next few years—work that complemented the resources already established in the registry of deeds, the church records, and in explorations of museum and archival collections.

Stephen Powell conducted the first archaeological survey along a fifty-metre-wide linear corridor for a second transmission line being cut by Nova Scotia Power through the area. He and his crew actually walked the corridor, side-by-side five metres apart, through present-day Birchtown, twenty-four kilometres to East Barrington. Coming up the hill to Birchtown, Powell found some intriguing features, including "a very interesting series of walls and enclosures, nothing like I'd ever seen before—perhaps some type of enclosures for animals." One had an opening and inside compartments, and he thought it was perhaps used for shearing sheep (such as the two sheep

Samuel Legare was caught eating in 1788). He found walls and cellar features he felt also might warrant further investigation.[5]

In 1993, Laird Niven began to survey a broader area of Birchtown, largely one threatened by the proposed Fox Ridge landfill. Stephen Powell worked with him. They found an actual pit house like the one Mr. Farmer told Clara Dennis about in the 1930s—an early form of shelter created by those first Black Loyalists. Niven said that after the survey, they were walking the old power-line cut. They passed a depression in the ground, with a really big rock in it, and he thought, "Hmm. Better go back and check that out." On testing, they found one little piece of ceramic. They took it back to Niven's mother's house, had a couple of beers, and washed it off. It was of the period, and the location made it almost certain to be Black Loyalist.[6] "That was really one of the highlights of my career," Stephen Powell remembers. "There was so much excitement when we put the first shovel-test in on that, and out came a piece of an English white stoneware, a press-moulded plate, that fits right in the 1780s–1790s time period. It was like—oh, definitely—who else could have been there?"[7]

According to Niven, the layout of Birchtown and its original division into lots still has yet to be determined. He had thought, when he first started this work, that he would find African expressions in the record, cultural carry-overs from an earlier time. He didn't, but he became fascinated by the differences among that first population at Birchtown—how some men and women became entrepreneurs and owned multiple lots of land, and others failed to thrive.

In 1994, Stephen Davis of St. Mary's University conducted an archaeological field school for his students in Birchtown. The thing he remembers most about investigating Black Loyalist history was the strong emotion he felt: "Only a couple of times in my career—and that's forty years now—did I ever feel attachment to the people whose sites I was digging. I could sense them, feel them, feel the angst." Their lives were so marginalized. The thing he hated the most, he said, was finding out how the disbanded soldiers had rioted and burned the black people out of Shelburne in 1784, burned their pitiful little possessions. "It was horrific, and something Nova Scotian history largely ignores."[8]

Laird Niven remembers something similar: "In 1994, on the last day of the SMU field school, Steve and the students left me at the pit house site so I could do some final excavating. I was working in the interior of the pit house, cleaning the soil away from the walls, which were dug into hardpan. It was quite eerie being out there alone, and as I trowelled the soil it fell away and revealed the shovel marks that were left by the Black Loyalist as he dug out his temporary home. It was a really strange feeling of being so close to the past—almost there, in fact—that I had to get up and look around to make sure I was still in the present."[9]

The Nova Scotia Museum, meanwhile, had launched a major two-year project, "Remembering Black Loyalists, Black Communities," largely funded by Canadian Heritage's multicultural program and the Nova Scotia Museum. Museum staff worked in partnership with the communities of Birchtown/ South Nova (through the Black Loyalist Heritage Society) and Tracadie/ Guysborough (through the Brownspriggs Historical Committee, later the Brownspriggs Heritage Society), as well as the Black Cultural Centre for Nova Scotia and the Learning Resources and Technology division and African Canadian Services division of the Nova Scotia Department of Education.[10]

This major project, running from late January 1998 through late January 2000, concentrated on research, public education, and community development under the supervision of an advisory group composed of Gloria Wesley Desmond and Pat Skinner in the north of the province, with Sharon Clyke-Oliver (later replaced by Marjorie Turner-Bailey) and Richard Gallion in the south; it included Henry Bishop, Black Cultural Centre; Robert Upshaw (later replaced by Patrick Kakembo), Nova Scotia Department of Education; David States, Parks Canada; and Gilbert Daye, Department of Canadian Heritage. Eventually, a travelling exhibit was launched, and is still touring. It now has a virtual equivalent on the museum website.

Under Carmelita Robertson's direction, the project began to collect oral histories from the communities in the form of tapes and transcripts as well as family genealogies; historical photographs, copied for the museum and the lenders; will abstracts and copies; cemetery inventories; deeds and grants of land; inventory forms for buildings associated with Black Loyalists and their descendants; and other items of interest. Marjorie Turner-Bailey, Gary Jacklin, and David Hartley did local research in Birchtown, and Monica Kennedy did the same in Tracadie.[11]

Laird Niven went back to Birchtown in the summer of 1998 under the auspices of this project, with field assistants Sharain Jones and Katie

Cottreau-Robins. Survey work and testing had been done there every year since 1993, so Niven concentrated on a more detailed investigation of particular features already recorded. Approximately sixteen thousand artifacts were recovered from three sites: an excavation at the Goulden and Acker properties on the shore, thought to have been the home of Black Loyalist colonel Stephen Blucke and which proved to be particularly rich; the testing of a probable Black Loyalist dwelling north of town; and the bisection of one of twenty-two odd rock mounds. Seventeen sites associated with Black Loyalists were documented and the fieldwork extensively photographed.[12]

TRACADIE, LINCOLNVILLE, BIRCHTOWN NUMBER II, ANTIGONISH AND GUYSBOROUGH COUNTIES

Under the auspices of the "Remembering Black Loyalists, Black Communities" project and the Brownspriggs Heritage Society, a second archaeological initiative was undertaken in Antigonish and Guysborough Counties in 1998, led again by Stephen Powell. With field assistants Katie Cottreau-Robins and Sharain Jones, Powell surveyed Crown land granted to seventy-four Black Loyalists in 1787, as well as other areas within the two counties later settled by their descendants. "It was in May—May 11 to June 5—one of the hottest Mays I can remember," Powell says. "The worst blackflies in Nova Scotia—probably the worst in the world."[13]

The most exciting aspect of the project was that it was the first survey in the area, as well as the earliest with a focus on Black Loyalists outside Shelburne County. "The strength of the project was the community involvement," Powell continues. "We had several local contacts, more-than-enthusiastic helpers. James Desmond, for example, was with us almost every day, and he had so many places he wanted to show us, that I just changed the focus from a survey to just going where James took us....And every time he took us somewhere, we found something." Other help in the area came from Everett Desmond, George Ash, Russell Morris, Tony Cotie, Angus Cotie, Alfred Cotie, Alonzo Reddick, Cecile Reddick, Elsie Elms, George Elms, Russell Elms, and Gerald Elms. "Sixteen areas of archaeological interest were recorded during the course of the survey," Powell notes. "The main locations investigated were East Tracadie, Rear Monastery, Upper Big Tracadie, areas adjacent to Highway 16, Lincolnville, and Birchtown." This last was a more recent settlement of the same name as the original one in Shelburne County.[14]

On the original Brownspriggs grant, Powell's team found only one site that might have dated to the time of the grant, which was shown them by Tony Cotie: "One shell-edged rim of a ceramic was found, which could date to 1790–1810. It's still a leap to say that it's a site associated with an original Black Loyalist grantee, but odds are good." Follow-up archaeology was recommended but has yet to be done.[15] The other sites were in what was then called the Tracadie Backlands, from Rear Monastery through to Lincolnville, areas given out to Black Loyalists after the government re-assigned most of the original grant lands to others. These later Backland sites, cleared and built on by descendants of the Brownspriggs grantees, dated from the mid to late 1800s. Some are on property still owned by people with Black Loyalist ancestors, with the same surnames as on the grant. James Desmond, growing up in the area, arranged introductions and access to sites, which were recorded and shovel-tested.

Finally, "because it was there," they explored a second Birchtown, the abandoned site in Guysborough County where Black Loyalists and their children's children had lived, leaving only in the early 1900s. "It was an absolutely fascinating cultural landscape: old roads, cemetery, dozens of cellars, a schoolhouse foundation, stone walls, all now deserted," Powell says, adding that it would need a three-year archaeological study to do it justice.[16]

One of the happy results of new research and increased community awareness in Antigonish/Guysborough has been the creation of the Afrikan Canadian Heritage and Friendship Centre, established in 2001 under the aegis of the Strait District School Board. The Guysborough County Heritage Association website now has a page devoted to the centre, as well as a link on Lincolnville and a brief profile of the Black Loyalist Graveyard in Monastery.

Sharain Jones, herself a descendant of Black Loyalists from Tracadie, worked on both the Birchtown and Tracadie digs. She completed her undergraduate degree in anthropology at St. Mary's University, Halifax, and has a masters degree from the University of Leicester, where her thesis was on the material culture of Black Loyalists in Nova Scotia. She says she became fascinated by the story of her ancestors—"people who looked like me"—when

Carmelita Robertson, her first cousin, began working at the Nova Scotia Museum. For the first time, she saw that oral histories and photographs of her ancestors "mattered to academia and museum studies." Sharain Jones is now director of the Sam Waller Museum in The Pas, Manitoba.[17]

Katie Cottreau-Robins, now the provincial archaeologist for Nova Scotia, went on to do a master's thesis on "Domestic Architecture of Black Loyalists, 1783–1810." She considered how the "finely-honed skills" of Black Loyalists (carpenters, bricklayers, masons, sawyers, etc.) would have translated into building their own homes in those early years, in that much harsher new environment. She has finished a doctoral dissertation about the daily lives of those Black Loyalists who came here as slaves—work which has led her to consider the Loyalist era here as the age of slavery in the province.[18]

A number of descendants of Black Loyalists have been working individually on their own genealogies. Bud Cromwell, for example, has made many trips to South Carolina and found there two unique documents mentioned in this book, Henry Middleton's 1779 list of escaped Black Loyalist slaves and his post-war updated claim for reimbursement.

Gloria Ann Wesley, poet, writer, and former wife of James Desmond, has authored *Chasing Freedom*, a young adult novel about a Black Loyalist girl coming to Nova Scotia from South Carolina. In 1997, Wesley was instrumental in bringing together the descendants of Brownspriggs grantees for a moving memorial ceremony at dusk along the shore of Tracadie Harbour, where they recited the names of their ancestors. Lesley Ann Patten filmed this ceremony for her documentary about the search for Black Loyalist roots in Nova Scotia and South Carolina, *Loyalties* (Ziji Film & Televsion Production and the National Film Board, 1998). This is yet another interesting manifestation of modern interest in Black Loyalist history.

PORT MOUTON

Port Mouton wasn't archaeologically surveyed until 2002, when Mike Sanders took an initial look at the area, under the auspices of another heritage group. "The Mersey Heritage Society's six-day survey," he says, "identified several abandoned roads, nine suspected dwelling sites, and many former clearings with perimeter stone piles." Although it initially seemed a lot to have survived over two centuries, he noted that "finds seem remarkably few when you consider that the site once had approximately three hundred buildings and quartered more than twenty-five hundred people." One of the saddest features was the Loyalist cemetery, with its "dozens and dozens of dead," and only a rough rock for each headstone.[19]

Basically, Sanders's group was just doing a ground survey, but they did put in a single one-by-one-metre test pit, next to a feature that proved to be a house foundation. "It was fantastic," Sanders recalls, "when we started to see artifacts that confirmed the [1783–1784] age, and that the house had been burned by fire." More archaeological work, obviously, here, too, will be necessary.

More historical research is also needed. The only substantial study to date, Mike observed, is one done in 1947 by Thomas Raddall, who researched Port Mouton and collected local oral histories, but that was mainly concentrated on the men of Tarleton's Legion. (Raddall's research has proved both helpful and flawed, as discussed in chapter 8.)[20]

I asked Mike Sanders what it felt like, being down there in the woods at Port Mouton. He said he often thought of how bleak and miserable it must have seemed to those new settlers, coming to a higher northern latitude and landing in an uncleared wilderness, "where the ground was either extremely rocky, or hopelessly wet"—not to mention lacking proper supplies, with winter coming on.[21]

On March 31, 2006, the Black Loyalist Heritage Society suffered a horrific setback. Someone firebombed the little office that had been built to house the society's offices, their boardroom, and the storage for all their historical research and family genealogies. I asked Elizabeth Cromwell if she could tell me what happened, as I had been down in South Carolina at the time. "That was a night to remember," she said. "Someone called and said, 'Your building's on fire.' We couldn't believe it. Someone had already called the fire department. We got over there, and sure enough the building was on fire. The fire had been set from the verandah that ran across the front of the building....We stood and watched. Well, there was nothing they could do. It's a wooden structure, and by the time the fire department got there, the fire had pretty much destroyed the front of the building." She said the firefighters did their best, carrying out as much stuff as they could save, adding, "I watched it for a while, and finally I…I just had to leave. I just couldn't stay there." Her husband, Everett, kept vigil while the fire burned until late that night. Other members of the society arrived as well as people from Shelburne generally, and they all stood in front of the flames and wept. Even the firefighters were saddened, and worked quietly: "It was almost like it was a funeral. It was quite moving."[22]

The next morning, there wasn't a thing about it in the news, anywhere.

Elizabeth Cromwell told me that one of the things that kept running through her mind was, "How did our people stand this, when it was going on all the time? How did they stand this when they had to be afraid?" The fear generated by the threat of fire persisted for a long time. All the board members felt it. I asked her if anyone was ever charged with the hate crime, and was told the police thought they knew who did it and had charged them, but it never went to trial: "And what followed was even more damaging, because we received a continual litany of threats over our answering machines." The society had to write to the minister of justice and get the RCMP involved. Many of the calls, they found out, were coming from the United States, from white supremacist groups. "It set us back a bit, you know," Cromwell says. "I think we were pretty disturbed at the time. And there was the question, well, what do we do now? Can we continue this? And I think we just said, we can't stop. We can't give up. We cannot let that stop us."[23]

The work continued, and now, five years later, funding is almost complete for a state-of-the-art museum in Birchtown. "I look back now," says Elizabeth Cromwell, summing up, "and I think perhaps it hasn't been so long. At one point, you realize that there's so much to do. And we had a lot to learn, because there's process. I'm not saying that there weren't delays and roadblocks in our way, because I think that there were, sometimes. We had to change projects in order to get funding to keep the doors open, and that slowed us down somewhat, but, you know, I'm happy about where we are now. I'm really pleased that the designs and the thing for the new building are done. The exhibits are being worked on. I think the story will be told, and I think it will be a very beautiful place."

I asked Beverly Cox, director of the Black Loyalist Heritage Society and Marjorie Turner-Bailey, a board member, what, in their minds, were the best things to come out of this modern search for roots. Marjorie, a nurse and former Olympic medalist, told me, "It's a great psychological uplift for young people...it gives them strength to go far in those exercises and to help." Bev Cox pondered the question for a while: "I think it's the fact that people are being made more aware of the plight of the black people in this province, and that they've come a long way, and their history is just as important as any Caucasian history—and that we need to celebrate our history just as well as anybody else does." The most moving thing, she said, was that the group had discovered that people outside the Black Loyalist communities were interested in offering practical aid and sympathy: "I think that as a black community, we kind of stay together, and work through our struggles, but sometimes we just need to ask for help....Through this process, we have found that there are people who are just waiting on the sidelines to say, 'Yes. I will help you....' There are people out there who are very socially conscious, who are willing to step up and say, 'This is a very great project. Your history is just as important as ours, and we need to all celebrate it.'"[23]

My hope is that this book about the Black Loyalists who came to Nova Scotia from Georgia and South Carolina will contribute, in some small way, to this great movement toward understanding, reconciliation, and celebration. My respect and appreciation goes out to all who have contributed to make it so.

Acknowledgements

Deepest thanks to Carmelita A. M. Robertson for suggesting this project, and for spectacular research, especially for finding the Book of Negroes, Boston King's memoir, and the first Royal Navy muster roll. Supplementary researchers for this project were Sharain Jones in Nova Scotia, the Bahamas, and England; Katie Cottreau-Robins in Nova Scotia and England; Sarah Whitehead in England and South Carolina; Jessie Cohen in South Carolina; Satya Ramen in Ontario; Rachael Colley Whynot, Elizabeth Peirce, and Joleen Gordon in Nova Scotia. Cicely Berglund did online research on medical topics.

In Canada: Thanks to the Government of Canada, Department of Canadian Heritage, Multiculturalism Program, for a timely grant, covering the cost of photocopies and scans of pertinent documents on the Black Loyalists for a collection now housed at the Nova Scotia Museum. This collection has contributed greatly to research for the book; my special thanks to case officer Marcelle Gibson. Thanks to Jim Burant and Carole Cloutier, Library and Archives Canada, Ottawa; Laurier Turgeon, Université Laval, Quebec; Peter Larocque, New Brunswick Museum, Saint John; Walter

Cromwell and Lawrence Hill in Ontario. Special thanks to Dr. Ingeborg Marshall, Newfoundland, and to two other generous funders who wish to remain nameless.

In Nova Scotia: Thanks to Elizabeth Cromwell, Everett Cromwell, Beverly Cox, and all the staff and researchers with the Black Loyalist Heritage Society, Birchtown; Marjorie Turner-Bailey, Lockport; Lloyd Boucher, Tony Cotie, James and Gloria Desmond, and the communities of Tracadie and Lincolnville; Pat Skinner, Antigonish; Henry Bishop, Black Cultural Centre; Jocelyn Gillis, Antigonish Heritage Museum; Frances Nixon, James House Museum; Eric Ruff, Yarmouth County Museum; staff at the Guysborough County Museum; Linda Rafuse, Queens County Museum. Special thanks to George C. Cromwell, Dartmouth, for finding me Henry Middleton's slave list; and to Charlie Dillman, Middle Musquodoboit, for showing us the foundations of slave cabins on his property. Julian Gwyn and John R. Reid elucidated Royal Navy sources. Jeani Mustaine provided an insider view of the Henry Laurens project. Sass Minard helped check Book of Negroes data, and Elizabeth Peirce copy-edited the British entries. Janet Baker found books on joint-stock companies and the Norway rat (brought first to New York City by Hessians in 1776). Christiane Graham and Brigitte Petersmann did German translation. Maritime Marlin did the travel, and M. A. Mercer did the taxes.

Archaeologists Stephen Powell, Stephen Davis, Katie Cottreau-Robins, Sharain Jones, Laird Niven, Mike Sanders, Bruce Stewart, Heather MacLeod-Leslie, and others literally dug up data and shared information. Special thanks to Trudy Sable, whose photographs of West Africa showed me that part of the world.

Thanks to the staff of the Nova Scotia Museum and the Maritime Museum of the Atlantic, as always, particularly David Christianson, Scott Robson, Deborah Trask, Deborah Scott, Marie Elwood, Sheila Yeoman, Jemal Abawajy, Carmelita Robertson, and research associate Joleen Gordon; Leslie Pezzack, Fred Scott, Andrew Hebda, Alec Wilson; Sheila Stevenson, Linda Silver, Judith Shiers-Milne, and Dan Conlin, as well as students Rachael Colley Whynot and Tammy Poirier, and volunteers Elizabeth Peirce and Christine Hobin. Mike Osmond transcribed the oral histories. Executive director David Newlands made me a standing offer of museum help, where possible, for this book (written after I retired). Special thanks to the two staff people who contributed most of all: Penny Harvey for years of data entry, among other things, and Roxanne MacMillan for vast numbers of interlibrary loans, the lifeblood of research. At Learning Resources and Technology, Roger Lloyd and Richard Plander did a lot of the photographic printing generated by the Black Loyalist Exhibit project, and much of the photography; Ray Whitley did everything else.

Thanks to the Nova Scotia Archives staff: Margaret Campbell, Lois Yorke, Barry Cahill, Garry Shutlak, Philip Hartling, Gail Judge, Anjali Vohra, Barry Smith, and Georges Dupuis. Thanks to filmmaker Lesley Ann Patten and her crew who created a documentary on Carmelita Robertson's and my search for South Carolina Black Loyalists (*Loyalties*, Ziji Film & Television Productions and the National Film Board of Canada, 1999). Thanks to Alyson McCready, Black Loyalist descendant, for questions that made me think.

In Great Britain: Thanks to Richard Groocock of the National Archives of Great Britain (Public Record Office), Kew (pristine scans and perfect photocopies); Kristopher McKie, National Archives of Scotland, Edinburgh. Special thanks to Carol A. B. Whitehead, Dulwich, for food and shelter, and some really helpful ideas about transportation.

In the United States: Thanks to Vincent Carretta and Tony Horwitz, Virginia; Marianne Martin, Colonial Williamsburg Foundation; Kristy Haney, University of Virginia Library; Henry Louis Gates Jr, Massachusetts; Grace Ellis, Irene Scott Gilland, and the Duke University Library, North Carolina; Helen O'Neill, Associated Press, New York; Jane Fitzgerald and John Vandereedt, National Archives, Washington; William L. Clements Library, University of Michigan; Marilyn Pettit, Brooklyn Historical Society, New York; Cecil Giscombe, University of California.

In South Carolina: Thanks to the late George C. Rogers Jr, University of South Carolina; and the late Frances Webb, for whom I once worked at the Charleston Museum. Alexander Moore, as director of the South Carolina Historical Society and acquisitions editor at University of South Carolina Press, helped me through years of research; Steve Hoffius, Home House Press, gave superb editorial feedback. Thanks to Mike Allen, US Parks Service at Fort Moultrie, and to the rangers at Fort Moultrie who made me sing "Farewell to Nova Scotia" for them; Pat Bennet and Carole Jones, Charleston Library Society; Angela Mack and Joyce Baker, Gibbes Museum of Art; Al

Sanders (best office), Martha Zierden, Anne Fox, Jennifer Scheetz, Sharon Bennet, and Julia Logan, Charleston Museum; Michael Trinkley, Columbia; Charles Lesser and Steven Tuttle, South Carolina Department of Archives and History; Cat Evans, College of Charleston; Harlan Green, at both the Charleston County Public Library and the Avery Institute; Nic Butler, at both the South Carolina Historical Society and the Charleston County Public Library (best research stories); the staff of the South Carolina Historical Society; Jon Poston and Karen Emmons, Historic Charleston Foundation; A. H. Keller, Circular Congregationalist Church; Nicole Green, City of Charleston and Old Slavemart Museum; Wevonneda Minis, *Charleston Post and Courier*; Barbara Doyle and Mary Edna Sullivan, Middleton Place; the staff at Drayton Hall; Charleston County Public Library's South Carolina Room staff: Lish Thompson, Marianne Cawley, Katie Gray, Amy Quesenbery, Liz Newcomb; Kendra Wilson and Kevin Corcoran in the main library. And special thanks to Dale Rosengarten at the College of Charleston Library.

Don Burbidge shared information on the Linings. Ralph Bailey and Charles Philips took us up the eighteenth-century Ashley River and environs. Gary S. Wilson and the late John H. Wilson, creators of the Early South Carolina Newspaper Database, contributed much of their time and research gratis. Della Carter and her father, John Wesley Carr, who together own part of what was formerly John Lining's plantation on the Ashley River, showed me indigo still growing wild there. John DeVeaux pointed out the old route between Fort Moultrie and the back-beach spot where General Charles Lee wanted William Moultrie to build a bridge, and introduced his parents, whose house on Sullivan's Island may have the tabby (a concrete of sand and crushed oyster shells, often seen in eighteenth-century construction) foundation of old Fort Moultrie's west flanker running underneath it. My cousin Lawrence Walker Jr. arranged for us to see Mulberry Plantation and disseminated my research, on CDs, for me in South Carolina to anyone who wanted it. I also thank Ben Miller, manager at Mulberry Plantation; Robert Hortmann at Medway Plantation; and the staff at Boone Hall. Winfield Towles took me to Beaufort and Huntington Island. Norma Ballentine showed me Dewees, Hamlin, and Copahee Sounds, Harriott Pinckney's plantation, and the Congregationalist cemetery up Highway 17. Thanks also to Norwood Smoak, Roy Williams, Anne Baker Leland Bridges, and Catherine Tupper

Faires. Special thanks to Julia Garrison, for taking me to the South Carolina Department of Archives and History, Columbia, for reading drafts and for timely rescues; I only wish she had lived to read this book.

Most fervent thanks to Melissha Ilene Richardson and her entire family: Miss Rosa Teretha Bell, Tony Lee, Katrina Renea, Shontea Patrice, Emmy Amanda, Chaquetta Saimon, Kyle Donvaye, and Kristen Rachel; prophetess Helen Kinloch, the late Shirley Broughton, Keisha Richardson Rattley, Jimmy Richardson, and Dorothy Richardson.

Grace Ellis, Thomas Hoge, Ethel Nepveux, Robert McCully, Jo Hutcheson, and Margaret Humphreys provided leads, stories, maps, and help of other sorts, as did Helen and Joseph Maturo, Helen Maturo Sease and Elizabeth Maturo Hutton. David Humphreys shared family research. Wade and Anne Everett drove me all around the backcountry so I could see landscapes, battle sites, Georgetown, and the Black Mingo swamp. Tim Everett drove me around Charleston cemeteries; David and Katrina Everett packed the research files (all forty-seven feet of them) for shipment to Nova Scotia. Bart Everett connected me with websites for satellite photography. Edward Ball shared photos of Sierra Leone and research on Ball slaves; Elizabeth G. Ball navigated me through the Registry of Mesne Conveyance in Charleston. Jessie Cohen did impressive research; I learned a lot from her. Sarah Whitehead and Ryerson Christie helped me all the time, and I could not have done this work without a South Carolina base at my parents' house. The first thing I did when I started my research was to call my mother, who told me everything about everybody, even unto the tenth generation. She did not live to read even the final draft, but the book owes much to her information and her insights.

Elsewhere: Thanks to the National Archives of Sierra Leone, Freetown; to Sierra Leone's Freetong Players; and to Christine Ross, National Museum of the Gambia, Banjul. Thanks to Cassandra Pybus in Australia (great book!).

Charleston, South Carolina
Halifax, Nova Scotia
1996-2012

Abbreviations

NEWSPAPERS

DHVG	Dixon and Hunter's *Virginia Gazette*, Williamsburg, VA
EGMA	*Essex Gazette*, Essex, MA
JPVG	John Pinkney's *Virginia Gazette*, Williamsburg, VA
MCLA	*Morning Chronicle and London Advertiser*, London, UK
PDVG	Purdie & Dixon's *Virginia Gazette*, Williamsburg, VA
PVG	Purdie's *Virginia Gazette*, Williamsburg, VA
RG	*Royal Gazette* (1781-1782), Charlestown, SC
RVG	Rind's *Virginia Gazette*, Williamsburg, VA
SCAGG	*South Carolina & American General Gazette* (1764–1781), Charlestown, SC
SCG	*South-Carolina Gazette* (1732-1775), Charlestown, SC
SCGCJ	*South Carolina Gazette & Country Journal* (1766–1775), Charlestown, SC
SCGGA	*South Carolina Gazette & General Advertiser* (1783–1784), Charlestown, SC

INSTITUTIONS AND BOOK SERIES

BM   British Museum, London

CCPL   Charleston County Public Library, Charleston

DAR   *Documents of the American Revolution*

LAC   Library and Archives Canada, Ottawa

LC   Library of Congress, Washington, DC

MPA   Middleton Place Archives, Charleston

NAS   National Archives of Scotland, Edinburgh

NAUK   National Archives of Great Britain (PRO), Kew, Richmond, Surrey

NAUS   National Archives of the United States, Washington, DC

NCDAH North Carolina Department of Archives and History, Raleigh

NDAR   *Naval Documents of the American Revolution*

NSA   Nova Scotia Archives, Halifax

SCDAH South Carolina Department of Archives and History

SCHS   South Carolina Historical Society

UTL   University of Toronto Library, Toronto

UVAL   University of Virginia Library, Charlottesville

WCL   William L. Clements Library, Ann Arbor

Notes

INTRODUCTION

1 Deborah Trask, personal communication to Ruth Whitehead, October 1999. Trask found "Frank Doane records that Thomas Doane saw the British fleet," as a pencilled note in a typescript, "The Old Meeting House," 1932, New England Historic and Genealogical Society, Boston. Trask says there is indeed a clear view out to sea from this grave in Nova Scotia.

2 NSA, Executive Council Minutes, 1777, fol. 343; in, Walker, *Black Loyalists*, 7. I have not been able to find any mention of exchanging black people in these documents.

3 Guy Carleton to George Washington, 12 May 1783, Colonial Office 5/109, folio 313, NAUK.

4 Wilson, *Loyal Blacks*, 23–24.

CHAPTER ONE

1 Importation of slaves from Africa was outlawed in the US after 1807, but smugglers still brought over cargos of people up until the end of the US Civil War (1865).

2 Gates Jr., *Wonders*, 131–32.

3 Hakluyt, *Voyages and Discoveries*, 66–68.

4 Ibid., 105–107.

5 Hewatt, *Rise and Progress*, 1:43.

6   Ibid.; Donnan, *History of the Slave Trade*, vol. 2, *Eighteenth Century* (1931), 243.

7   Donnan, *History of the Slave Trade*, vol. 2, *Eighteenth Century* (1931), 271–72.

8   Ibid., 327–29.

9   Ibid., 264–70.

10 Ibid.

11 Ibid., 632–642.

12 Kiple and Higgins, "Mortality Caused by Dehydration," in Inikori and Engerman, eds., *Atlantic Slave Trade*, 323.

13 Donnan, *History of the Slave Trade*, vol. 4, *Border Colonies* (1935), 370.

14 Newton, *Journal of a Slave Trader*, 75.

15 Donnan, *History of the Slave Trade*, vol. 2, *Eighteenth Century* (1931), 352, 485.

16 D'Antonio, "New Mosquito," 65–69.

17 Wilson and Grim, "Slave Trade and Hypertension," in Inikori and Engerman, eds., *Atlantic Slave Trade*, 339–59.

18 Salley, *Original Narratives*, 142–43, 151.

19 Donnan, *History of the Slave Trade*, vol. 4, *Border Colonies* (1935), 241–242.

20 South Carolina Historical Society, *Shaftesbury Papers*, 165–167.

21 Ibid., 165–67, 173-174; Salley, *Warrants for Land*, 4.

22 Leland and Ressinger, "Ce Païs," 26–27, 30.

23 McCord, *Statutes at Large*, 1–17.

24 Bates and Leland, *Proprietary Records*, 17–19.

25 Salley, *Warrants for Land*, 52–54. Donnan posits that first evidence of blacks in the province is in a letter that Henry Brayne wrote in November 1670 to Lord Ashley, saying his servants included "one negro man" (*History of the Slave Trade*, vol. 4, *Border Colonies* [1935], 242). Evidence of black presence in Carolina actually goes back further, to a black man who together with a Berber slave and a Native Cuban deserted the expedition of Hernando de Soto in 1540 (Sauer, *Sixteenth-Century North America*, 168). The warrants for land, however, contain the first actual names. The "roll call of the enslaved" begun here, of course, refers only to black persons, and does not include the earlier and contemporary enslavement of North American Natives (and blacks) by other Natives.

26 Braund, *Deerskins and Duffels*, 29, 31, 33, 42, 72.

27 Deagan and MacMahon, *Fort Mose*, 19–20.

28 Donnan, *History of the Slave Trade*, vol. 4, *Border Colonies* (1935), 256, 483.

29 Ibid., 295, 295n.

30 Smith Family Papers, 30/4, SCHS. Moore and Simmons, *Abstracts of the Wills*, 6, 8–9, 33. Waring (*History of Medicine*, 10) writes: "In 1684 there appeared the first notable general sickness, a serious epidemic of a disease which was probably malaria…"

31 Donnan, *History of the Slave Trade*, vol. 4, *Border Colonies* (1935): 295. For Lining biography, see Ibid. 295. For malaria, yellow fever, and smallpox, see Waring's *History of Medicine*, 1:37–39. Slave ships were incubators for pathogens, even European

viruses. A smallpox epidemic in 1738 "entered the colony via the *London Frigate,* a Guinea slave ship. There were at least 2,298 cases with 321 reported deaths" (Ibid., 37).

32 Hewatt, *Rise and Progress,* 50.

33 Milligen-Johnston, *Colonial South Carolina,* 109. This intense summer heat was followed by an autumn hurricane. Milligen-Johnston (20–21) also pens a vivid description of a roaring great tornado that opened the Ashley River "to the Bottom," laying the channel bare.

34 Merrens, *Colonial South Carolina,* 268.

35 Donnan, *History of the Slave Trade,* vol. 4, *Border Colonies* (1935), 265–72.

36 Ibid., 306–307.

37 Ibid., 323, 326, 357, 362.

38 *SCG,* 6 July 1765; *SCG,* 19 February 1741; *SCG,* 16 December 1778.

39 *Papers of Henry Laurens,* 4:192.

40 Donnan, *History of the Slave Trade,* vol. 4, *Border Colonies* (1935), 305, 323, 330, 407, 426.

41 Ibid., 436–37, 469.

42 Ibid., 470.

43 Merrens, "Journal of Ebenezer Hazard," 190.

44 Mann, *1493,* 323.

45 Donnan, *History of the Slave Trade,* vol. 2, *Eighteenth Century* (1930), xiii.

46 Sanders and Anderson, *Natural History Investigations,* 12.

47 Frazier, "Journey for a Song: Music Links Georgians to Africa," *Charleston Post and Courier,* March 16, 1997.

CHAPTER TWO

1 *SCGCJ,* 31 July 1770.

2 Ibid., September 30, 1766.

3 Whitehead and Robertson, *Life of Boston King,* 14.

4 "*L'Abondance,* inspected New York, July 31, 1783," Book of Negroes, Carleton Papers (British Headquarters Papers), PRO 30/50/100, NAUK.

5 Waring Family Papers 30/4, SCHS; Waring, "Waring Family," 81–92; Whitehead and Robertson, *Life of Boston King,* 3.

6 Whitehead and Robertson, *Life of Boston King,* 15–16.

7 Gordon, *David George,* 30.

8 Ibid., 169.

9 Ibid., 170.

10 Ibid.

11   Ibid.

12   Ibid., 172.

13   Ibid.

14   Ibid., 30, 173.

15   Marrant, *Narrative*, 2, 4. In the 1730s, Whitefield was a cofounder, with John and Charles Wesley, of Methodism; he made ten missionary trips to North America before he died in 1770 (Carretta, *Equiano the African*, 165).

16   Ibid., 5.

17   Ibid.

18   Wilson, *Loyal Blacks*, 23–24. His age in 1783 and his owner's name come from the Book of Negroes, where only his first name, Warwick, is given; he escaped from Jellot in 1778.

19   Ibid.

20   Weir, *Colonial South Carolina*, 177–178.

21   Laurens, *Papers of Henry Laurens*, 7:328–29.

22   Melissha Richardson, audio interview with the author, November 1997, author's collection.

23   Ferguson, *Uncommon Ground*, xlii.

24   Melissha Richardson, audio interview with the author, November 1997, author's collection.

CHAPTER THREE

1   Book of Negroes, Carleton Papers, PRO 30/50/100, NAUK; Marriage Bonds, Book 1700, 1173, NSA.

2   *RG*, 26 May 1781.

3   Will of John Callaghan, *Transcripts of Wills and Inventories of Charleston County*, Will Book A, 1783–1786:199, CCPL; Inventory of John Callaghan, 15–16 May 1781, WPA Transcripts, 100:325–28, CCPL.

4   George Dener to Jane Callaghan, bill of sale for a slave named Jack, 24 October 1781, Series S213000: Vol. 002Q, 306, SCDAH.

5   Inventory of John Callaghan, 15–16 May 1781, WPA Transcripts, 100:325–28, CCPL.

6   Bill of sale, Alexander Barron to Jane Callaghan, 9 September 1782, Series S213000, Vol. 002Q, 358–60, SCDAH.

7   *Papers of Henry Laurens*, 3:203–204; 4:633; 6:762–63.

8   Book of Negroes, Carleton Papers, PRO 30/50/100, NAUK; Muster Roll, *Clinton*, 1 July to 31 December, 1783, ADM 36/9966, NAUK.

9 "Return of Negroes and their families mustered in Annapolis County between the 28th day of May and the 30th day of June 1784; Copied from the Muster Roll," MG 15, vol. 19, #36, NSA.

10 Rowland, Moore, and Rogers, *History of Beaufort County*, 86.

11 Hayne, "Records Kept," 233–34.

12 Daniel DeSaussure vs. Valentine Lynn, 26 January 1763, South Carolina Court of Common Pleas, Judgment Rolls, Series S136002, Box 58A, No. 122A, SCDAH; Daniel DeSaussure vs. Valentine Lynn, 20 May 1765, South Carolina Court of Common Pleas, Judgment Rolls, Series S136002, Box 62A, No. 111A, SCDAH.

13 James Welsh vs. Valentine Lynn, 25 April 1771, South Carolina Court of Common Pleas, Judgment Rolls, Series S136002, Box 90A, No. 85A, SCDAH.

14 Smith, "Radnor, Edmundsbury and Jacksonburgh," 46–47.

15 Alexander Fitzgerald vs. Valentine Lynn, 21 September 1772, South Carolina Court of Common Pleas, Judgment Rolls: Series S136002, Box 94A, No. 222A, SCDAH.

16 Joshua Lockwood vs. Valentine Lynn, 23 September 1777, South Carolina Court of Common Pleas, Judgment Rolls: Series S136002, Box 104C, No. 32A, SCDAH.

17 Merrens, "Journal of Ebenezer Hazard," 177, 181, 187.

18 Jacob Valk vs. Valentine Lynn, 21 January 1778, South Carolina Court of Common Pleas, Judgment Rolls, Series S136002, Box 109B, No. 10A, SCDAH.

19 Will of Valentine Lynn, dated 29 August 1781, proved 15 September 1781, Will Book WW, 1780–1783: 152, CCPL.

20 Merrens, "Journal of Ebenezer Hazard," 187.

21 Book of Negroes, Carleton Papers, PRO 30/50/100, NAUK.

22 "Judith Ladson, a free Negro woman, memorial for 6.50 acres on Charleston Neck, Berkeley County, September 15, 1733," Land Transfer Records, Series S111001: Vol. 3: 438; "James Fogartie to Richard Perroneau, a free Person of Colour, lease and release of land, 1781–1782," Series S363001, Vol. 05E0: 129. For slave purchases and sales by free blacks, see Series S213000, Vol. 05F0: 98 and Series S213000, Vol. 002Q: 424.

23 McCowan, *British Occupation of Charleston*, 105.

24 "Muster Book of the Free Black Settlement of Birchtown, Muster 3d & 4th July 1784," MG 9: B 6 (1), B 9–14, NSA. Accessed on microfilm. This muster includes some people formerly living at Port Mouton, before the spring fire of 1784.

25 "List of the blacks in Birch Town who gave in Their Names for Sierra Leone in November 1791," ledger pps. 361–66, 437–447, CO 217/63, NAUK.

26 Book of Negroes, Carleton Papers, PRO 30/50/100, NAUK.

27 Inventory of Thomas Shubrick (1756–1810), Inventory Book E, 1810–1819, CCPL.

CHAPTER FOUR

1   *SCG*, 9 February 1734.

2   *SCG*, 4 May 1752.

3   *SCG*, 27 November 1755; *SCG* 30 August 1770.

4   *SCGCJ*, 4 October 1768.

5   *SCAGG*, 27 January 1775.

6   Donnan, *History of the Slave Trade*, vol. 2, *Eighteenth Century*, 469.

7   Boswell, *Life of Samuel Johnson*, 618–619, 624–625.

8   *Papers of Henry Laurens*, 8:353.

9   Shyllon, *Black Slaves in Britain*, ix. F. O. Shyllon's account of this trial is one of the best for anyone who wishes to examine it in depth.

10   Ibid., ix-x, 165.

11   Wilson, *Loyal Blacks*, 2.

12   Adams, *Works of John Adams*, vol. 3, *Autobiography, Diary, Notes of a Debate in the Senate, Essays* (1851), 428.

13   *PDVG*, 30 September 1773. Emphasis mine.

14   Ibid., June 16, 1774. Emphasis mine.

15   *HVG*, 2 August 1775.

16   Commager and Morris, *Spirit of 'Seventy-Six*, 25.

17   Wilson, *Loyal Blacks*, 3.

18   *Papers of Alexander Hamilton* (1961), 1:47.

19   *EGMA*, April 25, 1775.

20   Clark et al., *Naval Documents*, 1:372.

21   Ibid., 758.

22   Ibid., 792, 801–802, 1103.

23   Ibid., 948.

24   Dartmouth Manuscripts, NCDAH. In *NDAR*, 2:792–97.

25   Varick Transcripts, George Washington Papers, LC. In *NDAR*, 4:376.

26   Haldiman Papers, BM; Wentworth to Moylan, 15 April 1776, George Washington Papers, LC. Both in *NDAR*, 4:489, 829.

27   "Extract from a Letter," *Morning Chronicle and London Advertiser*, 12 June 1776.

28   Butterfield, Garrett, and Sprague, eds. *Adams Family Correspondence*, 390.

29   Marble, *Information from Deaths*, 2:143–146.

30   Hansard, *Parliamentary History of England*, 1103–105.

31   Coke, *Royal Commission*, 211.

32   Reynolds to George F. Norton, 22 September 1775, William Reynolds Letter Book, LC; in *NDAR*, 2: 183.

33   Dunmore to Hillsborough, May 1, 1772, CO 5/1350, folio 46, NAUK. In *DAR*, 5:94–95.

34 Major Adam Stephen to Richard Henry Lee, February 1, 1775, Lee Papers, UVAL. In *NDAR*, 1:77.

35 LC Transcript, Mss. of Earl of Dartmouth, American Papers, CO 5/1353, NAUK. In Clark et al., *Naval Documents*, 1:259–61.

36 Ibid.

37 Muster Roll of the *Mercury*, 13 July 1775, under "Supernumeraries Borne for Victuals only Pr Order Vice Adm'l Graves," ADM 36/7738, NAUK.

38 Dunmore's Proclamation, UVAL. In Clark et al., *Naval Documents*, 2:920–922.

39 *MCLA*, 20 January 1776. In Clark et al., *Naval Documents*, 2:1307–1308.

40 *JPVG*, 9 December 1775.

41 *PVG*, 17 November 1775.

42 Clark et al., *Naval Documents*, 2:1309–311.

43 *DHVG*, 2 December 1775. This "inscription on their breasts" is much more likely to have been stamped on a tin or pewter badge, worn on the chest, rather than embroidery or appliqué on a uniform, as some have interpreted it. The Ethiopian Regiment wasn't given uniforms, nor were uniforms customarily embroidered with mottos.

44 Clark et al., *Naval Documents*, 3:621–22.

45 Account of Hamond's part in the Revolution, 1774–1777, Hamond Papers, UVAL.

46 Orders Received 1775–1776, Hamond Papers, UVAL; Captain's Log, *Kingfisher*, ADM 51/506, NAUK. Both in Clark et al., *Naval Documents*, 3:625, 1187.

47 Muster Roll, *Roebuck*, January 1, 1776, to February 29, 1777, ADM 36/8638, NAUK.

48 Orders Issued, Hamond Papers, UVAL. In Clark et al., *Naval Documents*, 3: 1188, 1349–1350. Note: the *Mercury's* muster shows "M. Gl H'y Clinton" came aboard January 12, "Pr O'r V'ce Ad'l Graves," accompanied by Francis Lord Rawdon, Captain Duncan Drummond, Captain George Martin, secretary Richard Reeves, a surgeon, a chaplain, three men described as "Gen'l Clinton's retinue," ten servants, and a pilot. They would all be discharged into the transport *Palisser* at Cape Fear, North Carolina, on April 18 (Muster Roll, *Mercury*, ADM 36/7738, NAUK.) For more on Moore's Creek, see Morrill, *Southern Campaigns*, 3–13.

49 *Narrative of Captain Andrew Snape Hamond*, No. 5, 16–31 May 1776, Hamond Papers, UVAL. In Clark et al., *Naval Documents*, 5:320–22.

50 Captain's Log, *Roebuck*, ADM 51/796, NAUK; Captain's Log, *Otter*, ADM 51/663, NAUK; Hamond Papers, No. 5, UVAL. All in Clark et al., *Naval Documents*, 5:320–22.

51 Clark et al., *Naval Documents*, 5:485.

52 Muster Roll, *Roebuck*, January 1, 1776, to February 29, 1777, ADM 36/8638, NAUK.

53 *PVG*, 19 July 1776.

54   Letters and Orders, 1775–1778, Hamond Papers, UVAL. In Clark et al., *Naval Documents*, 5:1138–139.

55   Master's Log, *Roebuck*, July 14, 1775, to July 14, 1777, ADM 52/1965, NAUK. These people were not mustered into her books.

56   Clark et al., *Naval Documents*, 6:51.

57   Hamond Papers, No. 5, UVAL. In Clark et al., *Naval Documents*, 6:172–174.

58   Tatum, *American Journal*, 249, 244, 250.

59   Harrington, "African Cemetery," 324–26.

60   Clark et al., *Naval Documents*, 1(1964): 815; 2(1966): 1270.

61   Hyde Parker to Shuldham, ADM 1/484, NAUK. In *NDAR*, 4:75.

62   Muster Roll, *Scorpion*, November 1776 to June 1778, ADM 36 /8378, NAUK.

63   "Moores Creek National Battlefield," National Park Service, last modified 3 December 2012, http://www.nps.gov/mocr.

64   Clark et al., *Naval Documents*, 4:369, 428. The *Glasgow Packett* came in on the 12th, and the *Kitty* arrived on the 16th.

65   Clark et al., *Naval Documents*, 4:1182–183.

66   Ibid., 1183.

67   Ibid.

68   "Return of Negroes and their families mustered in Annapolis County between the 28th day of May and the 30th day of June 1784; Copied from the Muster Roll" [hereinafter Annapolis Muster], MG 15, Vol. 19, #36, NSA.

69   Ibid.

70   Wilson, *The Loyal Blacks*, 34.

71   Annapolis Muster, Vol. 19, #36, MG 15, NSA.

72   Ibid.

73   Black Pioneer Murphy Stiel to Sir Henry Clinton, Sir Henry Clinton Papers, Vol. 170, Item 27, WCL.

74   Wilson, *Loyal Blacks*, 64.

75   "Inquisition…on the Body of Jenny, an Indian Woman, wife of Andrew a black," Carleton Papers, 9401: 1–4, MFN 10,121, NSA.

76   Coke, *Royal Commission*, 197.

77   *John Peebles' American War*, 338–40, editor's note.

78   Cunninghame of Thorntoun Papers, "Indenture for Ned," February 19, 1782; GD 21/158, "Peebles Diary," January 22, 24, 1782, NAS.

79   Shelburne County Court Cases, RG 60 Shelburne, Vol. 48.2, 28–29 August 1791, NSA.

80   "New York Census," *RVG*, 9 September 1773; "Return of persons who came off from Virginia with Maj-Gen. Mathew in the Fleet the 24th May 1779, showing names of the ships and the white men and the numbers of women, children and blacks," Vol. 52, No. 63, British Headquarters Papers, UTL.

81   Captain's Log, *Perseus*, March 25, 1776, to July 17, 1780, ADM 51/688, NAUK.

82   Ibid.

CHAPTER FIVE

1   *SCG*, 7 November 1775.

2   Clark et al., *Naval Documents*, 1:346–48.

3   Marrant, *Narrative*, 1–15. Both Vincent Caretta and I checked the *Scorpion*'s musters (ADM 36/8377–8378, NAUK), and John Marrant's name isn't there. Perhaps he used an alias, or just his first name, or perhaps he was actually on the *Scarborough*, also in the area at the time. He appears to have served on a number of ships in his six years of service (Vincent Caretta to Ruth Whitehead, personal communication, October 2001).

4   Clark et al., *Naval Documents*, 1:931; Muster Roll, Mercury, January 1774 to April 1776, ADM 36/7738, NAUK.

5   Clark et al., *Naval Documents*, 1:717.

6   *Collections of the South-Carolina Historical Society*, Charleston, South Carolina Historical Society, 1857-1897, 3: 87–91.

7   Coke, *Royal Commission*, 198.

8   Clark et al., *Naval Documents*, 2:1314.

9   *SCAGG*, 12 December 1776.

10   Crow, "Letters of Thomas Pinckney," 30.

11   Gibbes, *Documentary History*, 13–14.

12   Moultrie, *Memoirs*, 1:174–179.

13   Captain's Log, *Experiment*, ADM 51/331, NAUK.

14   Captain's Log, *Solebay*, ADM 51/909, NAUK. In Clark et al., *Naval Documents*, 5:797–98.

15   Clark et al., *Naval Documents*, 5:653, 800.

16   Captain's Log, HMS *Sphynx*, ADM 51/922, NAUK. In Clark et al., *Naval Documents*, 6:1074.

17   Clark et al., *Naval Documents*, 6:1468.

18   Whitehead and Robertson, *Life of Boston King*, 16.

19   *Papers of Henry Laurens*, 11:276–77.

20   Ibid., 345–46.

21   Muster Roll, *Daphne*, May 24, 1777, ADM 26/9486, NAUK.

22   Buchanan, *Road to Guilford Courthouse*, 26.

23   Frey, *Water from the Rock*, 84.

24   *Papers of Henry Laurens*, 15:20–21.

25   Rhodehamel, *American Revolution*, 499.

26   Ibid., 500.

27   Gordon, *David George*, 173–174.

28   Pass for Ned and Jemimah and their children, recorded at Halifax, 13 March 1783, RG 1, vol. 170:336, NSA.

29   Pass for Michael Thomas and family, recorded at Halifax, 14 March 1783, RG 1, vol. 170:338, NSA.

30 John Buchanan's otherwise excellent study of the war in the Carolinas (*Road to Guilford Courthouse*) begins with an account of the attack on Sullivan's Island in 1776, and then skips straight to Clinton's invasion in 1780. Simon Schama (*Rough Crossings*) and Cassandra Pybus (*Epic Journeys*) never mention Prévost's invasion of South Carolina at all.

31 "A List of Negroes belonging to Henry Middleton which were taken from his several Plantations," Henry Middleton Papers, MPA.

32 *Letters of Eliza Wilkinson*, 26–30.

33 Ibid., 67–71.

34 Jones, "Black Hessians," 292.

35 Ibid., 292, 300n. Jones had access to Hessian Archives in Marburg, Germany; his article goes into greater detail than is here possible. Here are the German lyrics:

> *Es traf bloss eine grosse Zahl; Von Negren bei uns ein*
> *Doch ohne Kleidung, ohne Brod; Sind sie vegnuegt mit Reis*
> *Der Schwarze kennet keine Not; Veil er vom Glueck nicht weiss.*

Loosely translated, the lyrics state: "Just now there are a large number of Blacks with us, without either clothes or bread; they make do with Rice. The Black Man knows no other life, and therefore doesn't suffer."

36 Prévost to Clinton, 21 May 1779, Carleton Papers 2011:1-11, MFN 10,121, NSA; Prévost to Clinton, 4 July 1779, Carleton Papers 2019:1-3, MFN 10,121, NSA. In 1785, two years after the war, Charles Cotesworth Pinckney addressed a committee of the House of Representatives about the importation of slaves, stating that it had been slaves who had saved Charlestown from Prévost in 1779: "He thought the strength of this country constituted its riches; that this sort of strength once saved this city, in the war, was the case when Prévost over-ran the county: 'twas true he only looked at us and went away, but what was this owing to—why to the number of bastions hastily thrown up, a service performed entirely by the negro pioneers" (Donnan, *History of the Slave Trade*, Vol. 4, *Border Colonies*, 482).

37 Ramsay, *History of South Carolina*, 1809.

38 Gordon, *Life of David George*, 38.

39 Ramsay, *History of the Revolution*, 32–33.

40 Ramsay revised this account later (1809) in his *History of South Carolina from Its Earliest Settlement in 1670 to the Year 1808*, removing a few of the more sensational details, most notably that of the soldiers with bayonets and cutlasses. This wasn't the only occasion in which Ramsay toned down his reported atrocities.

41 Ramsay, *History of the Revolution*, 32–33. Emphasis mine.

42 Lepore, "Goodbye, Columbus." I can't find evidence of the transport *Free Briton* evacuating Charlestown, as Lepore says; this vessel *did*, however, assist in the evacuation of New York in 1783.

43 Schama, *Rough Crossings*, 133. Schama does not cite Ramsay, or anyone else for that

matter, as a source for his statement. For the number of black people who left in 1782, see Barnwell, "The Evacuation of Charleston," 26. (See also chapter six in this book.)

44 Book of Negroes, Carleton Papers, PRO 30/50/100, NAUK.

45 Phillipsburg Proclamation, 30 June 1779, Clinton Papers, WCL.

46 Pass for John Williams, recorded at Halifax, June or July 1783, Commissioner of Public Records, RG 1, vol. 170:341, NSA.

47 Captain's Log, *Perseus*, September 17, 1780, to September 30, 1781, ADM 51/4289, NAUK.

48 Ibid.

49 Morrill, *Southern Campaigns*, 206.

50 Siege of Savannah, 30 July 1779, Regimental Order Book, LC; Paybook Campbell's 71st Regiment, GD 174/2/2172, NAS; Pybus, *Epic Journeys*, 38.

51 Gordon, *Life of David George*, 174–185. The account says she washed for Clinton, but this is obviously a misunderstanding on the part of the people who interviewed him in England. She perhaps was Prévost's laundress. During the winter of 1779, Clinton was not in Georgia more than a few days, certainly not long enough to provide a washerwoman with an income.

52 Ewald, *Diary*, 195-196.

53 Ibid., 197.

54 *John Peebles' American War*, 338–40.

55 Ibid., 340.

56 Ibid., editor's note. Peebles formally indentured Ned in 1782, as discussed in chapter 4 of this book.

57 Ewald, *Diary*, 226.

58 Uhlendorf, *Siege of Charleston*, 243.

59 Marrant, *Narrative*, 1–15.

60 Whitehead and Robertson, *Life of Boston King*, 16–17.

61 Morrill, *Southern Campaigns*, 76.

62 Whitehead and Robertson, *Life of Boston King*, 18, 19.

63 Gordon, *Life of David George*, 185.

64 Ibid.

65 Ibid., 175. Paterson was the first commandant at Charlestown, replaced by Nisbet Balfour, replaced by Alexander Leslie, replaced by Isaac Allen.

66 Wickwire and Wickwire, *Cornwallis*, 221. Kings Mountain is actually in North Carolina; the battle named for it actually happened a few miles to the south, over the border in York County, South Carolina.

67 Cornwallis to Cruger, 16 January 1781, PRO 30/11/106, NAUK.

68 Wickwire and Wickwire, *Cornwallis*, 254–55.

69 Buchanan, *Road to Guilford Courthouse*, 276, 326.

70 Wickwire and Wickwire, *Cornwallis*, 266.

71 Rogers, "Letters of Charles O'Hara," 171.

72 Buchanan, *Road to Guilford Courthouse*, 380.

73 Balfour to Cornwallis, 21 May 1781, PRO 30/11/6, NAUK.

74 Gibbes, *Documentary History*, 77–79.

75 Rogers, "Letters of Charles O'Hara," 160.

76 *RG*, 2 May 1781.

77 *Heads of Families*.

78 *RG*, 14 November 1781.

79 Wright to Balfour, 5 January 1781, PRO 30/11/62, NAUK.

80 *RG*, 26 December, 1781.

81 Wright to Balfour, 5 January 1781, PRO 30/11/62, NAUK; Commissioner of
    Sequestered Estates John Cruden, Tortola, to the Honorable George Nibbs,
    Magistrate of Tortola, 16 March 1783, folio 379, CO 5/109, NAUK; John Cruden to
    the Honorable J. Fahia, President of the Council, Tortola, 24 March 1783, folio 377,
    CO 5/109, NAUK; John Cruden to Major C. Nesbit, Barbados, 25 March, 1783, folio
    375, CO 5/109, NAUK; Gibbes, *Documentary History of the American Revolution*, 147.

82 *RG*, 12 January 1782.

83 *RG*, 26 December 1781.

84 Pass for Thomas and Hannah Williams, recorded at Halifax, late 1782 or early 1783,
    Commissioner of Public Records, RG 1, vol. 170: 333, NSA.

85 Wilson, *Loyal Blacks*, 47.

86 Marrant, *Narrative*, 15.

CHAPTER SIX

1   MacMaster, "Yorktown Campaign," 394; Frey, *Water from the Rock*, 164.

2   *Richard Henry Lee*, 218, 221–22.

3   Ibid., 230–31, 242–43.

4   Ewald, *Diary*, 305–306.

5   Ibid.

6   *Diary of Josiah Atkins*, 32.

7   Fenn, *Pox Americana*, 131–32. If Cornwallis made a conscious decision to use Blacks
    as carriers of disease, inoculating those free of the disease and sending them off to
    infect others, he had a lot of material with which to work. Thomas Jefferson wrote
    to William Gordon after the war in 1788 his estimation: that of the 30,000 Blacks
    fleeing to the army, "about 27,000 died of the small pox and camp fever" (*Papers of
    Thomas Jefferson*, 13: 363–364).

8   O'Hara to Cornwallis, 5 August 1781, PRO 30/11/89, NAUK.

9   Cornwallis to O'Hara, 7 August 1781, PRO 30/11/89, NAUK.

10 O'Hara to Cornwallis, 9 August 1781, PRO 30/11/70, NAUK.

11 O'Hara to Cornwallis, 10 August 1781, PRO 30/11/89, NAUK.

12 Ross to Patenes, 20 June 1781, PRO 30/11/87, NAUK.

13 Ross, *Correspondence*, 112.

14 Ross, *Correspondence*, 117–18.

15 Ewald, *Diary*, 335–36.

16 Clinton, *American Revolution*, 586.

17 Ewald, *Diary*, 336.

18 Dann, *Revolution Remembered*, 240–242.

19 Ibid., 244.

20 Scheer, *Private Yankee Doodle*, 241.

21 Ibid., 241–42.

22 Cornwallis to Clinton, 15 October 1782, folio 256, CO 5/103, NAUK. In Davies, *American Revolution*, 11:243.

23 Riley, "St. George Tucker's Journal," 391.

24 Dann, *Revolution Remembered*, 245.

25 Davies, *American Revolution*, 21:244.

26 Ibid., 22:252–253.

27 Ibid., 21: 6–7.

28 Ibid., 20: 255–256.

29 Dann, *Revolution Remembered*, 245.

30 Denny, *Military Journal*, 45.

31 Ewald, *Diary*, 343.

32 *Richard Henry Lee*, 2:270–71, 273.

33 Book of Negroes, Carleton Papers, PRO 30/50/100, NAUK.

34 Denny, *Military Journal*, 48–49, entry for November 1, 1781; Feltman, *Journal*, 28.

35 Moultrie, *Memoirs*, 2:354.

36 Davies, *American Revolution*, 21:116, 119.

37 Moultrie, *Memoirs*, 2:340. Entry for *Two Sisters*, inspected at New York on June 13, 1783, and bound for Saint John; Entry for *London*, inspected April 23–27, bound for Port Roseway, Book of Negroes, Carleton Papers, PRO 30/50/100, NAUK.

38 Davies, *American Revolution*, 21: 136.

39 Frey, *Water from the Rock*, 174.

40 Moultrie, *Memoirs*, 2:355–356.

41 Gibbes, *Documentary History*, 153, 156, 164.

42 *RG*, 7 September 1782.

43 Whitehead and Robertson, *Life of Boston King*, 19.

44 Moultrie, *Memoirs*, 2:343.

45 Ibid., 344. Emphasis mine.

46 Ibid., 351–52.

47 Shelburne County Court Cases, Court of General Sessions, Vol. 49.4, 1791, February n.d., May 23, July 5, July 15, November 3, RG 60 Shelburne, NSA. I know the Warings and Postells intermarried in the eighteenth century because we share a family tree.

48 Folio 379: Commissioner of Sequestered Estates John Cruden, Tortola, to the Honorable George Nibbs, Magistrate of Tortola, 16 March 1783, CO 5/109, NAUK.

49 Folio 377: John Cruden to the Honorable J. Fahia, President of the Council, Tortola, 24 March 1783, CO 5/109, NAUK; Folio 379: John Cruden to Major C. Nesbit, Barbados, 25 March 1783, CO 5/109, NAUK.

50 Davies, *American Revolution*, 21:140; Barnwell, "Evacuation of Charleston," 26.

51 Muster Roll, *Belisarius*, November 1 to December 31, 1782, ADM 36/9592, NAUK; Captain's Log, *Belisarius*, August 29, 1781, to October 18, 1783, ADM 51/97, NAUK.

52 Muster Roll, *Belisarius*, November 1 to December 31, 1782, ADM 36/9592, NAUK.

53 Captain's Log, *Belisarius*, August 29, 1781, to October 18, 1783, ADM 51/97, NAUK.

54 "Halifax Ship Arrivals, 1782," MG 7, Vol. 3A, 1784–1785, NSA; Master's Log, *Ceres*, August 2, 1781, to January 30, 1783, ADM 52/2217, NAUK.

55 Gordon, *Life of David George*, 174–75.

56 Birchtown Muster, MG9 B6 (1) B 9-14, LAC.

57 Moultrie, *Memoirs*, 2:357–60.

58 Muster Roll, *Belisarius*, November 1 to December 31, 1782, ADM 36/9592, NAUK.

59 Captain's Log, *Belisarius*, August 29, 1781, to October 18, 1783, ADM 51/97, NAUK.

60 Schoepf, *Travels*, 224–28.

61 Ibid., 229–31.

62 Ibid., 253, 260–62.

63 Ibid., 259, 260, 262.

64 *SCGGA*, 6 May 1783.

65 "A list of Negroes belonging to Mr. Henry Middleton taken from his Plantations," Henry Middleton Papers, MPA.

66 *Papers of Henry Laurens*, 16:363–64.

CHAPTER SEVEN

1 Muster Roll, *L'Abondance*, November 1782 to March 1784, ADM 36/9857, NAUK; Master's Log, *L'Abondance*, December 13, 1782, to March 16, 1784, ADM 52/2135, NAUK.

2 Muster Roll, *Clinton*, November 1782 to March 1784, ADM 36/9966, NAUK; Master's Log, *Clinton*, June 29, 1779, to June 30, 1781, ADM 52/1665, NAUK.

3 Whitehead and Robertson, *Life of Boston King*, 21.

4 Ibid., 19–21.

5 Ibid., 20–21.

6 Crary, *Price of Loyalty*, 360–61.
7 Whitehead and Robertson, *Life of Boston King*, 21.
8 Wilson, *Loyal Blacks*, 48.
9 Fitzpatrick, *Writings of George Washington*, 26:38, 40–41, 45–46.
10 Ibid.
11 Ibid, 34–35.
12 Gibbes, *Documentary History*, 243.
13 Michaelis to Beckwith, New York, 4 October 1783, Carleton Papers 9294:1–11, MFN 10,121, NAUK.
14 Crary, *Price of Loyalty*, 362.
15 Wilson, *Loyal Blacks*, 56.
16 John Vandereedt, NAUS, email to the author, 22 February 2006.
17 Hodges, *Black Loyalist Directory*, xv.
18 Whitehead and Robertson, *Life of Boston King*, 21.
19 *Collections of the New Brunswick Historical Society*, 4(6): 144.
20 Book of Negroes, Carleton Papers, PRO 30/50/100, NAUK.
21 Master's Log, *L'Abondance*, December 13, 1782 to March 16, 1784, ADM 52/2135, NAUK; Muster Roll, *L'Abondance*, ADM 36/9857, NAUK.
22 Master's Log, *L'Abondance*, December 13, 1782 to March 16, 1784, ADM 52/2135, NAUK; Muster Roll, *L'Abondance*, ADM 36/9857, NAUK; Vessels Inspected 29–31 July 1783, Carleton Papers, PRO 30/50/100, NAUK.
23 Muster Roll, *L'Abondance*, ADM 36/9857, NAUK; Birchtown Muster, MG9 B6 (1) B 9-14, LAC.
24 Muster Roll, *L'Abondance*, ADM 36/9857, NAUK.
25 Ibid.
26 Ibid.
27 Master's Log, *Clinton*, June 29, 1779, to June 30, 1781, ADM 52/1665, NAUK.
28 Master's Log, *L'Abondance*, ADM 52/2135, December 13, 1782 to March 16, 1784, NAUK.
29 Ibid.
30 Muster Roll, *L'Abondance*, ADM 36/9857, NAUK.
31 Master's Log, *Clinton*, June 29, 1779, to June 30, 1781, ADM 52/1665, NAUK; Muster Roll, *Clinton*, July 1, 1783, to December 31, 1783, ADM 36/9966, NAUK.
32 Muster Roll, *Clinton*, July 1, 1783, to December 31, 1783, ADM 36/9966, NAUK.
33 Master's Log, *L'Abondance*, ADM 52/2135, December 13, 1782 to March 16, 1784, NAUK.
34 Master's Log, *Clinton*, June 29, 1779, to June 30, 1781, ADM 52/1665, NAUK; Muster Roll, *Clinton*, July 1, 1783, to December 31, 1783, ADM 36/9966, NAUK; Master's Log, *L'Abondance*, ADM 52/2135, December 13, 1782 to March 16, 1784, NAUK.
35 Master's Log, *Clinton*, June 29, 1779, to June 30, 1781, ADM 52/1665, NAUK; Muster Roll, *Clinton*, 26 July to 2 September 1783, ADM 36/9966, NAUK.

36 Master's Log, *L'Abondance*, ADM 52/2135, December 13, 1782 to March 16, 1784, NAUK; Master's Log, *Clinton*, June 29, 1779, to June 30, 1781, ADM 52/1665, NAUK.

37 Ewald, *Diary*, 359.

38 Ibid., 359–60.

39 Bell, "Hessian Conscript's Account," 141.

40 Vessels Inspected 30 November 1783, Book of Negroes, Carleton Papers, PRO 30/50/100, NAUK.

41 Master's Log, *L'Abondance*, ADM 52/2135, December 13, 1782 to March 16, 1784, NAUK.

42 Muster Roll, *Ceres*, January 1 to February 24, 1784, ADM 36/9693, NAUK.

43 Master's Log, *L'Abondance*, ADM 52/2135, December 13, 1782 to March 16, 1784, NAUK.

44 Book of Negroes, Carleton Papers, PRO 30/50/100, NAUK.

45 Master's Log, *L'Abondance*, ADM 52/2135, December 13, 1782 to March 16, 1784, NAUK.

CHAPTER EIGHT

1 Whitehead and Robertson, *Life of Boston King*, 21, 24.

2 Dennis, *Down in Nova Scotia*, 359.

3 Shelburne Muster, Birchtown Muster, MG9 B6 (1) B 9-14, LAC.

4 Ibid.; Book of Negroes, Carleton Papers, PRO 30/50/100, NAUK.

5 Book of Negroes, Carleton Papers, PRO 30/50/100, NAUK.

6 County of Shelburne Court of General Sessions (Cavan), RG 60 Vol. 2.6, 2.9, October 1784, NSA; County of Shelburne Court of General Sessions (Grand et al.), RG 60, Vol. 3.6, no date, 1784, NSA.

7 Birchtown Muster, MG9 B6 (1) B 9-14, LAC.

8 County of Shelburne Court of General Sessions (Hill), RG 60 Vol. 25.3, October 16, 1787, NSA; County of Shelburne Court of General Sessions (Postell), RG 60 Vol. 49.4, February to November 1791, NSA.

9 Fergusson, *Clarkson's Mission*, 89–90.

10 County of Shelburne Court of General Sessions (White), RG 60, Vol. 37.3, 26 September 1788, NSA; County of Shelburne Court of General Sessions (White, Gordon), RG 60, Vol. 38.4, no date, 1788, NSA.

11 County of Shelburne Court of General Sessions (Fours et al.), RG 60, Vol. 29.7, March 23, 1787, NSA.

12 County of Shelburne Court of General Sessions (Legree, Van), RG 60, Vol 43.6, January 1, 1789; January 5, 1789, NSA.

13 County of Shelburne Court of General Sessions (Vann), RG 60, Vol. 44.6, January 8, 1789, NSA.

14 County of Shelburne Court of General Sessions (Snipe et al.), RG 60, Vol. 36.4, June 30, 1788, NSA.

15 County of Shelburne Court of General Sessions (Fitzgerald, Legree), RG 60, Vol. 49.1, August 4, 1791, NSA.

16 County of Shelburne Court of General Sessions (Legare, Vann), RG 60, Vol. 43.6, April 14, 1789; Ibid. (Fitzgerald, Legree), RG 60, Vol. 49.1, August 4, 1791, NSA.

17 Whitehead and Robertson, *Life of Boston King*, 25.

18 Marrant, *Journal*, 47.

19 Whitehead and Robertson, *Life of Boston King*, 25–28.

20 Fergusson, *Clarkson's Mission*, 117.

21 Ibid., 16.

22 "Petition of Thomas Peters a free Negro," CO 217/63, NAUK (ledger pps 58–59, corrected in pencil to 60–62); Robertson, *King's Bounty*, 100.

23 Fergusson, *Clarkson's Mission*, 53, 59, 99, 103–104, 167.

24 Ibid., 36.

25 Fergusson, *Clarkson's Mission*, 51, 116.

26 Whitehead and Robertson, *Life of Boston King*, 29–30.

27 Raddall, "Tarleton's Legion," 21, 22.

28 Ibid., 29.

29 Book of Negroes, Carleton Papers, PRO 30/50/100, NAUK.

30 Ibid.

31 Raddall, "Tarleton's Legion," 29.

32 Ibid., 34.

33 Ibid., 34–35.

34 Ibid., 35.

35 Birchtown Muster, MG9 B6 (1) B 9-14, LAC.

36 Hart, *County of Guysborough*, 57–58.

37 Ibid., 63.

38 Ibid., 192.

39 Book of Negroes, Carleton Papers, PRO 30/50/100, NAUK.

40 Hart, *County of Guysborough*, 201.

41 Robertson, *Black Loyalists*, 118; Powell, *Archaeological Survey of Tracadie*, 30.

42 Book of Negroes, Carleton Papers, PRO 30/50/100, NAUK.

43 Inventory of Ralph Izard, beginning March 12, 1761, *Inventories of the State of South Carolina: Charleston County*, 1758–1761, 85B: 832–36, CCPL.

44 "On the Muster Roll of the Departments of the Army and Navy, set down at Chedabucto, June, 1784," Lawrence Collection, Ward Chipman Papers, Vol. 24, Loyalist Musters, 1783–1784, MFN 10,163: 275, LAC.

45 Norma Ballentine to the author, personal communication, 27 April 2005.

46 Book of Negroes, Carleton Papers, PRO 30/50/100, NAUK.

47 "Will of John Sauseau, proved March 19, 1731," Will Book 2, 1729–1731: 88–89, CCPL; Gregorie, *Christ Church*, 31–32, 36.

48 Clark, *Loyalists in the Southern Campaign*, 183, 184, 521.

49 "Baptismal Records for Christ Church Anglican, Guysborough, NS," MFN: 11, 390, NSA.

50 "On the Muster Roll of the Departments of the Army and Navy, set down at Chedabucto, June, 1784," Lawrence Collection, Ward Chipman Papers, Vol. 24, Loyalist Musters, 1783–1784, MFN 10,163: 275, LAC.

51 "Baptismal Records for Christ Church, Anglican, Guysborough, NS," MFN: 11,390, NSA.

52 Book of Negroes, Carleton Papers, PRO 30/50/100, NAUK. *SCG*, 1 August 1761; *SCG*, 1 June 1765.

53 *SCG*, 2–30 November 1769; 2–16 August 1770.

54 *SCAGG*, 17 October 1776.

55 *Papers of Henry Laurens*, 11:391.

56 Book of Negroes, Carleton Papers, PRO 30/50/100, NAUK.

57 Records of Christ Church, Anglican, Guysborough, MFN # 11,390, NSA.

58 Smith, "Old Charles Town," 11–12; Holcomb, *Marriages*; Waring, *History of Medicine*, 254–260; Will of John Lining, Will Book 1760–1767: 20, CCPL. (Name is spelled "Sinning" in the typed 1930s transcript.)

59 SCG, 13 June 1761.

60 Uhlendorf, *Siege of Charleston*, 70; Ewald, *Diary*, 33, 39, 47; *John Peebles' American War*, 350.

61 Records of Christ Church, Anglican, Guysborough, MFN # 11,390, NSA.

62 Sutherland, "Wallace, Michael," in *Dictionary of Canadian Biography Online, 2000*.

CHAPTER NINE

1 Carmelita Robertson, video interview with the author, 4 January 2012, author's collection.

2 Ibid.

3 Elizabeth Cromwell, Beverly Cox, Marjorie Turner-Bailey, video interview with the author, 2 November 2011, author's collection.

4 Ibid.

5   Stephen Powell, video interview with the author, 19 December 2011, author's collection.

6   Laird Niven, discussion with the author, 3 January 2012.

7   Stephen Powell, video interview with the author, 19 December 2011, author's collection.

8   Stephen A. Davis, discussion with the author, 3 January 2012.

9   Laird Niven, email to the author, 12 January 2012.

10 Whitehead, *Shelburne Black Loyalists*, 5–7. Also quoted in Powell and Niven, *Two Black Communities*, 6; Robertson, *King's Bounty*, 7. For an expanded version of the project statement, by project manager Deborah Scott of the NSM, see Powell and Niven, *Two Black Communities*, 2–9.

11 Ibid.

12 Ibid., 7–8; Powell and Niven, *Two Black Communities*, 49.

13 Stephen Powell, video interview with the author, 19 December 2011.

14 Powell, "Archaeological Survey," 4.

15 Stephen Powell, video interview with the author, 19 December 2011.

16 Ibid.

17 Sharain Jones, discussion with the author, 17 December 2011.

18 Katie Cottreau-Robins, discussion with the author, 4 January 2012.

19 Mike Sanders, video interview with the author, 21 December 2011.

20 Raddall, "Tarleton's Legion," 1–50.

21 Mike Sanders, video interview with the author, 21 December 2011. He later added to or changed some of the information in his interview (email to the author, 6 January 2012).

22 Elizabeth Cromwell, audio interview with the author, 2 November 2011.

23 Beverly Cox, Marjorie Turner-Bailey, audio interview with the author, 2 November 2011.

Bibliography

Adams, John. *The Works of John Adams, Second President of the United States, with a Life of the Author*. Edited by Charles Francis Adams. 10 vols. Boston: Little, Brown, 1850–1856.

Atkins, Josiah. *The Diary of Josiah Atkins*. Edited by Steven E. Kagle. New York: Arno Press, 1975.

Barnwell, Joseph W. "The Evacuation of Charleston by the British in 1782." *South Carolina Historical and Genealogical Magazine* 11, no. 1 (1910): 1–17.

Bates, Susan Baldwin, and Harriott Cheves Leland, eds. *Proprietary Records of South Carolina: Abstracts of the Records of the Register of the Province, 1675–1696*. Vol. 2. Charleston: History Press, 2006.

Bell, Winthrop. "A Hessian Conscript's Account of Life in Garrison at Halifax at the Time of the American Revolution." Vol. 27 of *Collections of the Nova Scotia Historical Society*, 125–46. Halifax: Nova Scotia Historical Society, 1947.

Boswell, James. *The Life of Samuel Johnson*. Ware, UK: Wordsworth Editions, 1999.

Braund, Kathryn E. Holland. *Deerskins and Duffels: The Creek Indian Trade with Anglo-America, 1685–1815*. Lincoln: University of Nebraska Press, 1993.

Buchanan, John. *The Road to Guilford Courthouse: The American Revolution in the Carolinas*. New York: John Wiley, 1997.

Butterfield, Lyman H., Wendell D. Garrett, and Marjorie E. Sprague, eds. Adams Family Correspondence, Vol. 1. Series 2 of *The Adams Papers*. Cambridge: Belknap Press, 1963.

Caretta, Vincent. *Equiano the African: Biography of a Self-Made Man*. Athens: University of Georgia Press, 2005.

Clark, Murtie June. Vol. I of *Loyalists in the Southern Campaign of the Revolutionary War.* Baltimore: Genealogical Publishing, 1981.

Clark, William Bell, William James Morgan, William S. Dudley, and Michael J. Crawford, eds. *Naval Documents of the American Revolution.* 11 vols. Washington: Department of the Navy, 1964–2005.

Clinton, General Sir Henry. *The American Revolution: Sir Henry Clinton's Narrative of His Campaigns, 1775-1782.* New Haven: Yale University Press, 1954.

Clinton Papers, William L. Clements Library, Ann Arbor, Michigan.

Coke, Daniel Parker. *The Royal Commission on the Losses and Services of the American Loyalists, 1783 to 1785, Being the Notes of Mr. Daniel Parker Coke, M.P., One of the Commissioners During That Period.* Edited by Hugh Edward Egerton. New York: Burt Franklin, 1971.

Commager, Henry Steele and Richard B. Morris, eds. *The Spirit of 'Seventy-Six: The Story of the American Revolution as Told by Participants.* 2nd ed. New York: Harper & Row, 1967.

Crary, Catherine S. *The Price of Loyalty: Tory Writings from the Revolutionary Era.* New York: McGraw Hill, 1973.

Crow, Jack L., ed. "Letters of Thomas Pinckney, 1775–1780." *South Carolina Historical Magazine* 58, no. 1 (1957): 24–25.

Dann, John C., ed. *The Revolution Remembered: Eyewitness Accounts of the War for Independence.* Chicago: University of Chicago Press, 1977.

D'Antonio, Michael. "Making a New Mosquito." *Discover*, May 2001, 65–69.

Davies, K. G., ed. *Documents of the American Revolution, 1770–1783*, Colonial Office Series. 21 vols. Shannon: Irish University Press, 1972–1981.

Deagan, Kathleen and Darcie MacMahon. *Fort Mose: Colonial America's Black Fortress of Freedom.* Gainsville, FL: University Press of Florida / Florida Museum of Natural History, 1995.

Dennis, Clara. *Down in Nova Scotia: My Own, My Native Land.* Toronto: Ryerson Press, 1934.

Denny, Ebenezer. *Military Journal of Major Ebenezer Denny.* Philadelphia: J. B. Lippincott, 1859.

Donnan, Elizabeth. *Documents Illustrative of the History of the Slave Trade to America.* 4 vols. Washington: Carnegie Institution of Washington, 1930–1935.

Ewald, Johann. *Diary of the American War: A Hessian Journal.* Translated and edited by Joseph P. Tusten. New Haven, Yale University Press, 1979.

Feltman, William. *The Journal of Lt. William Feltman of the First Pennsylvania Regiment, 1781–82, Including the March into Virginia and the Siege of Yorktown.* 2nd ed. New York: New York Times & Arno Press, 1969.

Fenn, Elizabeth A. *Pox Americana: The Great Smallpox Epidemic of 1775–82.* New York: Hill & Wang, 2001.

Ferguson, Leland. *Uncommon Ground: Archaeology and Early African America, 1650-1800.* Washington: Smithsonian Institution, 1992.

Fergusson, Charles Bruce, ed. *Clarkson's Mission to America, 1791–1792*. Halifax: Public
Archives of Nova Scotia, 1971.

Fitzpatrick, John C., ed. *The Writings of George Washington from the Original Manuscript
Sources*. 38 vols. Washington: US Government Printing Office, 1931–1944.

Frey, Silvia. *Water from the Rock: Black Resistance in a Revolutionary Age*. Princeton:
Princeton University Press, 1991.

Gates, Henry Louis Jr. *Wonders of the African World*. New York: Alfred A. Knopf, 1999.

Gibbes, R. W. *Documentary History of the American Revolution*. 2nd ed. Spartanburg:
Reprint Company, 1972.

Gordon, Grant, ed. *From Slavery to Freedom: The Life of David George*. Hantsport, NS:
Lancelot Press, 1992.

Gregorie, Anne King. *Christ Church, 1706–1959: A Plantation Parish of the South Carolina
Establishment*. Charleston: Dalcho Historical Society, 1961.

Hakluyt, Richard. *Voyages and Discoveries: The Principal Navigations, Voyages, Traffiques,
and Discoveries of the English Nation*. Edited by Jack Beeching. London: Penguin,
1972.

Hamilton, Alexander. Volume 1 of *The Papers of Alexander Hamilton*. Edited by Harold C.
Syrett. New York: Columbia University Press, 1961.

Hansard, Thomas C., ed. *The Parliamentary History of England from the Earliest Period to
the Year 1803*. 36 vols. London: T. C. Hansard, 1806–1820.

Harrington, Spencer. "An African Cemetery in Manhattan." *Eyewitness to Discovery: First
Person Accounts of More Than Fifty of the World's Greatest Archaeological Discoveries*.
Oxford: Oxford University Press, 1969.

Hart, Harriet C. *History of the County of Guysborough*. 2d. ed., Belleville, ON: unknown,
1975.

Hayne, Isaac. "Records Kept by Colonel Isaac Hayne." *South Carolina Historical and
Genealogical Magazine* 10, no. 4 (1909): 233–34.

*Heads of Families at the First Census of the United States Taken in the Year 1790: South
Carolina*. Washington: Bureau of the Census, 1908.

Hewatt, Alexander. *An Historical Account of the Rise and Progress of the Colonies of South
Carolina and Georgia*. 2 vols. London: Alexander Donaldson, 1779.

Hodges, Graham Russell. *The Black Loyalist Directory*. New York: Garland Publishing,
1996.

Holcomb, Brent H. *South Carolina Marriages, 1688–1799*. Baltimore: Genealogical
Publishing, 1983.

Inikori, Joseph E., and Stanley L. Engerman, eds. *The Atlantic Slave Trade: Effects on
Economies, Societies, and Peoples in Africa, the Americas, and Europe*. Durham: Duke
University Press, 1992.

Jefferson, Thomas. *The Papers of Thomas Jefferson*. Edited by Barbara B. Oberg et al. 33 vols.
Princeton: Princeton University Press, 1944–2006.

Jones, George Fenwick. "The Black Hessians: Negroes Recruited by the Hessians in
South Carolina and Other Colonies." *South Carolina Historical Magazine* 83, no. 4
(1982): 287–302.

Kiple, Kenneth F., and Brian T. Higgins. "Mortality Caused by Dehydration During the Middle Passage." In *The Atlantic Slave Trade: Effects on Economies, Societies, and Peoples in Africa, the Americas, and Europe*, edited by Joseph E. Inikori and Stanley L. Engerman, 321–337. Durham: Duke University Press, 1992.

Laurens, Henry. *The Papers of Henry Laurens*. Edited by David R. Chesnutt and C. James Taylor. 16 vols. Columbia: University of South Carolina Press, 1968–2003.

Lee, Richard Henry. *The Letters of Richard Henry Lee*. Edited by James Curtis Ballagh. 2 vols. New York: MacMillan Company, 1911–1914.

Leland, Harriott Cheves, and Dianne W. Ressinger. "'Ce Païs Tant Désiré.'" *Transactions of the Huguenot Society of South Carolina*, no. 110 (2006): 1–41.

Lepore, Jill. "Goodbye, Columbus." *New Yorker*, 8 May 2006: 74–78.

MacMaster, Richard K., ed. "News of the Yorktown Campaign: The Journal of Dr. Robert Honyman, April 17–November 25, 1781." *Virginia Magazine of History and Biography* 79, no. 4 (1971): 393–402.

Mann, Charles C. *1493: Uncovering the New World Columbus Created*. New York: Alfred A. Knopf, 2011.

Marble, Allan Everett. *Information from Deaths, Burials and Probate of N.S, 1749–1799, from Primary Sources*. 2 vols. Halifax: Genealogical Association of Nova Scotia, 1990.

Marrant, John. *A Narrative of the Lord's Wonderful Dealings with John Marrant: A Black, Now Going to Preach the Gospel in Nova Scotia*. London: Gilbert and Plummer, 1785.

———. A Journal of the Rev. John Marrant, from August the 18th, 1785, to the 16th of March, 1790, accessed 11 January 2013, www.blackloyalist.com/canadiandigitalcollection/index.htm.

McCord, David J. *Statutes at Large of South Carolina*. Vol. 7, Acts Relating to Charleston, Courts, Slaves and Rivers. Columbia: A. S. Johnston, 1840.

McCowan, George Smith, Jr. *The British Occupation of Charleston, 1780–82*. Columbia: University of South Carolina Press for the South Carolina Tricentennial Commission, 1972.

Merrens, H. Roy, ed. "A View of Coastal South Carolina in 1778: The Journal of Ebenezer Hazard." *South Carolina Historical Magazine* 73, no. 4 (1972): 177–193.

———. *The Colonial South Carolina Scene: Contemporary Views, 1697–1774*. Columbia: University of South Carolina Press, 1977.

Milligen-Johnston, George. *Colonial South Carolina: Two Contemporary Descriptions by Governor James Glen and Doctor George Milligen-Johnston*. Edited by Chapman J. Milling. Columbia: University of South Carolina Press, 1951.

Moore, Caroline T., and Agatha Aimar Simmons. *Abstracts of the Wills of the State of South Carolina 1670–1740*. Columbia: R. L. Bryan, 1960.

Morrill, Dan. *Southern Campaigns of the American Revolution*. Baltimore: Nautical and Aviation Publication, 1993.

Moultrie, William. *Memoirs of the American Revolution*. 2nd ed. 2 vols. Eyewitness Accounts of the American Revolution Series. New York: New York Times & Arno Press, 1968.

Newsome, A. R., ed. "A British Orderly Book, 1780–1781." Pts. 1 and 2. *North Carolina Historical Review* 9, no. 3 (1932): 273–98; no. 4 (1932): 366–92.

Newton, John. *The Journal of a Slave Trader (John Newton) 1750–1754*. Edited by Bernard Martin and Mark Spurrell. London: Epworth Press, 1962.

O'Hara, Charles. "The Letters of Charles O'Hara to the Duke of Grafton." George S. Rogers, Jr., ed. *South Carolina Historical Magazine* 65, no. 3 (1964): 158–80.

Peebles, John. *John Peebles' American War: The Diary of a Scottish Grenadier, 1776–1782*. Edited by Ira D. Gruber. N.p.: Sutton Publishing for the Army Records Society, 1997.

Powell, Stephen. "Archaeological Survey of Tracadie and Surrounding Area: Antigonish and Guysborough Counties." Halifax: Nova Scotia Museum, 1998.

Powell, Stephen, and Laird Niven. *Archaeological Surveys in Two Black Communities, 1998: Surveying the Tracadie Area and Testing Two Sites in Birchtown*. Curatorial Report 92. Halifax: Nova Scotia Museum, 2000.

Pybus, Cassandra. *Epic Journeys of Freedom: Runaway Slaves of the American Revolution and Their Global Quest for Liberty*. Boston: Beacon Press, 2006.

Raddall, Thomas. "Tarleton's Legion." *Collections of the Nova Scotia Historical Society* 28 (1949): 1-50.

Ramsay, David. Vol. 2 of *History of the Revolution of South Carolina*. Trenton, NJ: Isaac Collins, 1785.

———. *History of South Carolina from Its Earliest Settlement in 1670 to the Year 1808*. Charleston: David Longworth, 1809.

Rhodehamel, John, ed. *The American Revolution: Writings from the War of Independence*. New York: Library of America, 2001.

Riley, Edward M. "Notes and Documents: St. George Tucker's Journal of the Siege of Yorktown, 1781." *William and Mary Quarterly*, July 1948: 375–95.

Robertson, Carmelita. *Black Loyalists of Nova Scotia: Tracing the History of Tracadie Loyalists 1776–1787*. Curatorial Report 91. Halifax: Nova Scotia Museum, 2000.

Robertson, Marion. *King's Bounty: A History of Early Shelburne Nova Scotia*. Halifax: Nova Scotia Museum, 1983.

Ross, Charles, ed. Vol. 1 of *Correspondence of Charles, First Marquis Cornwallis*. London: John Murray, 1859.

Rowland, Lawrence S., Alexander Moore, and George C. Rogers, Jr. *The History of Beaufort County, South Carolina*. Vol. 1, 1514–1861. Columbia: University of South Carolina Press, 1996.

Salley, A. S., Jr., ed. *Original Narratives of Early American History: Narratives of Early Carolina 1650–1708*. New York: Charles Scribner's Sons, 1911.

———. *Warrants for Land in South Carolina, 1672–1711*. Revised edition with a new introduction by R. Nicholas Olsberg. Columbia: University of South Carolina Press, 1973.

Sanders, Albert E., and William D. Anderson, Jr. *Natural History Investigations in South Carolina from Colonial Times to the Present*. Columbia: University of South Carolina Press, 1999.

Sauer, Carl Ortwin. *Sixteenth-Century North America*. Berkeley: University of California Press, 1971.

Schama, Simon. *Rough Crossings*. Toronto: Viking Canada, 2005.

Scheer, George E., ed. *Private Yankee Doodle: Being a Narrative of Some of the Adventures, Dangers and Sufferings of a Revolutionary Soldier*. Boston: Little, Brown, 1962.

Schoepf, Johann David. *Travels in the Confederation*. Alfred J. Morrison, trans. and ed. New York: Bergman Publishers, 1968.

Shyllon, F. O. *Black Slaves in Britain*. London: Oxford University Press for the Institute of Race Relations, London, 1974.

Smith, Henry A. M. "Old Charles Town and Its Vicinity, Accabee and Wappoo Where Indigo Was First Cultivated, with Some Adjoining Places in Old St. Andrews Parish." *South Carolina Historical and Genealogical Magazine* 16, no. 1 (1915): 1–15; 16, no. 2 (1915): 49–67.

———. "Radnor, Edmundsbury and Jacksonburgh." *South Carolina Historical and Genealogical Magazine* 9, no. 1 (1910): 46–47.

South Carolina Historical Society. *Diverse Accounts of the Battle of Sullivan's Island in His Majesty's Province of South Carolina the 28th June 1776*. Charleston: South Carolina Historical Society, 1976.

———. *The Shaftesbury Papers*. 2nd ed. Charleston: South Carolina Historical Society/ Tempus, 2000.

Tatum, Edward H., ed. *The American Journal of Ambrose Serle, Secretary to Lord Howe, 1776–1778*. San Marino: Huntingdon Library, 1940.

Uhlendorf, Bernhard A., trans. and ed. *The Siege of Charleston With an Account of the Province of South Carolina: Diaries and Letters of Hessian Officers from the von Jungkenn Papers in the William L. Clements Library*. Ann Arbor: University of Michigan Press, 1938.

Walker, James W. St. G. *The Black Loyalists: The Search for a Promised Land in Nova Scotia and Sierra Leone 1783–1870*. 2nd ed. Toronto: University of Toronto Press, 1992.

Waring, Joseph Ioor. *The History of Medicine in South Carolina, 1670–1825*. Vol. 1. Columbia: R. L. Bryan, 1964.

———. "The Waring Family." *South Carolina Historical and Genealogical Magazine* 24, no. 2 (1923): 81–92.

Weir, Robert M. *Colonial South Carolina: A History*. 2nd ed. Columbia: University of South Carolina Press, 1997.

Whitehead, Ruth Holmes. *The Shelburne Black Loyalists: A Short Biography of All Blacks Emigrating to Shelburne County, Nova Scotia, after the American Revolution*. Curatorial Report 94. Halifax: Nova Scotia Museum, 2000.

Whitehead, Ruth Holmes, and Carmelita Robertson, eds. *The Life of Boston King*. Halifax: Nimbus and the Nova Scotia Museum, 2003.

Wickwire, Franklin, and Mary Wickwire. *Cornwallis and the War of Independence*. London: Faber & Faber, 1970.

Wilkinson, Eliza. *Letters of Eliza Wilkinson*. Edited by Caroline Gilman. Eyewitness Accounts of the American Revolution Series. New York: New York Times & Arno Press, 1969.

Wilson, Ellen Gibson. *The Loyal Blacks*. New York: Capricorn Books/G. P. Putnam's Sons, 1976.

Wilson, Thomas W., and Clarence E. Grim. "The Possible Relationship Between the Transatlantic Slave Trade and Hypertension in Blacks Today." In *The Atlantic Slave Trade: Effects on Economies, Societies, and Peoples in Africa, the Americas, and Europe*, edited by Joseph E. Inikori and Stanley L. Engerman, 339–359. Durham: Duke University Press, 1992.

Index

Vessels Names and their Commanders	Where Bound	Negroes Names	Age	Description	Claimants Names	Residence	Na...
				(222)			is...
Ship Eliza Peter Stark	Port Mattoon	Suky	21	Stout Wench			Thig...
		Suky	21	Ordinary Wench M.			
		Penny	25	d.o			
		Katy	22	Stout Wench			
		Mary	17	Ordinary d.o			
		Billy	1	Infant			
		Elijah	1/2	d.o			
		Suky	1/2	d.o			
11th Octr 1783 Schooner Belsom Wm Rayon	Halifax	Kate	16	Stout Wench			D.r P...
		Will Hicks	12	Stout Boy M.			
		Solomon	23	Stout fellow			Capt...
		Dick	21	d.o Stout fellow			Lieu...
		Nancy	37	Stout Wench			Doct C...
		Bristol	25	Stout fellow			
Dutchess of Gordon James Holmes Mr	d.o	William Simpson	45	d.o			42.d...
		John Brown	30	d.o			
		Punch	25	d.o			
Brig Ben James Miller	d.o	Mingo Shiels	24	d.o			
		Sam McLeod	29	d.o			
Snow ... 14th Octr 83	d.o	Whitehaven	30	d.o			
Ship Cato 14th Octr 83	Annapolis Royal	Joe Freeman	35	d.o			Steph...
		Ben Peabody	33	ordinary fellow			
		John Dobie	50	Stout fellow			
		William Freeman	30	Ordinary fellow			
		Vigo	30	Stout fellow			
		James Brown	24	d.o			Isaac
		Titus	28	d.o			Steph...
		Abigail	20	Stout Wench			
		Massey Arten	31	d.o			Jacob
		Nancy King	19	Ordinary d.o			Nich...
		Joseph	30	d.o fellow			John...
		Timothy	33	d.o			Jacob
Ship Stratham B. Nicholson	d.o	Cato	35	Stout fellow			Godf...
		Rose Wainworth	30	d.o Wench with 2 Children 1 & 5 years of age			
		Ceasar	51	Ordinary fellow			M.r...
		Bee	14	fine Boy			
		Daniel	5	d.o			
		Hannah	30	Stout Wench with a Child 2 years old	2 Children 1 = 2 y.d and 1 mo old		
		Gesse Benson	24	Stout fellow			Ephr...
		Jenny	20	fine Wench w a Child 2 years old			Willi...
		Pam	57	fine Wench			Bart...
		Margaret	15	d.o			James
		James Jacksons	36	Ordinary fellow			John...
		Betsey Jackson	16	fine Girl			